SCANDINAVIAN ARCHITECTURE

THOMAS PAULSSON

SCANDINAVIAN ARCHITECTURE

Buildings and Society in
Denmark, Finland, Norway, and Sweden
from the Iron Age until Today

CHARLES T. BRANFORD COMPANY
NEWTON 59, MASSACHUSETTS

First U.S. Edition 1959

© 1959 Thomas Paulsson

Library of Congress Catalog Card Number 59–6290
Printed by Western Printing Services Ltd Bristol, England

PREFACE

SINCE the emergence of modern architecture in Scandinavia around 1930, its quality has aroused the continually growing interest of more and more people, especially in Great Britain and the United States. This interest does seem justified, for the Nordic countries have much to show the rest of the world. Many buildings are out-standing, but perhaps even more significant is the high average standard of architecture, higher than in most countries.

Against this background it seems rather strange that the literature in English about Scandinavian architecture should be so limited. Apart from a few publications about the more recent achievements, a complete history of Scandinavian architecture does not exist in the English language—nor in any one of the Scandinavian languages, for that matter. The general handbooks deal with Scandinavia in a surprisingly limited way. In the great classic work of Banister Fletcher the Nordic countries were not even included.

When the publishers asked me to fill this gap I was well aware of the size of the task; later I became aware of its stimulus. The goal was to publish a handbook that was as complete as possible and addressed both to the person interested in architecture and to the person interested in Scandinavia in general. At the same time the number of buildings included had to be kept within manageable limits, and I have held to the principle of including and illustrating only buildings which have original and primary values; versions and revisions which succeeded these are mentioned only briefly. In Part Six, because of the vast amount of good modern work, the treatment has had to be especially selective and is not intended to provide detailed accounts of individual buildings.

When analysing and classifying buildings I have regarded them as results of their practical, social, and aesthetic functions. They have, after all, been designed and built to serve as frames and forums for human life. I should like readers to see them, not as empty historical monuments, but as used and lived in by the people for whom they were originally intended. In this book purely technical questions are, for the most part, given secondary importance.

Since much of what has happened in Scandinavia has followed the same destinies as events in England and on the Continent, and was often the direct result of European events, I have when necessary made short excursions outside the Scandinavian frontiers. By so doing the coherence with the rest of Europe and its culture becomes clearer.

I have pointed out at the beginning of Part Three that during and after the Italian Renaissance the peripheral countries of Europe were under the influence of the more strongly creative centres, with the reservation that the process of selection was deliberate and not at all comparable to forced invasion from these centres. But still many forms have appeared in Scandinavia that were more or less identical with forms in their 'mother countries'. What then was Scandinavian architecture before 1930? The formalistic historian may deny that Scandinavia had an architecture of its own, since he only sees buildings that were imitations of other buildings. But one must remember that the 'imported' forms were used in a new and different context; they were the setting, the frame, for entirely different evaluations. To the Scandinavians such forms meant something quite unlike the original values held by those for whom they were created. This process, by the way, was repeated all over Europe and elsewhere when Renaissance forms appeared once again in the nineteenth century. And in this century, so far as Scandinavia was concerned, the creative impulses began to go the other way.

My wife has made the translation of the Swedish manuscript into English. I thank the staff of Leonard Hill Books for their great interest in the book and for the many valuable suggestions I have received.

Täby, Sweden
November 1957

THOMAS PAULSSON

CONTENTS

CONTENTS

PLATES

(On sources of illustrations, see end of list of text figures, p. xvi.)

Pl. 1 – 36 between pp. 80 – 81
Pl. 37 – 54 ,, pp. 96 – 97
Pl. 55 – 80 ,, pp. 128 – 129
Pl. 81 – 100 ,, pp. 176 – 177
Pl. 101 – 120 ,, pp. 208 – 209

ix

23 (*a*). Hover parish church, Denmark. *Nationalmuseet.*

    (*b*). Stora Herrestad royal church, Skåne. *ATA, Stockholm.*

24. Tyrvaa parish church, Finland. *Finland Architecture Museum.*

25. Østerlar parish church, Bornholm. *Danish Travel Assoc.*

26. Tveje-Merløse royal church, Denmark. *Nationalmuseet.*

27. Norre Alslev parish church, Denmark. *Nationalmuseet.*

28 (*a*). Kaga royal church, Sweden. *ATA, Stockholm.*

    (*b*). Holy Trinity, Uppsala, Sweden. *STF Bildarkiv.*

29 (*a*). St. Maria, Visby, bridal porch. *ATA, Stockholm.*

    (*b*). Stånga parish church, Gotland, porch. *ATA, Stockholm.*

30. Stånga parish church, Gotland, font. *ATA, Stockholm.*

31. Hattula parish church, Finland, interior. *Finland Architecture Museum.*

32 (*a*). Dalhem parish church, Gotland, stained glass. *ATA, Stockholm.*

    (*b*). Södra Råda parish church, Sweden, interior. *ATA, Stockholm.*

33 (*a*). Rone parish church, Gotland, interior. *ATA, Stockholm.*

    (*b*). Täby parish church, Sweden, interior. *ATA, Stockholm.*

34 (*a*). Borgund stave church, Norway. *Normann.*

    (*b*). Lom stave church, Norway, interior. *Normann.*

35 (*a*). Hoprekstad stave church, Norway, carved doorway. *O. Vaering.*

    (*b*). Urnes stave church, Norway, carved doorway. *O. Vaering.*

36. Hyllestad stave church, Norway, carved relief (Oldsak Collection, Oslo University). *O. Vaering.*

37. Olofsborg, Finland. *Wickberg.*

38 (*a*). Glimmingehus, Skåne. *Riksantikvarieämbetet.*

    (*b*). Malmöhus, Skåne. *Swed. Tourist Traffic Assoc.*

39. Hesselagergård, Denmark. *Jonals Co.*

40 (*a*). 'South Scandinavian' house, Setesdalen Valley, Norway.

    (*b*). Rosendal manor-house, Hardanger Fiord, Norway. *Neupert, Oslo.*

41 (*a*). Torup, Skåne. *Swed. Tourist Traffic Assoc.*

    (*b*). Skarhult, Skåne. *STF Bildarkiv.*

42 (*a*). Vadstena, Sweden, gable. *Swed. Tourist Traffic Assoc.*

    (*b*). Vadstena, entrance. *STF Bildarkiv.*

43 (*a*). Gripsholm, Sweden. *National Museum, Stockholm.*

    (*b*). Kalmar, Sweden, the well. *STF Bildarkiv.*

44 (*a*). Rydboholm, Sweden, painted panelling. *ATA, Stockholm.*

    (*b*). Gripsholm, Sweden, painted ceiling. *ATA, Stockholm.*

45. Kalmar, King Eric's State Chamber. *ATA, Stockholm.*

46 (*a*). Rosenholm, Denmark. *Nationalmuseet.*

    (*b*). Ulstrup, Denmark. *Nationalmuseet.*

FIGURES IN TEXT

Sources of illustrations (see also List of Books, p. 245)

Bugge: A. Bugge, *Norske stavkirker,* 1953.

Cornell: H. Cornell, *Den svenska konstens historia,* vol. I, 1944.

Dahlberg: E. Dahlberg, *Suecia antiqua et hodierna,* 1661–1716.

Lundberg, 1940: E. Lundberg, *Byggnadskonsten i Sverige 1000–1400,* 1940.

Lundberg, 1942: E. Lundberg, *Svensk bostad,* 1942.

Lundberg, 1948: E. Lundberg, *Byggnadskonsten . . . senmedeltid och renässans,* 1948.

Millech: K. Millech, *Danske arkitekturstrømninger,* 1951.

Thurah: L. de Thurah, *Hafnia hodierna,* 1748, and *Den danske Vitruvius,* 1749.

Wanscher: V. Wanscher, *Danmarks arkitektur,* 1943.

Abbreviations, sources in Stockholm

ATA: Antikvarisk-topografiska arkivet.

SAR: Svenska arkitekters riksförbund.

STF: Svenska turist föreningen.

Part One

THE EMERGENCE OF SCANDINAVIA

I

THE REGIONAL UNITY

FROM the point of view of the rest of the world, Scandinavia may appear to be a single regional unit. Yet this one region has produced within itself a variety of cultural idiosyncrasies to which the architecture of its several states bears witness. The numerous similarities, however, geographical and linguistic as well as cultural, are great enough to justify the writing of one book on Scandinavian architecture instead of four.

This unity has, of course, altered with the course of time. It was exceptionally strong when these coasts and forests were first being populated by related hunting tribes, but it is almost as strong now. Political structure has changed since the days of the hunters, since the time when each province formed one more or less independent kingdom, since the days of the Kalmar Union in the early fifteenth century when these countries were briefly united under one queen, to the autonomous nations of today. Of course the different countries have had their several histories. Sweden and Denmark have fought many a war between them, battling for the dominance of Scandinavia, but in the long run those many similarities and interests which they have in common have always conquered any separatist tendency.

The emergence of these common traits and interests grew from a common concern with the waters of the sea and the rivers as links and stepping-stones rather than barriers. Colonization in all probability started from the south along the coasts, and from there men penetrated inland along the rivers and across the lakes. Soon they became braver, and by way of numerous archipelagoes they colonized most of the shores of the Baltic. This often involved fighting with the Slavs. Skilful navigation during the Viking era spread Nordic culture abroad with a geographical sweep similar to the colonizing of the Greeks.

This uniting power of the waterways also explains the finer

regional division that one has to bear in mind for a full understand‑ing of Scandinavia. It was quite natural that the South Swedish provinces should be linked with Denmark by means of Öresund, 'the Sound' (see map, Fig. 1). North and east of Blekinge were vast wild areas of ridges and forests and these for a long time formed the natural frontier between Sweden and Denmark. It is for the same sort of reason that Norway later became Danish territory; it was easier for the Danes to sail across the Kattegat and Skagerrak than for the Swedes to cross the mountains. These turned their interest towards the east, colonizing the lands that later became Fin‑land and the Baltic states.

A regional division, then, can be roughly outlined which in many ways corresponds to the pattern of architectural differences. South Scandinavia comprised Denmark of today—that is, Jylland (Jut‑land) and the Danish islands with Bornholm—as well as the South Swedish provinces Skåne, Blekinge, and Halland. West Scandi‑navia included the present Norway and the Swedish provinces Bohuslän and, further north, Jämtland and Härjedalen. East Scandi‑navia consisted of the gradually united kingdoms of Svear and Götar, to which were added the coastal areas of Finland and the northern Baltic states with the islands Åland, Dagö, and Ösel. Then there was Iceland, from early times closely connected with Norway and later with Denmark; and finally, Gotland, which be‑cause of its excellent trading position in the middle of the Baltic soon became the point of exchange between the fur‑trading hunters of the north‑eastern forests and the salt and metal merchants from the northern parts of the Continent. With this wealth the prosperous town of Visby could maintain its independence against the peasant population of the rest of Gotland and the other Nordic kingdoms, until with the end of the fourteenth century and the travelling of trade along new paths, the island declined in importance.

South Scandinavia is a fertile, level country with few forests. By exporting large quantities of farm products it was long the leader in Scandinavia from a cultural point of view. A contributing factor was its proximity to the rest of Europe.

West Scandinavia was a poorer region. The country is inter‑sected with mountains and fiords, and farming was possible only in small areas, usually isolated valleys. Much of the Norwegian hinter‑land has had little contact with other cultures, and it was quite

4

FIG. 1. Scandinavia.

natural that many Norwegian valleys should preserve a certain independence along with retarded customs in building. This means that Norway can display a fine variety of local building traditions.

East Scandinavia occupied a middle position. It is neither completely flat nor sharply mountainous. Farming there, in contrast to that of Denmark, has been based on the small freeholder rather than the large-scale farmer. Swedish farming could not be carried out in the more rational—from a modern point of view—South Scandinavian way, and no export worth mentioning took place. What agriculture was to Denmark the export of copper and, later, iron ore and timber was to Sweden.

This definition of large regions has been deliberately simplified. Within each of these are smaller areas with their own character, such as the Swedish Bergslagen, Dalecarlia, the different Norwegian valleys, and so on. The importance and individuality of some of these regions will become apparent later in the book.

The political boundaries of today's Scandinavia do not exactly correspond to those mentioned above. The countries have regrouped politically; new means of transport and new methods of waging war have brought about new laws, no longer peculiarly regional. Norway, Finland, and Iceland have become independent states, and the Swedish culture in the northern Baltic states has been wiped out by Russian expansion. But, seen from an architectural angle, the regional laws have often been stronger than political boundary lines, with an existence independent of such barriers.

II

PREHISTORY AND COLONIZATION

THE thick layer of ice that for three long periods covered the greater part of northern Europe receded from Scandinavia last of all. This took a long time: around 12,000 B.C. the ice started to melt in South Scandinavia; 3,000 years later it was still melting in the middle of Sweden. The weight of the ice had been so heavy upon the land that when the ice finally disappeared South Scandinavia was under water. Having got rid of the ice, however, the land began to rise. This elevation, which is still going on today, was more rapid in the south and slowest in the north-eastern parts of the Scandinavian peninsula. Sweden and Norway were linked to the Continent by Denmark; the Baltic Sea was an inland sea with outlets through rivers running into the Atlantic.

It is supposed that Scandinavia was populated by hunters who went north following the receding ice. It is not known for certain who these hunters were and where they came from, and against the theory that they came from the south stands the fact that man had survived in the extreme north and north-west of Scandinavia all through the glaciation period just as the Eskimoes of today live close to the borders of the ice in Greenland. These early inhabitants left very vague traces of culture behind, few not only because of a severe climate but also because these were wandering hunters with no need for a settled community organization or any other form of organized environment.

A remarkable change took place about 3000 B.C. Parts of the land in the south became submerged anew, and the warmer waters of the Atlantic flowed into the Baltic through the Great and Little Belts and Öresund. This meant a change in the climate, and so it meant new and altered conditions of life. The nomadic hunter was replaced by the farmer who settled down and stored corn and kept cattle; he would stay in one place year after year and his children and grandchildren after him. And so was born a firmer organization of

7

society arranged according to a more practical attitude towards life and other men. The results were dwellings and storehouses—all since destroyed—and more ceremonious and permanent burial customs. These Stone Age settlers buried their dead in so-called chamber tombs. Their culture was able to establish itself and expand in spite of the resistance which undoubtedly was put up by the older hunting inhabitants. A comparison between the primitive weapons of the hunters and the skilfully designed flint-axes and knives of the new tribes is significant.

The Stone Age ended about 1500 B.C. and was succeeded by the Bronze Age, in its turn followed by the Iron Age around 500 B.C. Little is known about the building achievements of these two periods. We know their burial customs, however: while in the Stone Age men buried their dead in cairns and single tombs of stone, new customs were introduced in the Bronze Age, when tombs were large mounds of earth or stones, in which were laid weapons and ornaments.

During the Bronze Age there appeared an unmistakable desire for artistic expression. Above all this is clear in the rock carvings of Bohuslän and western Norway which are still well preserved. Unfortunately we cannot read all of the symbolic language, but parts of the carvings tell about hunting men and fighting youths, about large ships manned with many rowers, and there was a sun-and-fertility worship, natural reaction to a milder climate. By this time an amalgamation between the older and the younger peoples had no doubt taken place.

But again there came a change mainly due to the climate: the temperature fell, the struggle for life became harder once more. We can but guess what happened when the Iron Age developed around 500 B.C. We can assume that the Bronze Age people could not stand up to the severe Nordic weather that succeeded the Mediterranean-like climate that had been prevailing in Scandinavia. Teutonic tribes appear on the stage and it is very likely that they were the creators of Nordic Iron Age culture.

With the arrival of the Teutonic people a break in cultural progress occurs. Originally these were a barbaric nomadic race who surged westward in savage waves from their home country in the Don Basin. Because of their own nomadic existence they despised other people's organized societies and tried to destroy any culture that came in their way. Their path towards western Europe was a waste of plunder and burning. But like their southern relatives who soon adopted Roman civilization, the Teutons who settled in Scandinavia began to accept the habits and traditions of the original inhabitants. It is therefore not at all contradictory that the Iron Age people should have made ships similar to the ones pictured on the Bronze Age rock carvings. As was the case in southern Europe the Scandinavian Teutons also became farmers. They lived close to the land and grouped their dwellings in villages, finding that they needed each other to run the land as they needed each other in times of war and catastrophe. Each farmer had his land divided into several small fields; to start with, a farmer did not take more land than he thought manageable at the time. When later he became more prosperous, he had to look for new fields further away, beyond the land already occupied by others. This pattern of land ownership—which was practised in Sweden until the nineteenth-century Enskifte, or law of land redistribution—made the farmers dependent on one another's help. The cultivation of the land became a communal matter and all important tasks were carried out by the *byalag,* or council of men of the village.

The law of the Teutons was not a written law like that of the Romans, but an accumulation of rights based upon custom, like the English common law. The most eminent men of the village were the judges and out of those emerged one who became their chieftain and later on their king. The desire to follow him meant no submission; in the very much later Law of Västergötland we read that the leader was rejected quite often if he did not carry out his duties to the satisfaction of his men. The structure of the community was that of a collective democracy.

All production necessary for the household took place within the household itself, and so there was as yet no local trade. Many years were to pass before any market towns grew up. This, then, was the basic organization of a civilization in which the large household and its cultivation of the land absorbed the main creative power. It was not until much later that the church and town emerged as parallel factors in the community.

The first Teutonic settlers in Scandinavia must be regarded partly as colonists of the wilderness. The daily work on the farm, the administration of community matters, and protection against enemies and dangers took such a major part of the peasant's time and energy for so long that the Scandinavians were not ready to expand and attack the failing Roman Empire until several hundreds of years later than their neighbours to the south. The span of life was short. With the simple implements that farmers had, crops grew unwillingly and only after hard toil and labour. The Nordic songs and epics, composed in the form in which we know them long after the times described here, have an exceptionally laconic quality. A corresponding temperance and lack of extravagance is noticeable in the early architecture of Scandinavia. Perhaps the explanation is to be found in the hard life of its farmers.

III

THE IRON AGE HOUSE

DURING the first period of the Iron Age the Nordic Teutons came into little or no contact with Mediterranean culture. The Teutons in Germany were much closer to it; not only did they go ravaging across the Rhine several times before their northern neighbours went down that way, but they were also employed by the Romans in France and were sometimes allowed to farm Roman land in order to keep them quiet—a policy that only postponed trouble. It was not until the time of the birth of Christ that the Nordic races encountered the Romans; archaeologists call this period in Scandinavia the Roman Iron Age. Examples of Iron Age dwellings that have been found can be regarded as national and original.

The typical house (Fig. 2) was rectangular and can be described as consisting only of a high curving roof with the slope starting at ground level and built of a latticework of rafters held in position by ridge-pieces which were supported by slender poles and cross-beams.

FIG. 2.
Iron Age house, reconstruction.

The rafters and poles were either stuck down into the ground or rested against a low stone foundation to preserve them from rot. The house was covered by straw, turf, or rushes. If the house was a small one, it had only one row of poles with the ridge at the top in the middle, a double-aisled house. If larger, with two rows of vertical poles carrying two ridges, the house became triple-aisled. In order to prevent the two ridges from pressing towards each other by the weight of the roof the poles were held apart by transverse beams. Primitive dwelling places of this kind are of course no longer in use in Scandinavia, but there are barns and outhouses with a similar roof construction.

A related type of 'roof house' is still to be found in use in the Hebrides and Shetland Islands, but these have walled-in hearths with chimneys in one or both gables, while the Iron Age home had an open hearth in the middle of the house with a louver in the roof above it. Furthermore, the Hebridean home has built-up thick stone walls three or four feet above ground; there is a distinction between the wall and the roof. The grouping of houses in the original Hebridean villages, with their narrow strips of land where open ditches afford the only drainage, gives a fairly clear picture of the structure of a Scandinavian Iron Age village.

This type of house was the only one in existence until the century of the birth of Christ when the Scandinavians discovered the Roman Empire. These encounters grew lively with the coming of the Vikings.

Part Two

THE AGE OF THE PEASANTRY

IV

CIVILIZATION AND
OUTWARD TRENDS

THE Teutonic people who had settled in Scandinavia were better equipped to stand up to the harsh Nordic climate than the earlier inhabitants and with the help of their iron they could construct better ploughs and sow in a better-prepared ground. They had come to stay; and so the germ of culture and civilization began to grow.

The centuries just before and after the birth of Christ are wrapped in obscurity. The written references to Scandinavia that Greek and Latin historians have left behind cast a little light upon the times. Indigenous sources are much younger, with so much saga interwoven among the facts that one must interpret them with care.

After some time, kingdoms crystallized in Scandinavia. The process started in the south and west, where Denmark and Norway emerged—with very vaguely defined frontiers—and went on further north where the Götar and Svear established their own states, the Svear not until A.D. 500. These kingdoms fluctuated in size. Wars against frontier chieftains who could recognize no other ruler but themselves were common. Exactly when the kingdoms of Sweden, Norway, and Denmark were established is not known, but we do know that in the ninth century there were kings in Norway, and it is supposed that Denmark was united under one king even sooner.

In Sweden the Svear became the strongest element. They had settled long before in Uppland and Roslagen with Gamla Uppsala as their centre and had begun cultivating the soil that had risen from under the water. It was not until about A.D. 1000 that the rest of Sweden became part of the Svear kingdom, most likely in the reign of King Olof Skötkonung.

These first centuries of Nordic civilization were distinguished chiefly by a profound unrest; when not at war with each other, they became involved in the great transformations which were part of the attack against the Roman Empire. Their first slight acquaintance

15

with the culture of Rome, brought to them through neighbouring nations in the south, had profound effects upon their ways of living. We must regard these first centuries of the new civilization as a time of inner colonization. New land was tilled, the habits of the village became traditions, and society was more secure.

From a Continental point of view, influenced from the Mediter-ranean, this society to the north no doubt seemed young and bar-baric. Connections were at first peaceful; the Scandinavians traded fur and amber for precious metals, spices, and salt. A trade route was soon established from Novgorod by way of Visby on Gotland, Hedeby in Denmark, and so southward.

When the Scandinavian countries had established themselves and were beginning to live in relative tranquillity on what in our view would seem a very modest scale, within their own borders, the time had come for expansion. To start with, it was slow and insignificant: Norwegians and Swedes travelled to Iceland, the Swedes navigated the Baltic Sea and the Gulf of Finland; for instance, the Svear from Uppland founded Grobin in Latvia.

But other times were still to come; and the Northmen enter the history of Europe in the ninth century with the Viking campaigns. These campaigns are to be regarded as high-handed trading and colonizing enterprises. There were enormous riches to be obtained from the borderlands of the disintegrating Roman Empire, where trade—and raids—could flourish. The numerous rune stones erected by surviving sons or wives who were left behind often tell a tale of transactions involving the sword and a fight to the death.

The geographical situation of each of the Scandinavian kingdoms dictated the direction in which their several populations went. The Danes turned to England, which in the early eleventh century was to be ruled by Danish kings. Many outhouses and sheepfolds in northern England today bear witness, in type and general outline, to days of the Danelaw. When Alfred the Great, in the ninth cen-tury, forced the Danes back, they turned their attentions to France, where the new colony of Normandy was founded. The Norwegians sailed to Scotland and Ireland, to Iceland and Greenland, even perhaps to North America.

The Swedes at first helped their neighbours in the south to bring home the Danegeld, but soon they continued their earlier way east-ward. They sailed down the Russian rivers to Constantinople, and on their way left colonies along the Dnieper. Many tales have been told about the fame-seeking Northmen and their heroic deeds in the south, these tall men who never left their swords behind. We cannot deny—and here we have Arabic sources and actual finds of coins in our day—that the wealth they brought home was considerable, even when measured by our standards. Still more important, however, was the intangible booty of ideas brought back from the more developed societies of Europe and Asia Minor.

V

HEARTH HOUSE AND
GALLERY HOUSE

THE Iron Age roof house was a primitive affair in both construction
and function. It consisted of only one room where all household
tasks and all indoor life went on. When southern building customs
began to penetrate Scandinavia, it is not surprising that at first the
Northmen only adopted the most elementary ones; they did not
understand the others. Since it was the one-room house that they
chose to imitate, we cannot yet speak about any differentiation of use.
But constructively this house was really new.

This new house (Fig. 3) has been called the hearth house, from
the hearth in the middle of the floor with a vent hole in the roof
above it which also provided the only light, as there were no windows. The entrance was placed in the centre of one of the gables,
with the roof extended, and sometimes the walls, to form a porch.

This hearth house was built of timber in a corner-joint technique.
The walls were logs laid one above the other, each log being grooved
on the underside to fit into the log beneath. In the corners the logs
were joined together in the typical rough notches. The ridge-piece
was a horizontal log let into the gables, and supporting a roof of
sawn boards set close together and covered with birch bark to make
it waterproof. On top of this was another board roof to keep the
bark in place and prevent it from splitting. This type of timber
roof was mostly used in the northern regions. The outer boards
were supported at the eaves by wooden brackets, but were sometimes
joined together at the ridge in different methods of 'buttoning'. In
southern Scandinavia where timber was less plentiful, the roofs
were covered with turf to keep the birch bark in place—a technique
that is still in use.

This sort of construction, which is very simple, is also very solid.
The entire structure of such a house was an entity, and with the passing of the years the joints pressed more and more firmly together by

18

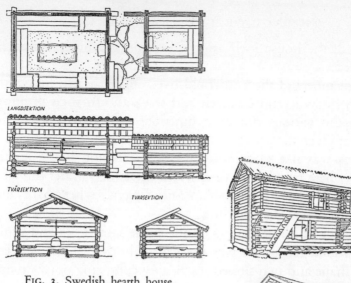

LANGDSEKTION

TVÄRSEKTION

TVÄRSEKTION

FIG. 3. Swedish hearth house.

FIG. 4. Swedish gallery house.

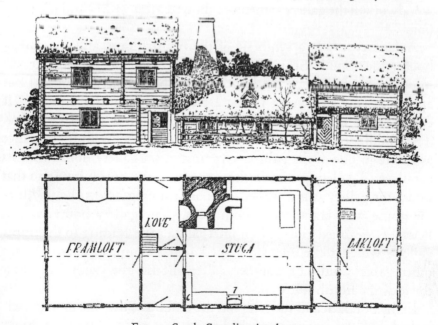

FRAMLOFT   KOVE   STUGA   BAKLOFT

FIG. 5. South Scandinavian house.

the weight of the house itself and so became absolutely watertight and insulated.

All the members of the household lived in the hearth house, the master with his wife and children and servants. In such primitive conditions, the various domestic functions had hardly been dif ferentiated or given their proper setting. But life in the Scandinavian hearth house was not so primitive as in the Saxon house on the Continent, where people and their livestock resided under the same roof, an embroilment unheard of in Scandinavia, where barns and storehouses were separate buildings.

Another type of house (Fig. 4) built at the same time and in the same corner joint technique was the gallery house. This was rect angular in shape and two storied, each story consisting of two rooms with no connection between them and entered from the outside, the upstairs rooms from a gallery running along the front of the house and reached by a wooden outdoor staircase. Originally the upper rooms were used for storage, but quite early they were furnished with wooden beds fixed to the walls. In Norway the houses were also equipped with hearths at a fairly early stage and the gallery house was then really used as a residence, not only as a guest house or summer residence. The small windows had sliding shutters and the carved woodwork of the gallery sometimes showed great variety and imagina tion.

A later type was a synthesis of the hearth house and the gallery house: the 'South Scandinavian house' (Fig. 5). It became the most common type in South and West Scandinavia, but did not appear in Sweden except in the extreme south, near Denmark. It consisted of three—sometimes only two—houses joined together. The middle section was a one room hearth house, with the entrance as before in one of the gables. Against this a gallery house with its cantilevered gallery protected the entrance of the hearth house so that under the gallery was a walled in room running across the width of the house with entrances at both ends. The gallery house was, as before, two storied and had an internal staircase leading to the upper gallery, which sometimes developed into a room, or *kove*. At the other gable would be another gallery house also with its gallery towards the hearth house.

In the South Scandinavian plan the outhouses became more closely linked with the main part of the house. It is believed that the gallery house in front, that is to say the house over the main entrance, was formerly used for storage only, but the house at the back was usually built on top of a brick cellar and contained an inner living-room. This increased complexity, then, signified a higher standard of housing. Naturally the fact that the inhabitants had more space for living, and for storage close at hand, meant a greater step towards a civilized life than the cramped hearth house alone could allow.

The roof of this house had a very slight pitch, as had the earlier types. According to some theories it was because these houses were so firmly established in rural Scandinavia that the steeper Gothic roof could never replace the flatter classic roof outside the towns. But one must also remember that in the cold North it was essential to keep the snow on the roofs for insulation.

In many old South Scandinavian houses fireplaces with chimneys were built in later. The vent hole in the roof is still there, now only serving the purpose of a skylight.

This style of house varied in detail in different parts of Scandinavia. In Skåne and Denmark, where it soon outnumbered all other types, an old roofing method derived from the Iron Age roof house still prevailed, and here people were more inclined to cover all the separate units under one roof. The separate elements are easily recognizable, however: the line between the hearth house and the gallery house runs along a transverse passage with entrances in both ends—this is the old built-in gallery.

Because of timber shortage South Scandinavia soon discovered another building technique. The use of thick timber, or whole logs, was restricted to the framework which supported the walls and roof, the space in between being filled with horizontally placed boards. This technique later developed into another, using still less timber, the so-called half-timber technique, where the frame was filled in with earth and plaster.

On Gotland there were two versions of the South Scandinavian house. The gallery house was either built alongside the hearth house, in which case the two units had separate entrances, or the gallery house was turned sideways as on the mainland and the two houses then had an internal communication by means of the built-in gallery.

In many Norwegian valleys another variation came into use, as for example in Setesdalen (Pl. 40a), where the gallery house at the

21

back of the hearth house had galleries running along three sides instead of just one. These houses display a remarkable diversity of rich ornament, a native performance that was perfected without benefit of outside 'influence'.

It is not known just when these house types were introduced into Scandinavia, but they are regarded as ultimately derived from Greek and Cretan cultures. The hearth-house plan conforms with that of the Greek *megaron,* originally a northern Greek type and not at all like the southern, Oriental *pastas* type. The similarity between the hearth house and more recent megarons such as Megaron B at Thermos is especially noticeable. The difference is in the number of rooms, the megaron having had two, the hearth house only one. The porch of the latter coincides with that of the megaron, whose entrance *in antis* always faced south and was sheltered by this outdoor room. The prototypes of the gallery house are said to have been the palaces of Crete with peristyle courtyards and galleried upper stories that also appeared to some extent on the Greek mainland.

It may be a bit difficult to see the prototypes of the simple Scandinavian houses in complicated classical buildings, whose functions the Northmen undoubtedly did not appreciate, but it has been pointed out that the farmhouses which still exist around the Mediterranean can provide the missing link. These farmhouses are often two-storied and all along one side runs a gallery, where most of the daily work of the housewife takes place, especially her work at the loom.

The more complex South Scandinavian house may well have had a much more winding and longer way to travel, but it also must have originated in classical times. It is interesting to speculate on its ancestry, by way of England and the Merovingians back to Rome and Greece. Why the Saxon house—which herded families, cattle, food, and fodder all together—was not acceptable to Scandinavians is not known. The Scandinavians must have had a higher regard for human beings than the Saxons, who were 'younger', culturally. In Scandinavia only the dwellings had any sort of heating. All other activities were relegated to independent outhouses or to quite separate parts of the main house.

In the hearth house the master sat in the place of honour among his family and servants. The furniture consisted of wooden benches fixed to the wall, beds, and tables. The walls were hung with tapestries which helped to keep out the draughts. Throughout the community, from rich farmer down to small freeholder, the pattern of living was the same—it was only a matter of difference in size. All around the house were barns, cattle-sheds, larders, etc. grouped together. In East Scandinavia these were all separate buildings, but in the south they were built together in ranges on three or four sides of a courtyard, as part of a compact whole.

VI

ROYAL ESTATES AND
TOWN BEGINNINGS

THE basis of the firmer structure of the Scandinavian community was mainly the power of the ruling kings. In order to strengthen his economic and political position a monarch set his own manor-houses about the countryside. The management of such an estate was entrusted to a steward especially appointed by the king. In Sweden place names with suffixes like -husby, -tuna, and -bo reveal the existence of such estates.

Another system that also aimed at a strengthened communal organization was the dividing of the country into hundreds, or, as they were called in the coastal districts, ledung. Each hundred was obliged to put one or more soldiers at the king's disposal.

Moreover, it was the king who supported the missionary work of Christianity. The missionaries lived in the king's house, or in the house of one of his men, and they held their sermons and baptized in the chapels that were built on the royal estates. Therefore we know for certain where the first churches were built. It must be noted that they were not built exactly on the old ritual sites. But the missionary was eager to compete with old pagan beliefs and traditions that were tough to root out, and he built his chapel as close to the pagan temple as he could and dared.

The fact that the agrarian household was self-supporting so far as the basic food and utensils and clothing were concerned did not now mean that there was no trade. The farmers depended on two things which they did not produce: salt and iron. To buy these they sold butter and cattle. Markets, then, grew up where such exchanges of goods took place. The kings, apparently, tried to control these markets from the beginning; it suited their finances and bolstered their status to do so. The king would grant the use of a field on one of his own estates as a market-place. The place name Sigtuna, which frequently occurs in Sweden, reminds us of these

24

ancient market-places, for some of them expanded during the eleventh century and became market villages, called Sigtuna-places after the town Sigtuna by Lake Mälaren. They all grew according to the same pattern, a concentration of farms around a road junction, close to which stood the parish church. The market-place at Lund in Skåne (Fig. 6) was situated north of the village proper, on a site now occupied by Lund Cathedral.

Similar market towns, a century younger, have names ending in -*köping* or -*købing*, derived from *kaupung*, which means 'buying field'. Such towns are Ringkøbing in Denmark and Söderköping in Sweden.

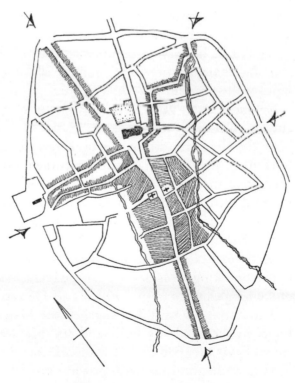

FIG. 6.
Lund, Skåne, in early
medieval times.

VII

ECCLESIASTICAL BUILDINGS
BEFORE 1500

DURING the eleventh century Scandinavia came into contact with Europe in more mature and less explosive ways than the Vikings had, and connections were established with other parts of Europe besides England and Normandy. From this time onward Scandinavia was part of Western civilization, and the stream of cultural influences drawn towards the north became richer and more complicated.

From the moment that Scandinavia took its part in European cultural affairs—assuredly a very minor part to start with—cultural and political developments there were analogous to those in other countries. There were the same three powers, each creating its own specific and important domain: the powers of feudalism, religion, and trade. The varying dominance and interaction of these powers and the changeful intensity of their effects on medieval life were signs of the times in Scandinavia, too.

Favoured by its geographical situation, more fertile soil and better climate, Denmark soon took the lead. The fact that they had been both absorbed and driven out by England and Normandy did not discourage the Danes, who now turned eastward. In 1219 they conquered the Estonians and Tallinn, the castle of the Danes, was founded there. Valdemar II ruled the Baltic and vast areas in North Germany. The Swedes, who already had a proprietary interest in the eastern shores of the Baltic further north, quite frequently collided with the Danes, who wanted, moreover, to unite all of Scandinavia under one king. Medieval Scandinavian history is largely the tale of the long duel between Sweden and Denmark.

The numerous wars that engaged the Danes, against their neighbours in the south, as well, and the peasants' revolts and private feudal fights they had to deal with, all tended to weaken the country. This gave the third medieval power, the Hanseatic League, towards the middle of the thirteenth century, its chance to get into the Nordic countries; the duel became a three-cornered fight. Hanseatic towns grew up all along the coast of the Baltic; later also, in other seas, they went as far north as Bergen in Norway. Through the Hanseatic League new elements appear in the field: the merchants and their towns, originally with a strong Germanic tinge, and fairly evenly distributed all over Scandinavia. The Hanse's hold over the towns along the Sound was probably firmer than in the purely Swedish towns on the Baltic.

During the Middle Ages the agrarian community was recon-structed. The aristocracy, or *frälse* as it is called in Swedish, emerged from the farmer class as a social class by itself. The pattern was the Continental feudal system: in return for certain services the yeoman was sure of protection from his feudal baron. In Sweden, however, the feudal system did not develop in quite the same manner as in Denmark. The farmers were granted freedom in Sweden from both king and Church provided they paid taxes to both. Thus a private feudal system was prevented—there were some exceptions. But the king, that is, the central State, was the foremost feudal lord, and an alliance was formed between king and farmer. This phenomenon runs all through Swedish history as a continuous thread: the king always depended on the farmers; not even in times of absolute monarchy has the king broken the law in his relation to the farmers. This was the background for the king's (and later his noblemen's) battle against the Church and its, very often, Danish interests. When in the year 1514 Sten Sture the Younger successfully besieged the castle of the Archbishop of Uppsala at Stäket, most of the men in his army were peasants.

The feudal system in Denmark had a more disintegrating charac-ter. Admittedly the king was usually stronger than the feudal barons, but he needed their good will. The two-front wars against the Hanseatic League and Holstein during the early fourteenth century were to a great extent financed by loans from German lords who received vast areas of Danish land as security for their money. The door was opened to Central European feudalism, Holstein noble-men reigned in Danish castles, the king could even be driven out of his country, and the farmers were oppressed. Later on these became serfs: in the middle of the fifteenth century, serfdom was a fact. It is to be noted that in Denmark the results of the Black Death were different than in England. Valdemar Atterdag, who reassembled the Danish kingdom, drew in all the estates under the Crown: because of the crying lack of working-power caused by the Black Death and the great immigration to the Hanse towns, peasants were forbidden to leave the farms on which they worked.

Long before Luther had nailed his doctrines on the Wittenberg church door, doctrines which would help to turn the cultural flow in Europe into a new course, there was a flourishing antagonism between the Church and the monarchy in Sweden. Generally speaking, one can say that the Kalmar Union in 1437 meant an advantage for the Church in Scandinavia, the power of the Nordic archbishops being considerably increased during this period. Copenhagen, which had been a free city governed by its inhabitants, fell back to the feudal position of a Danish bishopric. The union did not mean, however, that the battle between nationalism and internationalism in Sweden was ended, only that there was an interval. At last, after many attempts by his predecessors, Gustavus Vasa (ruled 1523–60) succeeded in crushing the three powers that obstructed a strong monarchy in Sweden: the Church, the feudal system, and the Hanseatic League.

The feudal barons in Scandinavia were never as well off financially as their counterparts on the Continent, and in splendour never reached southerly heights. There was no chivalric poetry worth mentioning, although there was no lack of good intentions. A certain amount of courtly life of an unpolitical character was carried on. Karl Knutsson (Charles VIII) on the Swedish throne did what he could to introduce the more refined customs of the Burgundian court. Christian I, who was ruling Denmark, rather shakily, at the time of the battle of Brunkeberg in 1471, in which the Danes were thoroughly beaten by the Swedish army, was not at all discouraged by this because it allowed him to go off and pay a visit to Bartolomeo Colleoni in Venice.

Because there was less wealth to squander, castles both profane and ecclesiastical were less gigantic and numerous than in Germany or France. But the layout of a Scandinavian castle in the Middle Ages—strategic position, defensive arrangements, and the dwelling within—entirely accorded with recognized feudal principles.

Of the three powers that each created its specific environment during the Middle Ages, the Church was not only the most important influence in Scandinavian history but also the first to leave its mark. After its appearance on Nordic soil during the ninth century, the Church was to dominate architecturally for several centuries. Not until the beginning of the fifteenth century, when the ecclesiastical building programme was more or less completed, did this activity diminish. During the fifteenth century some rebuilding went on; some choirs were enlarged, and in parish churches new windows and vaults were put in. But on the whole the power of the Church was worn out. It surged up later under a new impetus.

When describing buildings anywhere, one cannot treat them simply as styles following styles—an arid form of narration that in this case would only be an attempt to deprive Scandinavia of all originality. Stylistic description we cannot wholly do without, but I should like the monuments to be recognized as representing different building programmes, as results of the decided will of different sorts of patrons. To understand a church, or other building, we must know what various functions, and whose, it was meant to perform. Whether its walls are Saxon or Norman is a secondary question, however interesting that may be.

Here I must underline the fact that Scandinavia could not begin by creating her own building tradition, being such a remote part of the organization of the Church and doubtless from an educated ecclesiastic's point of view amounting to cultural wilderness. So much that came there from outside during the Middle Ages was new. Add to this the fact that poverty limits great enterprises, and all the experience that could be gained from them.

There as elsewhere, various bodies were concerned with building churches: the king and (at first) his missionaries; the bishops in their sees; the monks and friars and nuns; the merchant companies of the trading towns; and the peasants in their parishes. Obviously such diverse patrons looked to different models for inspiration. Since most things were imported to start with, it is necessary to recall a little of the architectural situation in eleventh- and twelfth-century Europe.

Four clearly distinguishable architectural regions, each in its turn, contributed to medieval Scandinavian architecture: in the south, Lombardy; in the north, the imperial nucleus in western Germany; in the centre, France south of the Loire valley; in the north-west, Normandy and England.

The English element was conservative at first, in the nature of such Anglo-Saxon churches as Boarhunt, Hants, with rectangular nave and choir, or Bradford-on-Avon, Wilts., which had lateral porches as well. This type of church had only narrow openings between the separate compartments. More complicated inspiration was later provided by the early twelfth-century cathedrals. The Norman element can be represented by St. Etienne at Caen, before the extension of the choir: a triple-aisled basilica with transept and three semicircular apses. Many early Nordic cathedrals were built on this plan.

The Lombardic region—the classic example would be S. Ambrogio in Milan—created in the twelfth century triple-aisled basilicas with or without transepts vaulted according to the Lombardic system with one vault in the nave corresponding to two in the aisles. The characteristic Lombardic decoration of blind arcades, applied column strips, and eaves galleries is noticeable on some Scandinavian cathedrals of the twelfth century. Already through the German-Roman alliance this style had penetrated northward along the Rhine, becoming 'Rheno-Lombardic', with new German values added to the old. The plan continued basically conservative, often adhering to the old tradition of the double-ended church with both eastern and western choirs between which antiphonal chanting was exchanged. Some of these were cathedrals built for the Holy Roman Emperor, as at Speyer, where the interior elevation included an imperial tribune, or throne. Outside, the emphasis was vertical, with an array of towers. A more conservative example was the abbey at Laach, begun at the end of the eleventh century.

Westphalia and Lower Saxony adopted and developed certain Lombardic features, which later influenced church-builders in Scandinavian trading towns at the beginning of the thirteenth century.

We are not concerned with the part of France north of the Loire valley, where local schools developed at an early stage an architecture much more complicated than the others. So far as Scandinavia was concerned, the Burgundian monuments were the best known and the most interesting. Auvergne, Perigord, etc. are of no importance in this connection. It was mainly through the Benedictine monks that the northerners learned of the style of Burgundian building. The so-called Cluny II and III became prototypes, and later on through the Cistercians, Fontenay as it stood originally and then as it was rebuilt in 1174 with a new choir.

Finally there are the parish churches, which clearly had to be very simple because the parishes were so poor. Each was the centre of its community. The priest was usually a relatively uneducated man who had learned the Latin mass by heart. His church was not only a religious centre but the main meeting house for secular activities such as markets, which were actually held in the church. The overwhelming majority of parish churches in Scandinavia, several thousands in number, were built before the middle of the thirteenth century—that is to say, in times of continuous war and upheaval, and before Stockholm itself (first referred to in 1252) was founded. This was a tremendous achievement.

Christianity in Scandinavia

In 826 a missionary by the name of Ansgar, sent out by the Franks to christen the barbaric heathen in the north, came to Hedeby in Denmark and three years later he was in Birka, the central town of the Svear on Lake Mälaren. In both places he established short-lived Christian communities. Thirty years later he returned to Birka to start another, just as short-lived, Christian church. So the long and slow process of christening the Scandinavians had started, a process that would last for several hundred years and would not win a full victory until about 1100, when the pagan temple in Gamla (Old) Uppsala was finally destroyed. Apart from royal respect for purely religious conversion, the missionary work was undoubtedly regarded as a political instrument; where the sword had fallen short, rulers or would-be rulers now tried the Cross.

The first German missionary wave, supported by the Pope, who established a diocese of Hamburg-Bremen in 831, was an attempt at political as well as religious expansion, but it did not work. The traditional links with English culture may account for the fact that, as time went on, there came English monks who knew better how to link the new religion with the old; to begin with, they let the Vikings imagine Christ and his disciples as a chieftain with his warriors. Nevertheless their work must have been strenuous; the gap was wide between the new teaching of human dignity and the old pagan ideas of slaves, blood-feuds, and offerings.

The rune stone of Jellinge says that in 980 King Harold of

Denmark made the Danes Christians; during the next century English bishops came over. In the eleventh century the Danish King Canute established his empire in Norway and England. Later in the century, the Christian ruler of Norway, Olav Haraldsson, who had fallen in battle in 1030, was canonized: it was decided to build the cathedral at Trondheim as a reliquary for his bones. In Sweden there was a Christian centre at Skara around the beginning of the eleventh century and the Christian positions were moved further north with Sigtuna—the new centre after Birka—as an outpost towards pagan Gamla Uppsala. In 1103 Scandinavia got her own diocese in Lund and the work was crowned when in 1130 the Bishop of Sigtuna moved to Gamla Uppsala.

Wooden chapels were built for the preaching and baptizing by the first missionaries on the royal estates, but what these chapels looked like we cannot know since none survived into modern times. Most of the first churches of which we have any knowledge were wooden buildings constructed according to the technique preferred in the neighbourhood where they stood, generally either of logs in the corner-joint method or timber-framed with a filling of horizontal boards. The commonest type of all was the stave church, although few outside the secluded valleys of Norway survived replacement in stone or brick in Romanesque and Gothic times.

FIG. 7. Hemse, Gotland, early stave building technique.

If it took time to christen Scandinavia it took an equally long time to develop her church architecture. The small stave churches at Hedared in Västergötland and Hemse (Fig. 7) on Gotland show that both plan and elevation were strongly traditional. To start with, a rectangular form was adopted, perhaps that of the heathen temple although we have no real evidence how that looked. The temples are thought to have had a centralized plan, with a painted wooden image of the god in the middle. But churches demanded a longitudinal approach to the altar, and the plan had to be changed. A small choir was added to the eastern part of the nave, as an almost separate compartment. These wooden churches soon arose all over Scandinavia. Often connected with the farms, they far outnumbered the churches we have today.

To build these first stave churches, standing posts were joined together to form the walls. The bases of the posts were buried in the earth; at the top they were fitted into horizontal logs, or wall plates, joined at the corners and connected by tie beams across the width of the church. These together with the corner posts gave stability and carried the roof. In smaller buildings the corner posts were some-times omitted; in larger ones there were added rows of dug-down posts, making the churches double-aisled or triple-aisled. The stave churches always had this roof truss, derived from the construction of the old roof houses; but the hearth house and the gallery house did not.

St. Maria Minor at Lund, built in the eleventh century, was one of the larger churches so built, with two rows of interior posts to make the nave and choir triple-aisled. The stave churches of Nor-way, which continued this tradition long after it was abandoned everywhere else, will be dealt with later in this chapter (p. 76).

It is believed that the first church at Husaby was a simple building of the same character as Hedared and St. Maria Minor. According to legend, King Olof Skötkonung of Sweden was baptized in the well of Husaby at the beginning of the eleventh century. Even if the legend is not true, the name of Husaby implies that the land was on one of the royal estates and that the church was built by the king.

By 1057 at the latest an immense tower of stone had been added to Husaby church, partly as a rallying-point in times of war. The tower is square with smaller circular turrets attached on the north and south, originally higher than the tower itself. The material was yellow sandstone, and the masonry technique rather primitive. In its original state the tower stood at an angle to the old church. In about 1090 the old stave church was pulled down and one of stone erected in its place (Pl. 1). The new upper story of the tower was then built to hold the bells.

The new church, of finely cut sandstone, is clearly derived from an English type of church. It has a nave without a transept, a choir or chancel with semicircular apse, and formerly a prominent south porch (Fig. 8), with two subsidiary compartments added on the north. A notable detail is the narrow opening between nave and chancel. This cross-vaulted stone church at Husaby represents a type that took deep root in the Scandinavian countryside.

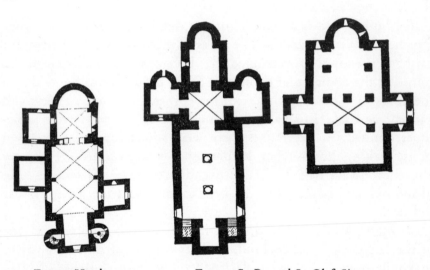

FIG. 8. Husaby.   FIG. 9. St. Per and St. Olof, Sigtuna.

A similar character is to be found in the plans (Fig. 9) of two churches at Sigtuna, St. Per and St. Olof (Pl. 2a), which today as ruins give evidence of the firm anchorage the Church had in eleventh-century Sigtuna. Both churches reveal a strong English and Norman influence—it was natural that this should be so. But neither is a direct copy of any foreign church. St. Per had a double-aisled nave with two piers down the centre, transepts consisting of an apsidal compartment either side of the crossing, and a choir with semicircular apse. St. Olof had a wide dwarfed nave (once perhaps longer) with transepts, and a triple-aisled choir with semicircular apse. The cruciform plan aimed at is not achieved by means of a regular transept but by added units on either side of the central tower. The passages between compartments of such churches were often narrow, making for a plan that was easily dissoluble into its constituent parts and not a true synthesis. Each of these two churches had a heavy central tower, a distinctly Anglo-Norman feature.

Irregularities and inconsistencies in plan were frequent. The central structural core was sometimes over-accentuated. Even at ground-floor level attention was drawn to the tower through more piers than were actually needed and which must have concealed much of the chancel from the people in the nave. This veiling of the priestly space from the laymen's space was characteristic of English churches, other than friars' churches, before the Reformation. The dressed native stone with which the Sigtuna churches were built became tradition in Uppland until bricks were introduced by friars and merchants from Germany.

St. Halvard's Cathedral in Oslo and the Benedictine church at Venge on Jylland in Denmark—built for English monks—are further examples of the firm entrenchment of this Anglo-Norman school in the whole of Scandinavia throughout the Missionary Age. A slightly older type is that of Botne church in Norway with neither transept nor apses.

In plan and elevation the Sigtuna churches set the fashion. The former cathedral at Gamla Uppsala (Pl. 2b) is an example, although once much longer than St. Per or St. Olof. Only the eastern part with the central tower remains, but from them we can see that once this was a considerable monument. Another example is Norrala in Hälsingland, and also the primitive Skånella in Uppland (Pl. 3a), which in spite of the small scale and the lack of transepts tried to copy the larger Sigtuna churches. The main impression given by these churches, whatever their scale, is of compact mass, small-windowed, low-roofed, set off by high towers.

To South Scandinavia Canute the Great brought English bishops, and probably English artisans as well, to Odense, Roskilde, and Lund; his grandchild Canute the Holy started and protected the extensive building of cathedrals in these places. Thus the first church buildings on a cathedral scale came under the same Anlgo-Norman influence as the earlier ones. There are only a few remains. Odense Cathedral was ravaged by fire in 1247 and has since been altered several times. Those at Roskilde and Lund had to give way to later ones: part of the old church is now included in the crypt of Lund Cathedral.

The plans varied somewhat. Roskilde had no transept, but a semicircular apse. Lund originally had a transept, with semicircular apses both in transepts and choir. It has been disputed at great length as to whether these cathedrals of Canute's were influenced in design by that of Bremen. It is much more likely that his English bishops turned to English builders, and the reverse might well have been possible: that Bremen was influenced by Anglo-Norman design.

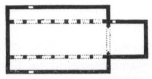

FIG. 10.
Dalby, original plan. Scale 1:1,000.

In about 1060 the king of Denmark, Sven Estridsen, started the building of an extensive church at Dalby (Pl. 3b, Fig. 10), about six miles east of Lund. The size of this royal church implies its function as a cathedral and it is known that a bishop, Egino, sent out by the Archbishop of Bremen, was at Dalby. A strange situation, this, with two bishops so close to each other as Dalby and Lund. The episcopal division of Scandinavia was hardly stabilized; there was, moreover, a certain amount of competition between English and German missions, the former led by the Danish kings, the latter by powerful political personalities in Bremen.

However, the Bishop of Lund soon died, in 1066, and Bishop Egino was moved there to take his place. His short stay at Dalby makes it very unlikely that either he or the archbishopric of Bremen could have had any influence on the design of the church. Its geographical situation corresponds to that of another royal church, Husaby—on the edge of a forest overlooking a plain—and there is evidence of Sven Estridsen's personal interest in the building.

The Dalby church of the eleventh century was much altered by later generations. Originally it was a triple-aisled basilica with square piers and a rectangular choir. The windows in the aisles and clerestory were small. Little is left of this church. During the next century the western part was extended: the addition was a baptizing church with nine cross-vaults and with a quadrangular tower on either side of it.

A transept was added, a new apsidal choir was built, and the intention was to put towers on either side of the choir, but these were never executed. Obviously the nearby cathedral of Lund stimu-lated great competitive effort, a rivalry that had by no means ended in the eleventh century, although the extensions at Dalby were not all carried out as planned. The twelfth-century work was supervised by an anonymous Scandinavian stone-mason from Lund, chiefly known for his baptismal fonts and called Byzantios because he was much influenced by the Byzantine elements in the sculptural orna-ment being produced at Lund.

In the thirteenth century the church was vaulted with brick vaults according to the Lombardic system, and in connection with this the piers were reinforced. Every second pier was enlarged and equipped with an attached column supporting the transverse ribs. The trans-verse ribs in the aisles were carried down by smaller pilasters. At the same time new clerestory windows were opened up. In the four-teenth century a south porch was added and the northern aisle was lengthened one bay in order to form a chapel. The two west towers have fallen down and nothing of them remains above ground, for they were never rebuilt; instead, the second story of the baptizing church was raised to make a central tower. The upper parts west of this tower have since been destroyed, leaving a strange silhouette today.

The Reformation meant catastrophe to Dalby church. During the seventeenth century the northern and eastern parts of the monas-tery which was connected with it were pulled down, and the north aisle of the church may have been destroyed at the same time. In 1686, building material for the German church at Malmö was needed: it was found in the apse at Dalby. Eventually, under the altered conditions of pressure, the choir fell down and, after a while, the eastern bay of the nave and remaining aisle as well. In 1758 it was felt that the church had suffered enough damage; the lead roof was sold and, for the money, both interior and exterior damages were repaired. The church of today is only a mutilated remnant, with little of the character of a triple-aisled basilica.

I have deliberately dwelt upon the long building history of this church, because in many respects it illustrates the fate of so many Scandinavian churches. Collapses, rebuilding, and additions have changed much of the medieval work. During the Middle Ages

37

when a church was going to be built, the community was some‑
times too poor to hire the best stone‑masons, and compromises had
to be made in technical matters. This poverty also meant that the
work took a long time. Therefore it happened again and again that
new ideas emerged during construction; the urge to follow the
fashion and create a modern building was stronger than reverence
for purity of style. In the fourteenth century, for instance, if the
neighbouring parish or town vaulted its church—and if the money
could be scraped together—it became an important matter of prestige
to do the same.

Churches similar to Dalby were the one at Bergen in Norway,
built at royal request, and the one at Vreta in Sweden, which was
built for King Inge the Elder on the model of the first cathedral at
Lund by Canute the Holy. Such royal foundations would have
been less pressed for money than many Scandinavian churches were;
nevertheless, there were two categories of 'king's churches', both
belonging to the Anglo‑Norman family: those with transepts and
semicircular apses, and those without. The differences cannot be
fully explained by other foreign influences, but rather by the relative
elaborateness or simplicity of a particular church's functions. In
general, the eleventh‑century church with a transept and semi‑
circular apses was designed to meet the needs of a more complicated
service.

Twelfth‑Century Cathedrals

The cathedral of Canute the Holy at Lund was a large enterprise
for medieval Denmark, designed to manifest the, by then, well‑
established Church. It was probably started in the 1080's and
planned with three aisles and four bays in the nave, projecting
transept with small eastern apses, a short choir and semicircular main
apse. This plan corresponds to Canute's other establishments in
Denmark. But new ideas emerged before the cathedral was finished,
and a more magnificent project evolved. The change was due to
external reasons.

In 1103 the Danish King Erik Ejegod arranged that Lund should
become the seat of a new diocese embracing the whole of Scandi‑
navia. This remarkable new diocese was the most extensive in
Europe and it was quite natural that the new archbishop, Asker,
should want a more magnificent building to represent his newly

extended power. The cathedral had to be replanned on more imposing lines, but the young Nordic countries had no such great building of their own for a model. Since this one was meant to be both royal and archiepiscopal, inspiration was sought in Germany, in the Emperor's cathedral at Speyer.

The first cathedral at Lund—that of Canute the Holy—was not many feet above ground in 1103. It was fairly easy to alter the plans, yet the design of the new church (Fig. 11) to a certain degree was necessarily bound by the dimensions and proportions of its predecessor. The old church is now part of the crypt, cruciform in plan and cross-vaulted on low free-standing columns and attached half-columns, sparsely decorated with different incised designs.

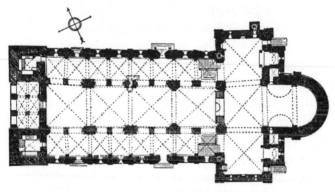

FIG. 11. Lund Cathedral. Scale 1:1,000.

To supervise the work a skilled stone-mason from Speyer by the name of Donatus, an Italian, was asked to come to Lund. He extended the nave to include four square bays, planned a porch in the western part and above it a royal tribune; the western parts were rebuilt later. He enlarged the main apse, along with other alterations in the choir and transept, justified by the enlarged scale of the church. It was also decided to vault the church according to the system used in Lombardy. Originally the cross-vaults must have been without ribs, as only the wall ribs from the very beginning had secondary supports. A change took place in the 1120's, when more builders from Speyer arrived. Before their arrival Donatus had worked in an old, severe style with unarticulated walls and geometrical, cubic capitals. The new style introduced stronger accents on ornamental details, the capitals were decorated with ornamental foliage, and attached columns appeared along the nave. The vaults

39

were rebuilt after a fire about 1200, and restored in the nineteenth century, so conjecture as to when rib vaulting was introduced is impossible. In accordance with Lombardic tradition, and unlike the Rhineland churches, Lund was at first planned without western towers. These were added by order of Archbishop Absalon, at the beginning of the thirteenth century.

After Donatus' death, probably in the 1130's, the supervision of the work was taken over by his fellow-countryman Regnerus, who also did not live to see his work completed. With Lund Cathedral a new spirit came into Scandinavian architecture, brought by the Lombardic builders from Speyer and taken over by the local masons. The exterior displayed the new Rheno-Lombardic style of exuberant decoration. The outer walls of the apse (Pl. 4) begin with a quiet theme, a blind arcade on column strips and corbels in shallow relief. The theme becomes more pronounced in the second story, where heavily profiled windows alternate with blank recesses within an attached arcade, and reaches full development in the eaves gallery of the third story. This eaves gallery—once crowned with a zigzag flourish of dormers—was toned down in the nineteenth century by Zetterwall, spiritual disciple of Viollet-le-Duc and 'restorer' of Swedish cathedrals. It has been said that this gallery might pre-date any in Germany, but the fairest way to look at this matter is to consider Lund as parallel to the Rheno-Lombardic churches of Germany, neither a leader nor a backward imitator: Speyer and Lund were collateral descendants of the same origins.

In common with Romanesque architecture on the Continent, the cathedral at Lund is richly decorated with sculpture on capitals, canopies, arches, and tympanums, to remind the illiterate medieval churchgoer of the content of the Christian story. While the west front was as usual the most important one, that façade is not left to us in its original state. The south portal (Pl. 8) remains as it was built during Donatus' time. The tympanum is framed by five concentric receding arches, each supported by attached columns, their capitals decorated with masks and plants and animal motifs. Some of the arches display a rich intertwining foliage with a conventionalized Nordic character; while others show more southern plant motifs such as the acanthus on the inner one, and on another, vines with bunches of grapes. The tympanum itself contains five circular panels: in the centre the Lamb with the Cross, symbolizing

John the Baptist, surrounded by the symbols of the four Evangelists. The relief is fairly high, producing a rich pattern of lights and shadows. Compared with the twisting ornament and demons of the surrounding arches and capitals, the tympanum has a static, divine character which arrests us with a hint of the tension between Good and Evil in the medieval cosmos.

With the building of Lund Cathedral southern building traditions were introduced for the first time into Scandinavia. Simplifying the matter, one could say that the building was Rhenish and the ornaments Italian with a Nordic flavour. This church came to play a dominant part in the spreading of these new ideas to the whole of Scandinavia. In the stone-masons' yards attached to the

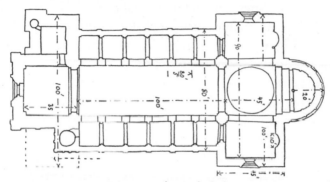

FIG. 12. Ribe Cathedral.

cathedral a great number of artists were trained who, after the work was finished, went off to carry on their trade in other parts of Scandinavia. Many went to Gotland. The plan of Lund was much copied, especially in Denmark where Ribe Cathedral was begun in 1130 and Viborg Cathedral ten years later. The small parish churches all around followed Lund and were soon equipped with half-columns, column strips, ornamented porches, and later with one or two west towers. One must not forget that Lund Cathedral was somewhat old-fashioned in plan compared to contemporary German churches. Master Donatus was educated in the severe and ascetic spirit of the early Cluniac churches, and never adopted the freer, grander style that included central towers and western choirs. The geometrical plan of the church was austere as well in its lack of elaborate differentiation between the parts.

The prototypes of the Danish cathedrals, Ribe and Viborg, beyond that of Lund, were Rheno-Lombardic, but at Ribe (Pl. 5, 6) the style was used more freely and independently. There is no crypt and the Lund plan has been shrunk, so to speak: the nave consists of only three cross-vaulted bays and the choir is greatly reduced, so that the apse is only separated from the nave by the crossing (Fig. 12). Each nave wall is supported by six arches, but these are not gathered in pairs in huge ornamental arched recesses as at Lund. Neither do small piers alternate with the main ones, since the aisles were planned to be vaulted from the beginning. The nave at Ribe was originally planned to have a flat wooden ceiling. The square piers along the nave have attached half-columns for the aisle ribs. The string-course running below the gallery adds horizontal emphasis: this was originally planned as an ornamental feature, but when it was decided to vault the nave, the moulding was enlarged to bolster the vaults. These are six-part vaults supported by column-strips ending in corbels above the piers. The transverse ribs and the half-columns of alternating light and dark blocks add to the vivid interior of this church, today more filled with daylight than Lund Cathedral because the clerestory windows were enlarged in the thirteenth century. This brightness is really alien to the earlier character of the building. Another alien feature for a Rheno-Lombardic building is the domed crossing, an alteration that does not appear on the exterior. It is not known what was the source of this dome, a feature more familiar in south-western France at this period.

The walls of the narthex are extremely thick, which probably means that a west tower was intended, although not carried out at the time. The present square western tower and the southern tower over the aisle, together with the spire over the crossing, are later additions. During the fifteenth century the two rows of chapels along the side aisles were joined with the aisles, making four side aisles, and giving the interior a rather odd appearance as the transept is so much narrower than the widened nave.

The exterior of Ribe Cathedral is not quite like its larger predecessor of Lund, either. The same themes were used, but the choice of language is varied. The apse stands on a stepped foundation, above which is the blind arcading of the first stage, a range of attached arches containing pairs of smaller arches on corbels and supported by half-columns with cubical capitals similar to those on Speyer Cathedral. The second story is plainer than the one at Lund, the third much simpler. The whole intonation of the twelfth-century building at Ribe is more severe and quiet than at Lund, where the Italian masons who had come from the Rhineland produced a richer variety of ornament with a softer handling of detail. The decorated archivolts around the west door at Ribe are rich but crude as if a native hand were feeling its way.

Viborg Cathedral, built entirely of granite, was probably finished towards the end of the twelfth century. It had two west towers, and two smaller towers at the east end. Later it was exhaustively restored.

Cathedrals of the Thirteenth and Fourteenth Centuries

These two centuries were just as important as the twelfth from a church-building point of view. During the middle of the thirteenth century, for instance, cathedral building was being carried on at Linköping, Strängnäs, Västerås, and Skara in Sweden, at Trond-heim in Norway, and at Roskilde in Denmark. In matters of style, each of these cathedrals became an individual with a distinctive character acquired during a long building history, each one a synthe-sis of accretions that are difficult to describe in chronological order. Those mentioned here are placed in the epoch which had the greatest influence on the building in question, with whatever recapitulations and looking into the future may be necessary.

It was never the same story as in the Île-de-France where, for instance, the cathedral at Reims was built in less than a generation and so stands out as a crystal-clear example of the pure Gothic style at that time. But this is not the only explanation why a thorough-going Gothic style never appeared in Scandinavia, either in French or in English shape. Much influence from these and other schools was eddying about but could not completely mould the buildings of a different social climate. The English and French Gothic expressed a new medieval spirit. The big change from the Romanesque period came with a synthesis between kings and towns. The wealth of the cities was the financial basis for such enterprises as building cathe-drals, while the aristocratic high-mindedness of court life fashioned an impressive, often ecstatic structure of feeling. Add to this the edu-cation on a high level which was emerging in the universities of Paris and Oxford and Cambridge.

Conditions in Scandinavia were different. Her kings lived a much less aristocratic life, and higher education was had 'on loan'. Admittedly, a city-culture was slowly developing in thirteenth-

43

century Scandinavia, but at first these were new towns, without traditions and built on virgin soil. Moreover, they acquired a strictly commercial character from their close relationship with the German Hansetowns. The churches in such towns would have seemed crude to a visitor from Western Europe. Universities were not founded in Scandinavia until the fifteenth century, at Copenhagen and Uppsala; meanwhile, an old habit of sending students to Paris was for a time changed to that of sending them to universities in Germany.

What then remained for Scandinavian borrowers from the 'International Gothic' was only its technique of construction, but not even that was used unchanged. In the Nordic countries, with the use of different building materials it was sometimes necessary to apply different construction methods from those used in France and England; this happened with the brick vaults at Uppsala, for example.

However, it goes without saying that a national building tradition could not possibly be created out of something entirely negative, out of a mere lack of the medieval spirit that ruled the rest of Europe. The lack was certainly not total—the Scandinavians tried hard to follow the evolution. The cathedrals themselves show that. Yet church interiors were never given such boldly pierced walls as was common in France, and so the related system of flying buttresses was also missing. Consequently the structure of these darker, more closedin cathedrals is not so apparent. It is as if the melancholy sense of fear contained in the Romanesque churches was never released in the sometimes almost overstrung ecstasy of the Gothic cathedral. Scandinavian emotions never reached such breathtaking heights, although they were no less intensely felt. The Nordic churches are more earthbound, their emotional scale in the minor key. It is as if the northerner could not grasp and experience the full extent of the divine relief that the Kingdom of Heaven afforded.

Bricks were introduced in Denmark in the twelfth century when the abbeys at Sorø (Pl. 16a) and Ringsted (near Sorø on Sjaelland) were built. An example of the interior visual effect that this material was to have is shown in our illustration of Løgumkloster (Pl. 17). The cathedral of Roskilde was rebuilt in 1190 entirely of bricks apart from the pillars and the crypt which were of granite. The sixty years that had gone by since the building of Ribe Cathedral brought

other new ideas besides the use of bricks. The monks who introduced these also introduced the Gothic building technique.

Roskilde Cathedral was the burial place of the Danish kings
because the town had been a royal residence since the days of Sven
Forkbeard, who had erected the first, wooden church. About 1080
a probably round, limestone church was built; a century later it was
replaced by the brick and granite cathedral. This inaugurated a new
era in Scandinavia, where it is the only one patterned on the fully
French Gothic. This is most clearly shown in the plan (Fig. 13)
which is that of a triple-aisled church with seven bays in the nave
and a double-aisled 'drawn-in' transept and semicircular east end
with ambulatory. A modular system was used throughout. In the

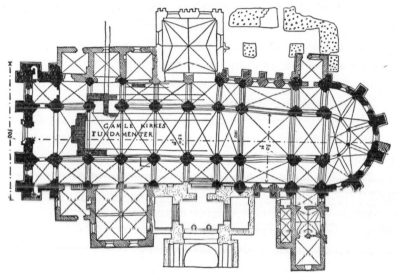

FIG. 13. Roskilde Cathedral.

choir, which is very similar to that of Tournai—explained by frequent connections between the two towns—the wall ribs are pointed,
but those of the nave arcade are not; yet, while rounded arches
appear in the triforium and clerestory, there are pointed wall ribs in
the emporium or main gallery over the aisles. ('Emporium' is the
term used by German and Scandinavian scholars for such a gallery,
once the meeting place for traders and deriving from the same Greek
root as the grandiose word for shop.) The nave elevation at Roskilde,
then, is four-storied. The pointed vaults are very shallow ones,
which in no way increase the vertical emphasis. The nave was
meant to be vaulted from the beginning: a consequence of the rib

vaults was that the old system of square bays with an extra pier for the aisle vaults could be abandoned. The nave arcade corresponded to the aisle arcades, for the rib vault was not dependent upon a square bay. The windows, grouped in threes, are early Gothic in character.

Choir stalls were carved in 1420 to resemble those at Lund. The needle-spired towers (Pl. 12) were only finished during the reign of Christian IV in the seventeenth century, although the original plan had included two west towers. Among the many chapels added to Roskilde Cathedral, that of Christian IV is the most prominent (see end of Chapter X). That of Frederick V, begun by Harsdorff in 1774, will also be mentioned (Chapter XX).

At Trondheim (Pl. 7) the picture is different. It was made a see in 1152 and an enlargement was planned for the church that had been started earlier and which in fact was the third on the site. The choir was vaulted about 1190, the nave about 1210. There was rebuilding after a fire in 1328; the exterior work still goes on. As a result of extremely lively cultural relations between Norway and England the twelfth- and thirteenth-century cathedral was a remark-able example of English church-building traditions at that time, with a particular resemblance to Lincoln Cathedral where rebuilding was going on from about 1190.

Compared to Lincoln the church at Trondheim has a somewhat simpler plan. The English cathedral is considerably larger than its little sister in Norway, with double choirs and transepts and a larger number of eastern chapels. The cathedral at Trondheim has an octagonal enlargement of the choir, or Lady chapel with an ambu-latory, and an eastern chapel in each of the arms of the transept. In the two interiors the language of form is much the same with certain exceptions. In the Norwegian cathedral the window tracery is not exactly the same as that at Lincoln; also, the vertical lines of the ribbed vault are somewhat more strongly stressed because the line of each group of gathered ribs is continued by a semi-detached colon-nette all the way down to the floor, whereas at Lincoln this was stopped by a corbel part-way down.

The long building history of Linköping Cathedral has been con-firmed after extensive archaeological excavations and investigations. An old stave church was replaced in 1130 by a church of the Anglo-Norman persuasion, with a transept and semicircular apses. About a hundred years later this church was considered too small and the choir was rebuilt with square sexpartite vaults, resembling those in St. Maria at Visby (see p. 69, although otherwise these two churches were not alike). Linköping choir has an ambulatory: the relics enshrined there required processional observance. There is little left of the Romanesque choir, apart from the façade of the south transept, which has an eaves gallery close to the roof and, above the heavily moulded doorway, three early Gothic windows in a style that was English and not French: separate lancets heavily profiled with attached columns in the embrasures.

In the 1240's Englishmen were asked to come and build the nave at Linköping (Pl. 10*b*). This was constructed as a hall church, not unlike the retrochoir at Salisbury (begun 1220) or the choir of the Temple Church in London (consecrated 1240). The walls of this nave were ornamented with blank arcading supported by attached columns; on the south wall, pointed arches suddenly re place the Romanesque. This, along with the many different styles of columns in the nave, suggests that there were numerous pauses in building during the thirteenth century. The church possesses almost every kind of column and window in existence during the Middle Ages. In spite of the many building periods, and in spite of the light choir and the eastern chapels added by German builders during the fifteenth and sixteenth centuries, it is the hall-nave that dominates the interior. The dark marble shafting against a light ground was a theme much developed in England.

The south door of the nave (Pl. 9) makes a rather heterogeneous impression: there is a theory that it was put together from different pieces. The attached columns on the sides are thicker and as a group broader than the more graceful arches they support. The central jamb is decorated with a richness of ornamental foliage. In the tympanum the Passion of Christ is framed by the Prophets in ten quatrefoils. A remarkable desire for realism is shown in these carvings, with a detailed setting-out of clothes, features, and so on that is at the same time artistically unified. The particular regional origin of the sculptor is unknown, but would most likely have afforded familiarity with North German work.

The outside of the church (Pl. 10*a*) before the present tower was added had a closed and compact character—below the oddly pinched-up roof—the buttressing entirely passive and not even that projecting very much.

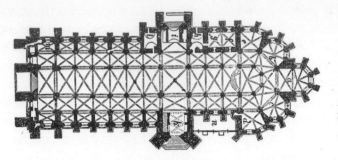

FIG. 14.
Uppsala
Cathedral.

When Uppsala Cathedral (Pl. 13*c*, Fig. 14) was begun around
1273, an English plan was adopted at first. The church was planned
with double transepts, but when in 1287 the Frenchman Etienne de
Bonneuil came to Uppsala to take over, the plan was changed and
the church was given a French apsidal end with an ambulatory and
chapels around the choir. A compromise, then, was made at an

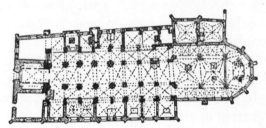

FIG. 15.
Strängnäs Cathedral.

early stage, an effort to unite two quite incompatible conceptions,
which from then on upset the proportions and the character of the
cathedral. Exactly how far the building had advanced when the
French architect arrived is not known. The large south window in
the transept as well as the clerestory openings are English in character, inherited from the early Norman style of such a building as

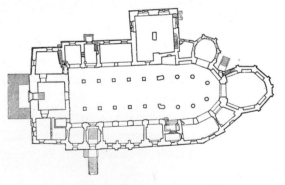

(Compara-
tive scale
not exact)

FIG. 16.
Åbo Cathedral.

Dryburgh Abbey, for example. The south transept façade has enormously heavy diagonal buttresses at the corners; this was also an
English feature. The chapels along the aisles were added later, as
were the high western towers.

Uppsala Cathedral has suffered other compromises in addition to
that of the plan, and as it stands before us today it sounds no dominant note. Both the early English and French builders began their
work in stone, but later on, partly for economic reasons, bricks became the material, which meant a different building technique, and
the visual effect was blurred. The nave, moreover, has the French
upward tendency, but the contained dissolution, as it were, that we
are used to finding in the multiple openings of the second story of a
French Gothic nave is not there. Instead, the blank wall on that
level above each pointed arch of the nave arcade is pierced only once,
with a small circular opening.

The west front was thoroughly rebuilt after a devastating fire in
1702; nothing definite can now be said about its original state. The
cathedral is the largest in Scandinavia, and the Swedes have so far
been unsuccessful in bringing its building history to a satisfactory
end.

In the thirteenth century the 'hall church' type of elevation (that
is, with the aisles as high as the nave and forming, as it were, one
space with it) was introduced, probably both by friars and by Hanse-
merchant patrons. There was an old tradition of hall churches in
Germany, even before the preaching friars adopted the type. But
there is also evidence at Linköping for importation by English
builders.

Influenced by the numerous merchant churches being erected
during the thirteenth century, the last cathedrals to be built in
medieval times were hall churches: for example, Strängnäs and
Västerås Cathedrals in Sweden and Åbo (Turku) Cathedral in
Finland (Figs. 15, 16). They are very similar in character and all
three are built mostly of brick.

Strängnäs Cathedral is the oldest, consecrated in 1291, on that
very day damaged by fire, and later repaired. Åbo is the youngest,
founded in about 1290, the choir vaulted in the middle of the fourteenth century and the nave about a century later. The choir vaults
at Strängnäs were built about 1450, and at Västerås some ten years
later. The chapels along the aisles of these cathedrals were not part

of the original plans, and now obscure the usual exterior shape of the hall type of church. Compared to Linköping, all three are markedly coarser and heavier in character. As at Uppsala, these cathedrals were equipped with west towers (Pl. 13) in the fifteenth century (the steeple at Västerås and the cupola at Strängnäs being added much later). Such towers belong to another category of church architecture and will be dealt with at the end of Chapter VIII.

Of an entirely different character from all the churches so far described is Kalundborg church in Denmark (Pl. 11, Fig. 17), begun in the late twelfth century, on a Greek cross plan, and probably founded by Esbjörn Snare, twin brother of Absalon, the famous archbishop and politician who organized several successful crusades against the Wends, the constant threat to South and East Scandi-navia. The central part of the church is crowned by a tower, which was rebuilt after a fire in 1314, and the new piers there were con-siderably more slender than the ones they replaced. The central tower has a square plan; the outer towers on each arm of the cross, probably dating from around 1170, are octagonal; they are all German in character. The central tower was destroyed by a fire in 1827 which also damaged several other parts of the church. It was then repaired between 1867 and 1871 but this restoration was only temporary and in 1916 a new restoration was begun. The aim was then to rebuild the church in its original state as far as this was known and possible. The illustration shows all four outer towers with eight small gables; originally only two of them had such gables, while the central tower and two of the outer towers had only four gables. An arid catalogue, but a bold impressive building.

The original plan of this brick church—combining a Greek cross with its function of a fortress—has been much discussed. Its func-tion as a fortress is natural; Kalundborg is situated at the Great Belt on Sjaelland and a fortified stronghold there could easily block access to northern Denmark. The plan of a Greek cross is explained when one considers that Absalon's successful crusades against the heathens south of the Baltic had not only a political aim but a religious one. His supremacy over the former Wendish island of Rügen was soon sanctioned by the Pope. The Greek cross was the symbol of Absa-lon's crusades against the Wends as it had earlier been for other European crusaders to Jerusalem. The cross is the symbolic dimen-sion of this church.

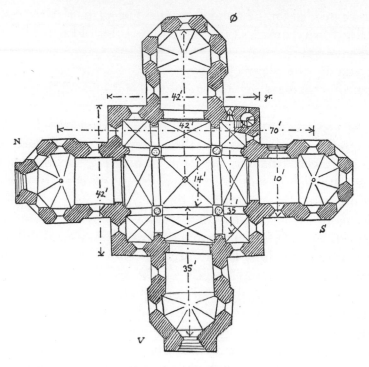

FIG. 17. Kalundborg.

Monks and Friars

Of all the monastic orders in the Middle Ages the Benedictines were the best organized, and they played a vital part in the spreading of culture north of the Alps. Without them the evolution of western Europe would have followed other paths. The ninth-century Bene- dictine monastery of St. Gallen, for which the rebuilding plan still exists, on vellum, became the prototype for the building of monas- teries throughout Europe.

The cloister was the centre of such an establishment. North of it was the nave of the abbey, to which it was linked by the south transept, and nearby was the monks' dormitory and the chapter- house. The house of the abbot or prior was north of the church —although in cold northern countries this was likely to be placed on the warmer side. South of the cloister were the refectory and kitchen. From such a nucleus there later grew other buildings: school, dispensary, infirmary, bakehouses, etc. Originally laymen were not allowed into the abbeys of the Benedictines. Their churches were basilican with transepts and three semicircular apses, the chancel extended for the monks' choir. The plan of Venge Abbey on Jylland in Denmark (Fig. 18) illustrates this old type of northern Benedictine abbey.

By and by the plans of abbeys were influenced by the pilgrim movement organized by the monks of Cluny. Pilgrims would await the procession in an antechamber to the nave, the narthex, and then the procession moved around the holy relics back of the altar by way of the ambulatory. Earlier apses were transformed into a series of chapels radiating from the ambulatory. In the great pilgrimage churches of southern Europe, doors and capitals were being richly decorated for the benefit of the pilgrims.

The monks from Cluny constituted a reform movement within the Benedictine Order. Their own ultimate, ideal church building was the so-called Cluny III, consecrated 1095. Its double transepts and numerous apses and chapels gave it an extremely complicated outline on the exterior, the final contradiction to the former simple architecture of that order. But in Scandinavia, even in churches which housed some holy relics, the crowds of pilgrims never grew large enough for such extensive enterprises as Cluny III.

Near the end of the eleventh century a new reformation movement from the monastery at Cîteaux in Burgundy turned against this worldly splendour. The Cistercians settled in the outskirts of civilization—Scandinavia must have been a perfect field for them. They started extensive agricultural enterprises and by selling the produce to nearby towns became rich enough to found new monasteries. They were hardworking ascetics, these monks; their rigorous spirit was so strong that their regime of life consisted almost entirely of prohibitions. This asceticism also meant that they turned their backs upon the building habits of the Benedictines. No towers or prominent chapels for them. Inside, decoration was omitted, crosses and chandeliers could at best be made of copper, the doors were painted white, and windows could only have clear glass.

Clairvaux, the abbey of St. Bernard the great Cistercian, stands no more, but as it was the prototype for the church at Fontenay of 1147, that church can give us a fairly clear picture of the original ideal of the Cistercians. It is triple-aisled with apsidal transept, unaccentuated crossing, and a rectangular choir and apses. Both nave and aisles were vaulted, and the attached columns supporting the nave ribs ended a few feet above the floor. The piers were plain. The exterior, too, was calm: no projections from the cruciform plan, and a simple roof covering both aisles and chapels. Then, under the pressure of the technical developments in Burgundy and in the Île-de-France, the choir at Clairvaux was rebuilt in 1170 with a semicircular sanc tuary with ambulatory and radiating chapels. It goes without saying that the Gothic vault was a condition for the vaulting of the irregu larly shaped spaces created in the ambulatory.

These two orders were the ones dominating Scandinavia (others such as the Knights Templar and the Carthusians never obtained a strong foothold) until the preaching friars, first the Franciscans and later the Dominicans, came to Scandinavia in the thirteenth century. These orders of friars grew up in the city states of Italy, where a new economic type of urban human being was developing—the man, in the textile industry for example, who earned solid coins with which he could do as he pleased, no longer so dependent on his customer as the old artisan had been on his feudal lord. The simple goodness of St. Francis appealed to a new tough sense of equality, and the common people were stirred by the element of mysticism in his life. Humbly the little brothers of St. Francis in their grey cowls carried on their charity work in the towns, preaching in the squares and streets. Their churches, simple from the first, developed the hall church type in various ways. The Dominicans were like them, but the Black Friars were more learned and put much stress upon spread ing knowledge to the people; the pulpit dominated the church. At first, the rule of the orders against donations made the friars poor and their churches plain, as plain as those of the Cistercians. Transepts disappeared and piers dwindled, so that as large a congregation as possible could hear the sermon.

Finally, there was the Scandinavian order of St. Birgitta, founded in the 1370's, not an urban order for it built its monasteries and nunneries in the country. In common with the friars, Birgitta, who had spent some time in Italy, held the hall church to be her ideal and directed that her own abbey at Vadstena be built accordingly. Her establishments were open for both men and women, who lived on either side of the abbey.

The monastic orders played an unprecedented role in linking Scandinavia with the rest of European civilization. Their disap pearance with the Reformation was a great loss.

Early in the twelfth century the Danish king, Erik Ejegod,

invited English Benedictine monks to Odense. There they took over existing churches and dedicated them to St. Alban and to Our Lady, not at first building any church of their own. A few years later, other Benedictines came and founded the monastery at Venge.

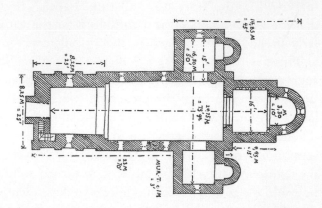

FIG. 18.
Venge, abbey church.

Venge Abbey (Fig. 18, Pl. 14a) is a single-aisled cruciform church with a two-storied transept which provided an upper gallery for the monks, a rectangular choir, and three semicircular apses. A tower has been erected over the south transept arm. Originally there was a west tower, which is clearly provided for in the plan by thickened walls and on the exterior by wall-buttresses. The passages between the nave, transepts, and choir are narrow, forming a sort of triumphal arch between the nave and choir. This arch is repeated, reduced in size, between the choir and the sanctuary, where the walls are decorated with blind arcades. There is no corresponding orna-ment on the exterior except a simple frieze moulding under the eaves of the main apse. The church was built of sandstone around 1125, the choir and nave being originally covered with a wooden ceiling.

In 1170 another Benedictine abbey was inaugurated, this time at Ringsted on Sjælland. It was the first abbey in Scandinavia to be built of bricks. As was the Cluniac custom, the church was given a large east end for the numerous priests and monks—the chancel is half as long as the nave—and a central tower. The nave is triple-aisled, and the transept has large chapels with apses. Originally it was intended to vault the aisles and chapels in the transept only, the rest to be covered with a wooden ceiling, but the plans were changed while building was going on and today large rib vaults with Lombardic transverse ribs cover the church.

At first bricks were laid in stretcher bond and grooved on the outside in order to look like the native stone. The local builders did not yet have the courage to use bricks in their original state. Having learned how to dress stone for reliefs and decorations, they dressed bricks for column bases, mouldings, etc. in the same manner, making each unit of sculptural ornament no bigger than a brick. At Ringsted, however, a specifically brick ornament developed. In the interior Romanesque decoration is common, either as *opus spicatum*— the bricks laid at a 45° angle with one corner exposed—or as an astragal moulding. Outside, this small convex moulding can be found on the gable of the transept, which is also decorated with blank arcades and sunk circular panels. Such themes could be endlessly varied and appear on nearly all brick churches in Scandinavia.

The years after 1160 were a busy period as well for the Cistercians, who were erecting two remarkable establishments in Denmark, at Sorø and Vittskøl—the latter was never completed—and in Sweden Alvastra monastery was built for the thirteen monks who arrived there in 1193. This monastery soon established subsidiaries at Nydala in Småland and Roma on Gotland. In Sweden the material used was stone, while in Denmark they used brick.

The abbey at Sorø (Pl. 16*a*) was an imposing building for its time with a nave of nine bays, over two hundred feet long. The plan is more strictly French than that at Ringsted, and a module has been used all through. In other respects one can see the influence of Fontenay: the eastern chapels are separate from each other and from the choir, but are covered by one unifying roof. Everything is planned to meet the needs of the Cistercian service. Only the ordained monks were allowed to enter the raised choir, while lay brothers and novices were restricted to the western part of the nave. The public were allowed to enter the abbey through the door of the north aisle. The stair between the south aisle and the dormitory remains today. The great Absalon, founder of Copenhagen, is buried in this church.

Alvastra also follows the plan of Fontenay, as do the subsidiary establishments at Nydala and Roma (Fig. 19), except that Nydala had wooden wagon vaults, and the choir windows were added later. At Roma the apses differed from the prototype in projecting slightly. Now one sees only the ruined nave arcades (Pl. 20*b*). The Swedish monasteries were more simple and serene inside than Sorø. Their

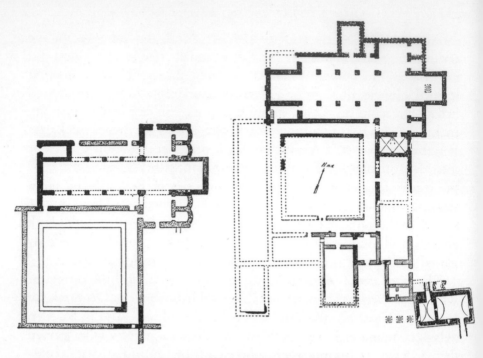

Abbey plans (comparative scale not exact).

FIG. 19 (*left*). Roma.   FIG. 20 (*below*). Varnhem.   FIG. 21 (*right*). Alvastra.

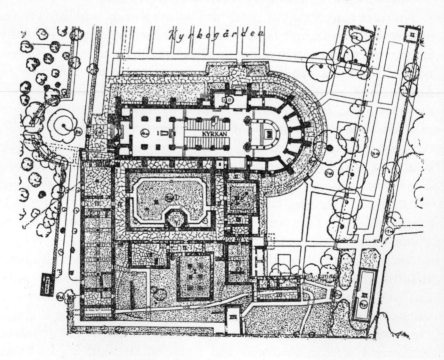

columns and unarticulated piers had no other visual function than to divide the different parts of these abbeys, and because they do not obtrude the experience of space is all the more intense. The interior of Sorø is more richly decorated in a somewhat Lombardic manner, although outside it is strikingly simple.

Quite another spirit rules in the Cistercian abbey church of Varn-hem in Sweden (Pl. 14*b*, Fig. 20), rebuilt after a fire in the thirteenth century. The rebuilding of the choir at Fontenay had its results, for Varnhem was given a semicircular sanctuary ringed with chapels. Moreover, the whole church was enlarged and more richly decorated, an unusual proceeding for Cistercians, made possible through large donations to the monastery by the Swedish kings. The transverse ribs of the nave vaults come to rest on elaborate corbels consisting of an odd cluster of half-colonnettes and half-pilasters. By stopping the vertical supports above the springing of the nave arches, the simplicity of the plain square piers and the round-headed arches is stressed, and there is even a certain tension between the richer mould-ings of the corbel capitals and the calm design below. The uni-formity is greater in the aisles, where simple cross vaults were used.

The choir and sanctuary, both raised a few steps, are architec-turally and sculpturally more elaborate, partly as a natural conse-quence of the irregular spaces formed by the ambulatory and sur-rounding chapels. Piers both circular and polygonal have fully developed capitals and the four piers at the crossing are clusters of columns. The exterior was somewhat changed by restoration in the seventeenth century when the buttresses were reinforced. But even before the restoration the exterior was complicated, especially the decoration of doorways such as the northern Porta Mortuorum through which the dead were carried out to the cemetery: over the moulded tympanum is a canopied portico supported by a colonnade.

Apart from the unusual enrichment at Varnhem, Cistercian monasteries usually display in their architecture an austere and special frame for a very austere and special form of divine service and religious life. More even than the earlier cathedrals and churches of Scandi-navia, they were ruled by the ascetic idea. It was not a question of retardation, but of discipline.

The monastery plans at Alvastra (Fig. 21), founded in 1143, and at Varnhem, founded just a few years later, accorded with the proto-type of St. Gallen apart from minor divergences in the grouping of auxiliary buildings. The prior's house is close to the south-east corner of the cloister. In England this was the case at Fountains Abbey and at Norwich, among others. Perhaps it was a question of climate, the north side of a church tending to be rather gloomy in the dark north. The smaller monasteries did not add so many secondary buildings outside the church walls.

As was the custom on the Continent, the nuns did not build new churches for their nunneries but took over old ones. At Vreta in Sweden (Fig. 22) they were given the old royal church, the choir of which was enlarged. At Sko in Sweden, their church resembles the architecture of the friars.

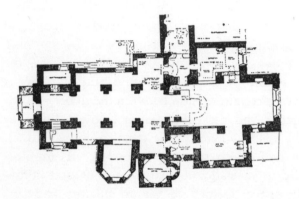

FIG. 22.
Vreta, abbey church.

In 1232 the first Franciscan monastery in Scandinavia was founded, at Ribe in Denmark. This shows how rapid was the rise of the Franciscans, whose church in Assisi had only been begun in 1228. Also from the first decades of the friars dates the present Viborg Søndresogn (Pl. 18), built of brick and originally belonging to the Dominicans. This hall church with rib vaults has no part more accentuated than another (the lateral extensions in our illustration being later chapels, not the original aisles). The choir is not raised, nor is the church divided into separate sections for friars and the public—this was a new sort of monk. All were equal in this preach-ing church—as in the later Protestant churches—and the sermons were given in the language of the people, forming a bridge between the Church's supremacy and the community. The outside of the Viborg building is decorated with a saw-tooth moulding and blind arcading on the gable ends, and along the sides with *opus spicatum*, the aforesaid 'spiky work' that lends texture to brick surfaces.

The Franciscan church at Odense, later pulled down, was originally double-aisled, that is, with piers down the middle. Here the difference between friars and laymen was somewhat emphasized, for the church had a rather large choir. There was less simplicity than at Viborg; times were changing and many wealthy merchants took special care to give donations to the Grey Friars, who presumably no longer minded, and this helped the building programme along. As time went on, these rich men started to erect their own chapels along the north side of the church, which thus eventually became triple-aisled. This also happened in the Black Friars' church at Aarhus in Denmark, where the chapels were added along

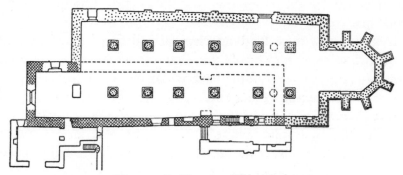

FIG. 23. St. Katarina, Visby. Scale 1:675.

the south side. Each chapel roof had its own stepped gable which, with the armorial ornament on the walls, was intended to show that gentry were buried within.

In 1233 the Franciscans pressed on to Visby, that lively trading centre on Gotland in the Baltic. Their church there, St. Karin or Katarina (Fig. 23, Pl. 21a), is now a ruin. At first it was a single-aisled, cross-vaulted church with the choir somewhat narrower than the nave and no sculptural ornament whatever. Then in the late fourteenth century the nave was widened to include side aisles of the same height, and the choir was enlarged. The polygonal apsidal end was added at the beginning of the fifteenth century and with its considerably longer windows stood in a certain contrast to the rest of the church.

The Dominican church at Visby, St. Nicolai (Pl. 21b), is also in ruins. It was founded in 1227, the plan being subsequently adroitly adapted to compete with the Grey Friars' church. The nave was extended after 1240 and the choir has many features in common with the choir of St. Karin's. But along the aisles are pilasters with attached columns for the aisle ribs, and the nave piers are simple square ones, not octagonal like the ones in St. Karin. On the whole there seems to have been much competition among the numerous churches of thirteenth-century Visby: they were enlarged, added to, and furnished with new vaults, all in virtuous rivalry with one another.

The hall character of St. Nicolai is not quite so marked as in St. Karin, for the aisles are a little bit lower than the nave. The vaulting technique was new: these could not quite be called cross vaults, for they have been so lowered as to appear almost flat. This with the plain piers gives an impression of poverty that is hardly counteracted by the mouldings on the walls. Discipline was at work here, too.

In contrast to these Gotland churches all friars' churches on the mainland were built of bricks, for example St. Maria at Sigtuna, of 1240–50 (Pl. 16b). A simple rectangular church with a rectangular choir, it was originally designed as a basilica, that is, with nave higher than aisles, but during the course of erection it became a hall church with rib vaults, whose outward thrust is mainly counter-acted by the thickness of the walls with the help of small buttresses, between which the windows are grouped in pairs. The exterior has a variety of brick ornament. The west door is set very deep in its concentric arches, with a plain niche on each side, and above is a tiny blind-arcaded strip of frieze. The western gable ornament shows where the roof was before it was raised. The Franciscan churches of St. Petri at Ystad, Sweden, of 1280, and Riddarholmskyrkan in Stockholm, of 1300, are both double-aisled hall churches of a simi-lar elevation but with remarkably higher and brighter interiors.

In 1430 King Eric of Pomerania founded a Carmelite monastery at Helsingør (Elsinore) by the Sound. The monks of this order devoted most of their time to charity and caring for the old and sick. Their church (Pl. 19), built after a fire in 1450, is an outstanding example of late Gothic in Scandinavia. The plan is a simple rectangle with no projecting choir, and the interior rises to a magnifi-cent height. The hall elevation is here abandoned, for the aisles are not more than half the height of the nave. Verticality is increased by the line of the ribs continuing down the columns, which have no capitals and are very slender. The whole building is covered by one unbroken roof line.

The stepped gables display a unique handling of common themes of decoration, and the west front is especially interesting. It is divided into the usual series of shallow vertical panels further divided in a spare, perpendicular way by sunk blank areas of subtly varied shapes. Such attached colonnettes stopped part-way down can be seen on the West Friesland churches of North Germany, and such perpendicular panels are characteristic of the Hanseatic Gothic of Lübeck. No other church gables in the whole of Scandinavia reach the sophistication and sensitivity of those at Helsingør, although there have been many attempts to copy them.

The monastery, well remembered by numerous benefactors, was not planned altogether according to rule. The cloister is north of the church, and the chapter-house with its rich ribbed vaults is to the east. The prior's house was at right angles to the cloister walk, while the monks' dormitory was above the chapter-house. This monastery, especially in the chapter-house and the refectory, is richly decorated with frescoes, of a character that belongs almost to a more secular century. The artist was probably a native Dane, but nothing certain is known about him. In the chapter-house are some keystones cut by the sculptor Adam van Düren: grotesque figures, and the Virgin with the Child, and Christ wearing the crown of thorns.

Convents of the Birgittine Order included Vadstena in Sweden and Maribo in Denmark, both founded at the end of the fourteenth century by Queen Margaret, and in Finland there was Nådendal. St. Birgitta gave careful instructions on how she wanted her churches built, explicitly directing that measurements were to be uniform, and that they were to be hall churches of limestone. In addition to these direct instructions, the rather complicated pattern of this order's services also influenced the interiors. These establishments were so-called double convents, open to both men and women; consequently the churches were equipped with two choirs. The public was allowed in the middle of the church, and the nuns had to have a secluded part from which they could not be seen. It was also necessary that there should be a connection between the two choirs. All this resulted in some rather complicated furnishing with several altars and iron grilles, partly still intact at Maribo.

At Vadstena, the striking simplicity of the original building is reinforced today by restorations in which later wall paintings were removed. Naturally the furnishing of the church must have drowned some of the simplicity of the vaults and pillars; at any rate, the contrast was undoubtedly great. The remaining auxiliary buildings of the convent are in the same spirit as the church. Birgitta had undoubtedly become well acquainted with the establishments of the Italian friars during a long visit to Italy.

The abbey church at Maribo (Pl. 15) differs somewhat from the mother church at Vadstena. The number of columns on a side was increased from four to seven, so that the open, hall character of the interior is somewhat lost, and the whole of the church was built of bricks—quite contrary to St. Birgitta's directions.

Parish Churches

Most of the Scandinavian churches are to be found out in the countryside, the parish churches. Their number is vast, amounting to several thousands still in the present day, and most of them were built in early medieval times. It is estimated that in present-day Denmark more than sixteen hundred churches still remain from the Middle Ages. Church-building activity was not less vigorous in other parts of Scandinavia.

This building activity was the result of a consolidation of Christian society in Scandinavia. Earlier a few strongholds had been established in missionary churches, cathedrals, and abbeys, but these were few and isolated. At the end of the eleventh century the ecclesiastical division of the countries into sees, chapters, and parishes took place. The countryside churches were either built on the personal initiative of the king or his feudal lords on the one hand, or as a result of the levying of *tiondet*, or tithes, introduced first in Denmark and then in Sweden at the beginning of the twelfth century. One-third of the tithes collected were granted to the bishop of the see—who, in other words, received over three per cent of the national income, and whose enormous power in medieval times must be seen against this background—one-third to the chapters, and the rest to the priest of the parish. From this it is evident that the tithes did not directly contribute to the erection of the churches, but only established the obligation. This was soon expressed in many different laws; the Östergötland Law stated that the king would start the parish church and the peasants would finish it, and a Danish law ordered that the farmer carry building material to the church on his cart before tilling his land in the spring. This was literally a heavy burden borne by the peasantry in early medieval times; nevertheless, the burden was carried and most parishes got their churches before the year 1200.

The process started in Denmark and spread north to Sweden and other parts of Scandinavia. Due to local unrest and other reasons it was delayed in the Mälar Valley; in Södermanland and Uppland the majority of the parish churches were built in the thirteenth and fourteenth centuries. The same was the case in Finland and on the east coast of northern Sweden.

Most of the parish churches standing today are not the unchanged monuments of an ancient culture. Many alterations and additions have been made, some of them soon after completion, or even during the time of erection. The technical knowledge of the builders was not always perfect; poverty and warfare contributed to the changing of plans, and where there was a lack of technical skill improvisation stepped in. That is why few parish churches, if any, are fully alike; they must be regarded as individuals, built for and by an individual parish and its people to serve its purposes. These purposes were many and all contributed in one way or another to give the parish church its form.

It is necessary to interpret the parish church as the frame for a service that was not established once and for all, and its form, more-over, was modified by the kind of community that built it, by different building styles from different epochs, by the materials used, by the ornamental art of nearby cathedrals, all fused in a unity with which the medieval peasant symbolized his Christian belief.

The divine service in the parish church had its roots in the rituals of the cathedrals, simplified partly for economic reasons since the parish had only one priest, possibly assisted by a few choir-boys. It is possible that the mass too was simplified; there were limits to what a poorly educated priest, usually of simple farming stock, could learn by heart. Besides the mass the other sacraments constituted the only service—the sermon was not introduced until the appearance of the friars.

This simplified service required a simple church. The prototype was introduced by priests from Anglo-Saxon England, that is to say before the Norman invasion of 1066. Examples of this type of church are Hover (Pl. 23a) and Gudrum (Fig. 24) in Denmark; Skårby (Fig. 25) and Skegrie in Skåne, Sweden; Skalunda and Häggesled in Västergötland, Sweden; Alstarhoug and Moster

(Pl. 22a) in Norway. It is a type of church that is mainly to be found in the west parts of Scandinavia, the parts that were the first to become Christian: Jylland, Skåne, Västergötland, and Norway. In Norway they were preceded by an even older form of church—the original Irish church, which consisted of only one rectangular room.

In their first shape these Saxon churches were rather primitive. The basic measurements were not always adhered to throughout. The chancel was separated from the nave by means of a narrow and crude chancel arch, which in the early churches was hardly recognizable as an arch. The altar was placed against the east wall of the chancel, which was slightly higher than the nave, where the community sat on simple chairs with the women on the north side and the men on the south. If there were two entrances to the church the women used the north door and the men the south door. The south entrance, because that was the men's side, developed into an ornamented porch, the bridal porch or *brudportalen*.

The plan was simple not merely because of poverty or inability to build more elaborate churches. This simplicity fully corresponded to the parish's needs; with only one priest, and a community that could be accommodated in the nave, there was no need for a transept. The chancel was usually wagon-vaulted, while the nave was covered by a wooden ceiling.

Of this early group of churches there were two varieties: those with towers and those without. If towered, the church was designed to serve an added purpose: apart from the priest and the village community, it was to provide space for the king or the feudal lord and their families. Due to social distance and barriers during feudal times the king and lord kept well apart from his people. A tribune, that is, a raised and separate pew or dais, was built in the west end of the church, in the tower—so that, apart from solving a social problem, the tower often served as the symbol for a royal church. There are, of course, exceptions to this rule, for a tower does not always indicate a royal church.

The royal church is a more ancient establishment than the parish church. The kings and lords wanted to set a good example, and many of the royal churches were built before the ecclesiastical division of the countries was established. Among the earliest churches of this kind in Sweden can be mentioned Bjälbo, Stora Herrestad (Fig. 26, Pl. 23b) in Skåne; Reslöve, Västra Vemmerlöv, and

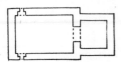

FIG. 24. Gudrum.
Scale 1:500.

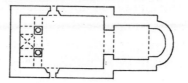

FIG. 28. Fjenneslev.
Scale 1:500.

Churches in Denmark (*above*) and Skåne (*below*).

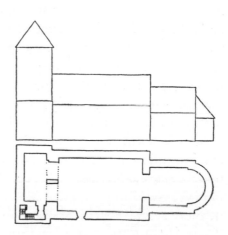

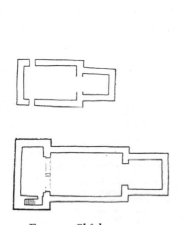

FIG. 25. Skårby.
FIG. 26. Stora Herrestad.
Scale 1:600.

FIG. 27. Loderup.
Scale 1:600.

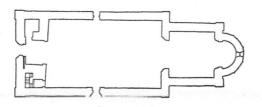

FIG. 29. Vä. Scale 1:600.

Gjellerup in Denmark, and Hvaler (Pl. 22*b*) in Norway. The distribution of these churches, roughly one in every hundred (or administrative district) especially near the oldest cities, bears witness to the king's deliberate order to have them erected. In other parts of Scandinavia, in the more eastern districts, they appear more sparsely and only on the earliest cultivated plains. On Gotland none was built, because of the independence of that island.

Towards the end of the eleventh century the parish churches and the royal churches underwent a change, which is evident above all in the plan. This change was originally caused by a change in the country that set the pattern—England. Through the Norman invasion the Anglo-Saxon plan with a straight east wall was abandoned in a very short time and churches were given instead a semicircular apsidal end. This fact is stressed by the fact that the Scandinavians were then focusing their interest on Normandy, whence this apsidal church had come. The change of the east end of the church did not imply any change in the function of the church—the ritual was still the same—only that the ideals or perhaps the fashion became different. Examples are Löderup (Fig. 27) in Skåne and Ravlunda, so full of ancient and 'fashionable' characteristics, in the same county, and Slaglille church on Sjælland. Among the royal churches of this type Tveje-Merløse (Pl. 26) in Denmark holds a unique position. A Swedish example is Vreta (Fig. 23), later adapted for nuns; in Norway, there is St. Halvard in Oslo. The tribunal openings at Tveje-Merløse stand in a rhythmical order, at the top designed as trefoils; there were other designs, large round arches as at Tirsted or a gallery as at Fjenneslev (Fig. 28), both of these in Denmark. When later the churches became ordinary parish churches many tribunes were destroyed. This was for instance the case at Askeby in Sweden.

The royal churches in the Mälar Valley were different. Skånella church (Pl. 3*a*), belonging to the Sigtuna group of churches, set the fashion and the central tower became the dominant characteristic. As was the case at Sigtuna these churches were built of granite and they also use the old cross-vaulting technique. Examples are Norrsunda and Färentuna. The style was adopted in parish churches but without the central tower, at Orkesta, Vidbo, Skogs Tibble, all in Uppland. An exception is Vaksala church near Uppsala where the tribune was placed in a west tower. These churches are the oldest in this part of Sweden and can be found only in the old cultural centres.

The apsidal churches were built in Scandinavia for about a century. Like the earlier Anglo-Saxon churches they were built in stone. Several materials were used. The great majority of the churches in Denmark, Sweden, and Finland were built of granite. Other kinds of stone, and bricks, were the material of only a third of the total number of medieval churches. Bricks were introduced towards the middle of the twelfth century in Denmark and about fifty years later in Sweden. At the beginning, bricks were used as structural material only, not as decoration.

The material that was at hand, and plentiful, came from the boulders spread all over Scandinavia during the glaciation period. To begin with, small undressed stones about ten inches in diameter were used, and later on, larger ones. As the size of the stones used increased it became necessary to dress them. They were halved and dressed but the natural form of the stones was kept. This technique was widely used in Uppland, although in Sjælland and Skåne it never developed. In west and north Jylland there is a fairly sharply limited area where the ashlar technique was used. Hover church is an example (Pl. 23a). There the use of granite became so firmly traditional that other materials could never penetrate. A particular reason for this was that the building programme there was almost fully carried out during the few short decades when this technique was in full bloom. The ashlar technique as represented in Jylland or at Lund was soon imitated in the churches built of crudely dressed stone. The joints of the stones were thickly plastered and more even joints drawn in the wet plaster. At the same time these churches display a rich variety of colours, with an exquisite handling of the different shades of the stones, reddish, greenish, bluish, etc. The most beautiful examples can be found among the thirteenth- and fourteenth-century churches in Uppland, further north in Sweden, and in Finland (Pl. 24).

On eastern Sjælland in Denmark some churches were built of chalk and in western Skåne near Hälsingborg and Lund there were sandstone churches. Limestone was used on the large plains mainly: near the Fiord of Roskilde and in eastern Jylland between the towns of Vejle and Horsens, in Sweden on the Västgöta and Östgöta plains. These are the most important building materials; others had a very limited use.

Towards the middle of the twelfth century the Anglo-Norman plan lost ground and had to give way for something new. Vä church in Skåne (Fig. 29) is a good example of the new spirit. In this royal church the different compartments—tower, tribune, nave, choir, and apse—were joined together to form a unity of quite another character than what had gone before. The measurements were more carefully observed with a deliberate proportion between nave and choir; the chancel arch no longer divided the church into two parts, and the apse was more closely related to the rest of the church. This not only shows a higher skill, the developing of a tradition, but proves that new ideals were replacing those from western Europe. These emerged from Germany and they meant a more intricate and complicated architecture, even for the parish churches. The influence was not always direct, more often via the great cathedrals at Lund and her sisters at Ribe and Viborg, to mention only a few. The new features are many, and one parish church might adopt a few, her neighbour others.

At Lund and Ribe the new vaulting technique from Lombardy was introduced. It not only facilitated the vaulting but also produced a certain regularity in the elevation and in the placing of the windows. This regularity is the new feature at Vä, where the original plan along simpler lines was abandoned during the course of erection when new signals came from Lund.

This influence from large cathedrals to parish churches is a frequent phenomenon. The influence of Lund was stronger than that of later cathedrals, since the impact of so many new features at once was enormous. It must be remembered that Lund was the centre of religious life in Scandinavia. The building of the cathedral was followed with the greatest interest, and a large number of bishops attended the reconsecration after its enlargement. And when Lund was completed, the stone-masons spread all over Scandinavia.

The royal church at Vreta (Fig. 22), probably founded by King Inge the Elder, was in its original shape an example of the 'principal' influence of Lund; the measurements at Lund were halved throughout.

A special feature at Lund is the shortened choir. This feature was adopted at the royal church at Kaga (Pl. 28a) in Sweden, which also adopted another feature from Lund, the added towers. Apart from the exuberant ornamentation at Lund the west towers were

the feature that most impressed her neighbours. The apsidal ornamentation was adopted, especially near Ribe, for example at Ballum.
The shortened choir appears at Svalöv, Höör, and Västra Tommarp,
all in Skåne. West towers can be found at Färlöv near Kristianstad
in Skåne where two towers were built, but sometimes the west
towers became one as at Stora Herrestad royal church (Pl. 23b). A
compromise was made at Rydaholm, where a large tower was
crowned by twin spires.

The influence of Lund was especially strong on Gotland; the
building of churches there had hardly begun before Byzantios
arrived from Lund. Together with influences directly from Westphalia he helped to create a quite specific kind of church architecture
on the island. The initiative on Gotland originally was taken in the
countryside; later it was the reverse—Visby took the lead. Byzantios
had learned the ashlar technique at Lund and brought it to Gotland:
there Vänge church is an example. When economic conditions
hampered such an extravagant and difficult technique, crudely
dressed stone became the substitute, as at Guldrupe. Both these
churches have a rectangular nave and choir with apsidal east end.
They also have towers, reminiscent of those at Lund, with two
coupled openings being the only articulation on the smooth tower
walls. On porches and tympanums was expressed an eager desire
for sculptural ornamentation.

Earlier in this book St. Katarina or Karin and St. Nicolai were
chosen to represent Visby (Pl. 20, 21). These two churches had,
however, much less influence on the surrounding countryside than
the church of the Germans, the present cathedral, St. Maria, and
St. Clemens and St. Drotten. St. Maria was rebuilt at the beginning
of the thirteenth century by Westphalians, and it was natural for the
German colony to want to change the church from a basilica into a
hall church, equipped with a west tower with galleries and a new
choir, flanked by two small octagonal towers (Fig. 30). These
towers are perhaps the strongest expression of the Westphalian spirit.
The rebuilding stood on the threshold of Gothic; the octagonal
towers have pointed arches while the new porch on the south side,
the brudportalen (Pl. 29a), is clearly Romanesque. This porch and
the towers were what influenced church builders around Visby the
most, so far as details go. The structural unity of the hall church
was adopted at once.

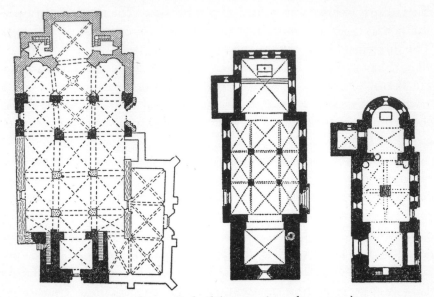

Three churches on Gotland (comparative scale not exact).
FIG. 30. St. Maria, Visby.   FIG. 31. Dalhem.   FIG. 32. Vall.

The church at Dalhem has a plan that is a simplified repetition of St. Maria (Fig. 31). The former has three bays, St. Maria five, but the new features are repeated, such as the large rectangular choir—here without the flanking towers—the west tower, and the south porch. A specific Westphalian feature is the spire. The same kind of tower is repeated at Öja. This plan was simplified in the churches of smaller parishes on Gotland such as Vall (Fig. 32), Stånga (Pl. 30), and Rone (Pl. 33a). The number of vaults was brought down from nine to four, supported in the middle by only one pier with capitals that varied during the course of time. These churches sounded a subdued echo on Scandinavian soil of the German imperial art.

Like the cathedral, the medieval parish church must be considered with its sculpture and other ornamental features, which were part of it, in order to be fully understood. But here these can only be dealt with in a fragmentary, incomplete way.

Principally the iconography of the church was obtained from the cathedrals, and the sculptural ornament in the Scandinavian parish churches corresponds to what is to be found on the Continent—the same motifs from Old or New Testament, or legends, here and there intermingled with motifs not entirely religious. The placing of these scenes was in general also the same, that is to say on and around the porches and on the capitals. Besides these, the baptismal fonts were ornamented and in the chancel arch there was a wooden image of Christ on the Cross, the rood as in English fourteenth-century churches. During later medieval times there was also a lively import of triptychs especially from northern Germany and the Netherlands. The impression of the churches on the visitor of today is often more barren than originally as many have lost their sculpture to museums.

Ornament in the oldest churches was rather scanty. The capitals were sometimes decorated, but were usually plain. The porches were accentuated with a simple moulding or column strip. Decora-tively the stress was laid on the baptismal fonts, which at the begin-ning of the twelfth century were being produced in great quantities. They stood, both spiritually and physically, at the entrance to the church. At Stånga there is a font made by Master Hegvald (Pl. 30). It is a typically archaic creation; Hegvald was not able to grasp all of the new spirit that swept Scandinavia during the twelfth century, for he was still partly tied to the old pagan tradition. It is true that the old Nordic ornamental tradition had withered, but the fact that it still existed at all prevented the artist from accepting the new style wholeheartedly. The epic desire to convey the new symbols is clearly visible, but the result is sometimes awkwardly drastic, and the animals on the lower part of the font have become burlesque creatures, perhaps from an excess of didactic fervour. Pagan belief was still closer than Christianity.

The cathedral at Lund also had an enormous impact on the orna-ment of parish churches. At once all possibilities were made clear to Scandinavian church builders. The consequences were rapid: tympanums, porches, and capitals were soon elaborately decorated. Like St. Maria at Visby, Stånga church on Gotland has its main entrance in the south wall (Pl. 29). Its decoration was carved in the middle of the fourteenth century, and the hundred and fifty years that had passed since St. Maria resulted in a much richer porch. The decoration is not restricted to tympanum and capitals only, but has spread also to the wall around the porch and the small gable above it, all arranged in a manner that would remind a visitor from France of Nôtre Dame de la Grande at Poitiers. The anonymous master of Stånga has been called Master Egypticus, an entirely misleading name, supposed to hint at his heavy style, which is not the most important aspect of his work. The porch is dedicated to Christ, with the Flagellation, Christ being taken down from the Cross, the Adoration of the Magi and, in the gable, the Resurrection. The tympanum shows the Crowning of the Virgin. A certain secular quality is apparent in these scenes; the epic is dominant and little is left of religious mysticism. All the characters are individuals with their own gestures and traits. The kings of the Adoration are noble lords from feudal courts, Christ's pain in the Flagellation is clearly visible in his tormented face.

Öja church had originally a wooden image of Christ on the Cross and a Mourning Mary, now at Visby Museum. They were carved by a master who was probably a native of Gotland educated at Reims in France; parallels with a sculpture of Joseph at Reims have been pointed out and are indeed visible; but the Swedish Mary is some, what more severe.

The first ecclesiastical buildings in which bricks were used were Ringsted, Sorø, the towers at Fjenneslev, and the round church at Bjernede in Denmark. So the new material first came into use on Sjælland and was at first limited to a few other areas: the south islands of Denmark, and western Schleswig as far south as Ejderen. Gumlösa church in Skåne from the end of the twelfth century is an early Swedish example. Like this church the earliest brick churches were built in accordance with the Anglo-Norman plan and decorated with Romanesque arches and soon also with blind recesses. In the fourteenth century the stepped gable appeared on towers and on the east end, and was a favourite feature often repeated in the following century, as can be seen at Norre Alslev (Pl. 27) and Kippinge in Denmark. One can also here see an influence from the church of St. Peder at Naestved in Denmark with its dominating and wide Late Gothic choir. This type also exists at Haderslev and Aarhus Cathedrals in Denmark, in a similar spirit to that at Linköping, Sweden.

Bricks were, however, most abundantly used in the Mälar Valley where the progress of Christianity was slow and church-building later, due to internal struggle and a strong local resistance. There the material was first used together with native stone; later it became the dominant material. Two sources gave inspiration to the builders of this region, the cathedrals of Strängnäs, Västerås, and Uppsala, and the friars' churches at Sigtuna, Stockholm, and elsewhere, hall churches on a simpler layout than the churches on Gotland. So a somewhat plainer plan was adopted. This is a remarkable phenomenon that goes to prove the strong influence that came from cathedrals and abbeys, although the layout of the latter was different, conditioned by a new service where the sermon was more important than the mass, while in the parish churches the service was unchanged and the altar was still the most important factor. Trönö church in Hälsingland, Sweden, built of granite, is an example of the simple rectangular type, Täby in Uppland (Pl. 33b) another. Össebygarn church was built of granite, with an apse, while Tegelsmora was built of granite in the lower parts but with pointed, steep gables of bricks where an elaborate ornamentation developed. A similar mixed technique is shown in Holy Trinity at Uppsala (Pl. 28b).

Uppsala Cathedral played the same part for central Sweden as Lund did for southern Scandinavia. The later part of its building history has been regarded as a victory for the basilical ideal. A strange translation of this took place at Södra Råda church in Värmland where the wooden ceiling became a trefoil in section (Pl. 32b), thus giving the illusion of a heightened middle part. A similar arrangement was originally to be found in the choir at Tensta in Uppland, where, however, the nave was covered by a wooden barrel vault. There are other features at Tensta coming from Uppsala, especially the diagonal buttresses, here on the west façade of the church.

Most churches in Uppland lack towers, the bells being hung in a detached wooden belfry, sometimes covered with tarred shingles similar to those used on the steep roofs of the churches. In the late fourteenth and in the fifteenth century numerous additions were made to these churches. Sacristies were built on the north side, vestibules on the south, and sometimes a wall was built around the churchyard with an attached entrance porch, or lichgate.

The brick churches in central Sweden were only seldom orna-mented with sculptures; the exteriors of these churches were instead decorated in the architectural spirit already mentioned. In the interiors, however, the vaults were richly decorated with frescoes done on dry plaster. Mural painting had already spread to Scandinavia in the Romanesque period; numerous schools developed through foreign influence and through the emergence of local traditions. Its aspects were just as varied as those of the suclpture. Here only certain ones can be mentioned.

One of the few Swedish churches which has kept its original wooden ceiling is Dädesjö in Småland. The ceiling was painted late in the thirteenth century with roundels containing Biblical and legendary scenes. The painter is not known. Runes appear in the painted text but are no guarantee for the nationality of the artist. The character of these paintings is a strange synthesis of a rather individual interpretation of the human figures with purely Byzantine features such as postures and costumes.

When during the thirteenth century new vaults were replacing the old wooden ceilings it meant new and more complicated compositions. The painted scenes were usually subordinated to the ribs (Pl. 31); sometimes 'artificial' lines were painted in the form of foliage. In late medieval times decorations became more abundant. The Romanesque motifs, acanthus and vines and so on, grew into trees and rich foliage, in which birds were often shown being attacked by evil powers. The tree could also symbolize Life. The earliest example of this is to be found in the east vaults at Strängnäs. These paintings date back to the end of the twelfth century and the same cathedral also tells of the complete dissolution of this style in the west vaults, where the organic conception is lost. The style spread to Finland, where Åbo Cathedral (Turku) is an example.

A distant relative of the original Uppland style appears on the stained-glass windows at Dalhem (Pl. 32a) on Gotland, executed in the middle of the thirteenth century. Added to the Byzantine spirit is a purely epic trend: the people actually act. In the Ascension angels are assisting Christ, yet at the same time they passively pose and turn to the onlooker.

The decorations at Södra Råda in Värmland are dated 1323 (Pl. 32b). They are found on the trefoil wooden ceiling and on the walls, showing in the east the Throne of Grace and in the west the Crowning of the Virgin. There are medallions and decorative borders and rows of statuesque figures in painted recesses with Gothic gables. The Legend of the Virgin is painted here as well. At Södra Råda French art appears in the North, for the postures are softened and divinity can be traced in the human features.

The medieval mural art reached its highest peak in Uppland in the fifteenth and sixteenth centuries. At Täby church (Pl. 33b), built about 1300, and with early Gothic vaults, we find an art quite different from that at Södra Råda. The paintings were done by a certain Master Albertus Pictor, according to his latinized name. He has been traced to Stockholm where he lived for the last fifty years of the fifteenth century. His art shows a different conception, funda-mentally a different religious spirit from the earlier painters we have seen.

In the chancel is a Pietà and in the same vault the Raising of Lazarus. In the second bay he painted the Annunciation, Jonah and the Whale, Saul and David, and other Old Testament scenes. In the third bay, among many other scenes, is the Deluge, in the last bay Cain and Abel, the Sin of Adam and Eve, the Massacre of the Innocents, etc. Thus the iconographical system is broken. Old Testament scenes are interrupted by scenes from the New Testa-ment, 'important' ones among 'unimportant'. The story of the Passion appears here and there, and not in its usual chronological order. The ribs are decorated with rhythmically twisting branches, usually vines. This freedom of the artist can be interpreted symboli-cally: he is no longer the humble servant of religion, but a painter who ought to have the right to arrange his pictures as he wishes and to lay the stress upon those he considers to be most valuable artisti-cally. This is verified if one studies the character of the different scenes. The starting point was the growing realism which appeared at Linköping Cathedral, a realism which had its roots in the emer-gence of a new type of human being, a more autonomous man dis-claiming the fear his forefathers felt for the Last Judgement. The new burgher culture was probably strongly felt by this Stockholm artist. His realism is sometimes on the verge of burlesque, as in the blood-stained sword of David and the lively mimic. Details are coarse, for instance the eyes and hands. Neither pictorial nor plastic effects were aimed at; there are no shadows, and sharp contours were drawn around people and objects. The contents are naïve, perhaps in an effort to make them easily understood—sometimes even a bit too easily.

In the south vestibule there are paintings by another artist. Here the style is more pictorial and lighter, less saturated colours have been used. The figures are characterized by a religion more deeply felt and have little in common with the people in Albertus' paintings.

The medieval parish church was not only the religious centre of the peasant community. The twelfth and thirteenth centuries, times of unrest with many Wendish harryings along the shores of the

Baltic, saw the growth of another building tradition related to the plans described above, that of the round church (as at Bjernede, Fig. 33). A similar trend has earlier been pointed out in regard to the centralized church at Kalundborg in Denmark. There are many examples of this type in Sweden and Denmark; Østerlar on Born-holm (Pl. 25) is one of the finest, and also the Norwegian church at Tönsberg. A compromise can be seen at Karise in Denmark,

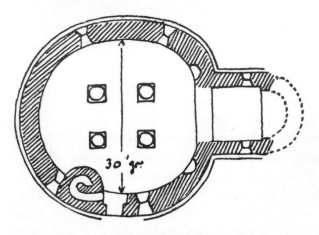

FIG. 33. Bjernede.

where the choir was extended and contains an upper defensive story. Another example is Köge church, also in Denmark, with a tower equipped with loopholes. The round church is a synthesis of the keep and its chapel, and is a purely Scandinavian creation which has nothing to do with Continental developments. On Öland a slightly different type of church emerged. It had two towers and the east tower above the choir was fortified.

The Stave Churches in Norway

Parish churches with a particularly strong regional flavour, developed in a separate tradition of their own, were the stave churches. Out of the old timber technique of Hemse (Fig. 7) and elsewhere there grew up in Norway a refined technique that was kept alive up to the sixteenth century. The refinement consisted in fastening wall boards—formerly posts stuck into the ground—to a ground-sill frame, which protected the bases of the boards more effectively against rot. The earlier frame construction with corner posts and roof truss as at Hemse combined with this new ground-sill to give a much stronger frame. Examples of this type of stave church were at Holtålen and Urnes (Fig. 34), both built during the later part of the eleventh century. It may be mentioned that there is an early example of this sort of thing still standing in England, at Greenstead in Essex, where the nave wall was formed by halved logs standing in a wooden ground‑sill.

The plans of the stave churches derived from the same Anglo‑Saxon plans that were being adopted in other parts of Scandinavia for churches of stone: the rectangular nave with a rectangular chancel. The west entrance was the most important one, where the porch with its ornamental features was built.

Just as other churches developed from double‑cell to basilican form, so did the stave churches. The earliest known example is the second stave church at Urnes (Fig. 34), built around 1125–40. The plan of this church is an extension of the first church on the site, which remained as part of it. The original ground‑sill frame was

FIG. 34.
Urnes I and II.

retained, carrying sixteen posts (considerably more than necessary for the construction) as an inner 'colonnade' supporting the roof, and the outer wall boards, instead of being placed between the posts, stood outside them in an outer ground‑sill frame connected with and supported by the older frame. Thus the spaces between the row of posts and the wall became side aisles; one might almost speak of an ambulatory, since this 'colonnaded' space surrounds the nave com‑pletely, just as it did in the original Roman basilican plan before the Christians adapted it. Here, however, the eastern space opens into the chancel.

As this type of church was so much larger than the earlier one it had to be equipped with buttresses. This was done by forcing naturally arched tree branches in between the vertical posts (which sometimes had carved 'capitals'); the result is Romanesque in charac‑ter. Cross‑pieces were also added on the inside of the outer wall. The steep rafters supported by the vertical posts have arched braces as well. Another church showing this construction is at Hoprekstad, also in the south‑western province of Sogn.

This sort of buttressing became still more complicated at Borgund, built about 1150. Here two kinds of arched braces were used and between them further cross-pieces. At Hoprekstad, at Borgund, and at Lom (Pl. 34*b*) among others, the interior of the nave was being given a horizontal division of stories that was analogous to the nave elevations of contemporaneous cathedrals. This became the tradi-tional elevation for stave churches, and there were no further basic structural changes.

Outside (Pl. 34*a*), Borgund church has all around the ground-floor walls an outer ambulatory or gallery with gables protecting the three entrances. The exterior shape of the building was thus made cruciform. This outer gallery served the double purpose of protect-ing the lower parts of the church against rot and providing a sheltered meeting place for the village people. Here is a remarkably rich ex-terior at Borgund. No less than six roofs grow out of each other: one roof over the gallery, one over the aisles, one over the nave, and the three little roofs of the belfry. The upper gables are decorated with dragons' heads reminiscent of pagan times. This sort of construc-tion, which gives the impression of growing straight up in the air around one central cell, became traditional.

In addition to the decoration inside these churches—carved capitals and shallow reliefs of dragon masks and twisted patterns with cut-out backgrounds—the exterior and especially the west front was richly decorated. The style of ornament is closely connected with that of the Viking rune-stones, and an Irish-Celtic character runs through it as well. As on the rune-stones, animal motifs were reduced in a lively, unstatic way to stylized forms, sometimes to such an extent that the various animals are difficult to separate from each other, especially when among them ornamental coils are interwoven. Under the influence of Late Roman ornament, foliage was added and this too was reduced to ropy patterns.

Such ornamental features are to be found surrounding the west door of Urnes stave church (Pl. 35*b*). It must be remembered that, when these were carved, Norwegians had been on terms of uneasy familiarity with Ireland for three centuries. The decoration at Urnes overflows the jambs and doorway arch to which it was more often confined. Here is told the tale of Zion (as a deer-like creature) fight-ing evil forces symbolized by snake-like creatures. The slender animal forms are twisting in S-curves, partly intertwined with one another. The carver's vigorous desire for expression appears in terms of design—as in the spiral 'hip and shoulder' lines—rather than in realism. Above, between, and underneath are the vines with endless wiry stems.

As for prototypes, there seem to be, apart from western influence, certain characteristics related to the work of Carolingian craftsmen in ivory, where the surface to be decorated was often 'open-worked'. The result here is similar, with carving almost in the round, although the relief itself is not very high, and the effect is that of a patterned surface on a dark background. It is a very expressive art, this Norwegian wood-carving. The coils are repeated in a regular rhythm that has been interpreted as analogous to the metre of Old Norse poetry.

On the west front of Hoprekstad stave church, of the late twelfth century, more ornamental vines appear (Pl. 35a). They grow up from the lower regions and mingle in the fierce fight between three dragons on the lintel. The subject of the carving was derived from pagan times: it is Ragnarök, the Last Day. From the point of view of style it is a further development of the doorway at Urnes. The rhythm is no longer as obvious. It is as if the fierceness had suppressed the earlier lyricism.

A quite overwhelming pattern of interweaving ornaments is to be found at Hedalen in Valdres, of about 1160. The motif is once more the battle of the dragons, in a less open design, more tightly knit and flat, full of crowded, curling forms. By and by, the desire to decorate swamped the original style. The south door of Heddals stave church, in the province of Telemark, of about 1250, for instance, is decorated with serpents and vines in a braid-like, shallow relief from which one can no longer pick out the different motifs.

On Hyllestad church in Setesdalen, of about 1200, there was an echo of the vigorous style of the previous century. The church itself is now pulled down, but the reliefs (Pl. 36) are in the Oldsak Collection at Oslo University. Here the vine coils contain human figures. The motif is taken from the tale of Favne, and in an archaic, naïve manner the story is told, starting from the lower parts of the right porch jamb: Sigurd has his sword forged, he tries it on the anvil, and he kills the dragon. On the left jamb, starting from the bottom, is the rest of the tale: Sigurd grills the dragon heart and hears the birds speaking, and finally he slays the treacherous Regin. It is the tale that Wagner was to celebrate as *Siegfried* and that Christians could tell about any dragon-slaying saint. Certain details of the human beings are particularly archaic. The eyes of figures in profile are seen as from the front, and details like clothes, beards, and hair are marked by geometrical incisions. The twisted ornament surrounding these scenes has in a sense lost its organic nature. The best of the figures is the horse Grane, with the birds sitting in the branches beneath him. That a heathen tale is told should not cause any surprise; in an associative manner the story was given Christian content. Good triumphed over Evil for every worshipper to see.

With all this analysis of the various aesthetic and functional aspects of the parish church, aimed at finding the forces that created it, one must not lose the structural whole, the unity, with which stone-masons and wood-carvers together with the people tried to symbolize their Christian belief and religion. The unity of these churches is difficult to pin down. One has a beautiful detached belfry, another a marvellous porch, a third perhaps an imposing tower, while others lie surrounded by old elm trees. The mood they convey, the values they guard, move slowly from the dark and sinister chapels of new-born Christianity to a melancholy and tender melody not without its primitive and awkward tones intermingled with a naïve feeling that rang out towards the end of the Middle Ages in a triumphal ecstasy filled with self-assurance and creative joy, materialized in the abundantly decorated and complicated Gothic vaults. The parish church represents the rustic soul of the medieval Scandinavian peasant. It speaks the same language and conveys the same feelings as its contemporaries, the great cathedrals; they are tuned in the same key, but the little church is transposed one octave.

1. 1. Husaby, Sweden (p. 33).

(b) Gamla Uppsala (p. 35).

(a) St. Olof, Sigtuna (p. 34).

(a) Skånella (pp. 35, 66).

(b) Dalby (p. 36).

Pl. 3. Early churches, central Sweden and Skåne.

Pl. 4. Lund Cathedral, Skåne, apse (p. 40).

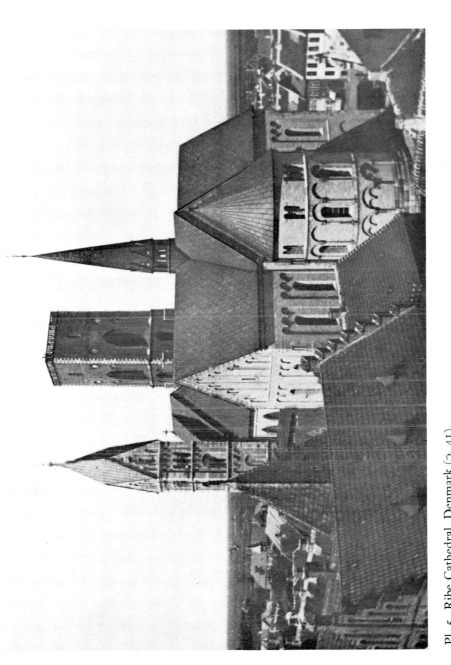

Pl. 5. Ribe Cathedral, Denmark (p. 41).

Pl. 6. Ribe Cathedral, Denmark (p. 42).

Pl. 7. Trondheim Cathedral, Norway (p. 46).

Pl. 8. Lund Cathedral, south transept door (p. 40).

1. 9. Linköping Cathedral, south door (p. 47).

(a) In the seventeenth century (p. 47).

(b) The nave (p. 47).

Pl. 10. Linköping Cathedral, Sweden.

Pl. 11. Kalundborg, Denmark (p. 50)

Pl. 12. Roskilde Cathedral, Denmark (p. 46).

(a) Västerås.   (b) Strängnäs.

(c) Uppsala in the seventeenth century.

Pl. 13. Swedish cathedral towers (p. 49).

(b) Varnhem. Sweden (p. 57).

(a) Venge, Denmark (p. 54).

Pl. 15. Maribo, Denmark, abbey church (p. 62).

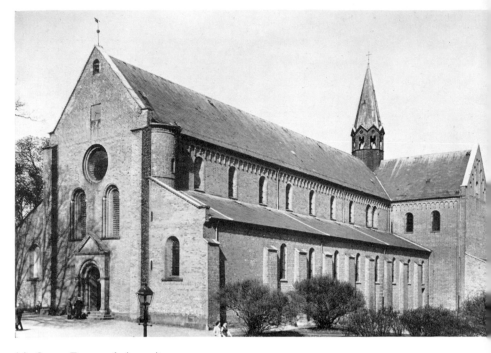

(a) Sorø, Denmark (p. 55).

(b) St. Maria, Sigtuna, Sweden (p. 60

Pl. 16. Brick churches.

7. Løgumkloster, Denmark (p. 44).

Pl. 18. Søndresogn church, Viborg, Denmark (p. 58).

Pl. 19. Carmelite abbey church, Helsingør, Denmark (p. 60).

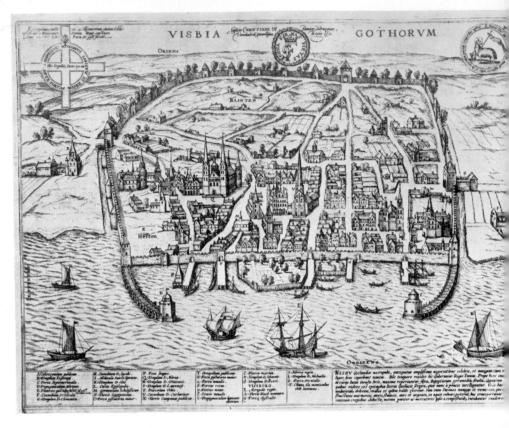

(a) View of medieval Visby (p. 90).

(b) Roma abbey church (p.

Pl. 20. The island of Gotland.

(a) St. Katarina, Visby (p. 59).

(b) St. Nicolai, Visby (p. 59).

Pl. 21. Two churches on Gotland.

(a) Moster (p. 63).

(b) Hvaler (p. 66

Pl. 22. Norwegian parish churches.

(a) Hover parish church (pp. 63, 67).

tore Herrestad royal church (pp. 64, 69).

Churches in Denmark and Skåne.

Pl. 24. Tyrvaa parish church, Finland (p. 67).

. Østerlar parish church, Bornholm (p. 76).

Pl. 26. Tveje Merløse royal church, Denmark (p. 66).

Pl. 27. Norre Alslev parish church, Denmark (p. 72).

(b) Holy Trinity, Uppsala (p. 73).

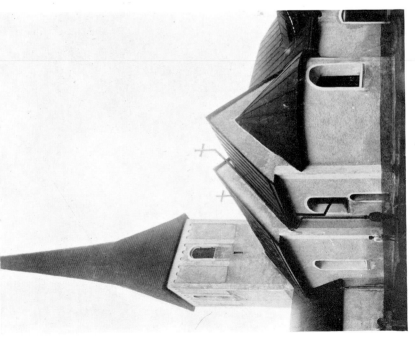

(a) Kaga royal church (p. 68).

Pl. 28. Two churches in Sweden.

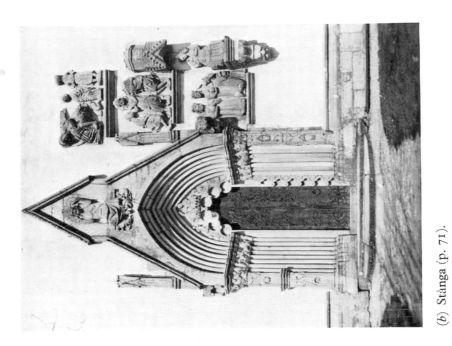

(b) Stånga (p. 71).

(a) St. Maria, Visby (p. 69).

Pl. 29. Church porches, Gotland.

Pl. 30. Stånga parish church, Gotland (p. 71).

1. Hattula parish church, Finland (p. 74).

(a) Dalhem, Gotland, stained glass (p. 74).

(b) Södra Råda, Sweden (p. 74).

Pl. 32. Church decoration.

(*a*) Rone, Gotland (p. 70).

(*b*) Täby, Sweden (p. 74).

Pl. 33. Parish church interiors.

(b) Lom (p. 78).

(a) Borgund (p. 78).

Pl. 34. Norwegian stave churches.

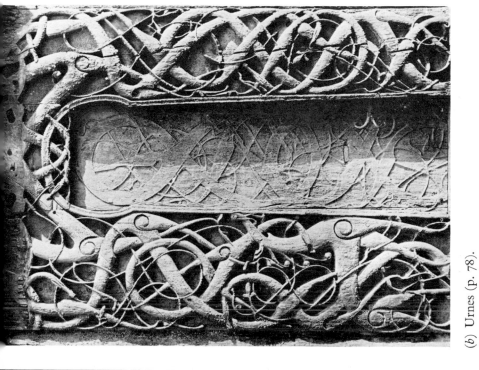

(a) Hoprekstad (p. 79).

(b) Urnes (p. 78).

Pl. 35. Norwegian church doorways.

Pl. 36. Hyllestad stave church, Norway, carved relief (p. 79).

VIII

DOMESTIC AND CIVIC BUILDINGS
BEFORE 1500

Medieval House Types

THE history of medieval houses in Scandinavia is the story of the spread of southern housing habits, allowing for the limitations of a poorer economic background. For obvious reasons the upper classes in society were the first to adopt new ideas and the peasants copied them. The very conservative habits of farmers meant that their houses were occupied almost unchanged for many hundreds of years, and enough of these remain today to give a fairly clear picture of the houses of the Middle Ages.

If possible the feudal baron built his house of stone. It was planned according to the two-room system known to have been at least as early as the ninth-century plan for St. Gallen. In the plan of the prior's house there, the first story above the ground-floor kitchen was divided in two: one living-room and one bedroom. For occasions of ceremony—natural consequence of feudal life—the story above that was built as a banqueting hall with a partly open south wall, or solarium. This banqueting hall at St. Gallen consisted of only one modest room, a simplification of the classic plan in which the recep-tion apartment had two rooms as well, with an inner withdrawing room for ceremonial occasions. This type of house, then, provided two upper stories, one for everyday life and the other for festivities, each divided into a private part and a communal part. When the desire for privacy grew stronger, a room of more intimate character was added to the ordinary bedroom, the wardrobe or closet.

In Sweden the principle of the house at St. Gallen is represented by Tynnelsö in Södermanland (Fig. 35) and by Torpa in Väster-götland (Fig. 36). The planning of Tynnelsö is entirely Conti-nental: on the ground floor the household department, on the next floor hall and bedroom, and on the top floor the banqueting hall. The ground-floor ceiling was cross-vaulted. Ceremony was more

G

dominant at Torpa, where the two upper floors consist of large halls, while the ground floor contains a vaulted bedroom and the house-hold department is dug down in the cellar. This indicates the frequent compromise with the old habit of living at ground level, probably tradition from the time of the hearth house. Another example of the two-room plan in Sweden is Alsnö. The Abbess's House at Vreta nunnery had a similar plan. The fortified house at Gurre in Denmark also has the two-room plan.

When, during the troublous times in Europe following the disintegration of Rome, people were forced to live in fortified houses, the two-room plan was used vertically in a circular or quadrangular tower, with the rooms on top of each other instead of beside each other. Above the ground floor was the living-room and over it the bedroom, where sometimes a closet was added in the thickness of the wall. Examples of such keeps in Scandinavia are the twelfth-century tower in Stockholm around which was built the castle Tre Kronor, and those at Gothem and Kalmar and Hälsingborg (the Kärna, Fig. 37). Such tower dwellings were always rather confined, and were only used in times of unrest and war, while in peacetime a roomier house of the two-room type beside the tower was used. Bishop Absalon's castle in Copenhagen and Hammershus on Bornholm each had these two main buildings in addition to all defensive arrangements. Nyborg Castle in Denmark, built about 1250, consists of three structures: residence, keep with room, and encircling wall. Håkonshallen in Norway was contemporary with it.

On the Continent the urge for feudal splendour resulted in yet another building, a hall of such magnificent dimensions that there was not room for it in the ordinary house. This separate banqueting house consisted of a hall and a withdrawing room; the latter, more private end of the building was always placed nearest to the private rooms of the dwelling house, either adjoining or connected by a gallery. The Holy Roman Emperor's palace at Goslar was an establishment of this kind, with the addition of a separate chapel, and marked the fullest northern development of the medieval household plan. A Scandinavian version was the Bishop's Palace at Trondheim in Norway, built about 1200 (Fig. 38), with two-room dwelling and hall house. The latter had two floors with two rooms on each floor. At Åhus in Sweden the Bishop's Palace is an example of

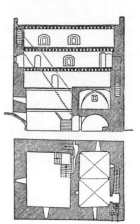

FIG. 35. Tynnelsö house.   FIG. 36. Torpa house.

T. MÅRTENSSON INV. GOTH·GUSTAFSSON DEL. 1934

Fig. 37. Hälsingborg keep, reconstruction.

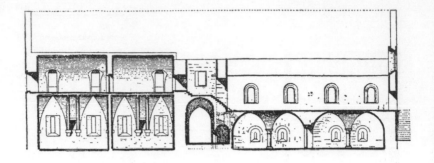

Fig. 38 (*above*). Bishop's palace, Trondheim.
Fig. 39 (*below*). Bishop's palace, Vadstena.

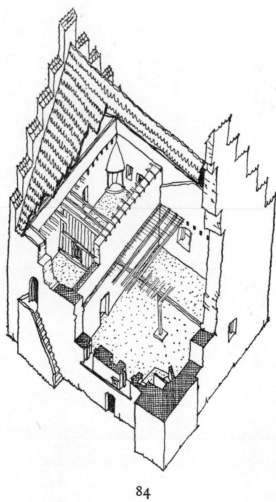

hall house and keep built together. This was a water castle on a small island, so that all had to be on a small scale: the tower is no bigger than a Continental closet.

A synthesis was often contrived of the various elements (transla' tions in stone of the timber technique) in these fortress houses, which makes it hard to tell sometimes whether a dwelling with two rooms developed out of a single-roomed tower with closet, or a tower with adjoining hall house, or the St. Gallen type of two-room plan. It was natural in a cold climate to pull the different structures together. In England such hybrids were frequent, enclosing within one build' ing chapel, residence, and hall. This habit in Scandinavia is repre' sented by the Bishop's Palace at Vadstena in Sweden (Fig. 39), which belonged to the bishops of Linköping. This consisted originally of a tower to which a house of the two-room type was added later; the ground floor of the latter had an entrance hall and an inner room, while the floor above had a large outer room and a small inner room. Some similarity to the old rural South Scandinavian house is obvious: the tower room at Vadstena corresponds to the hearth house, and the two-room house to the old adjoining gallery house. What is left out at Vadstena is the built-in passage, which would have provided a separate entrance but is here transformed into one of the two ground-floor rooms. This lack of a separate entrance space indicates a reduced residential standard, although this was an upper' class house. The separate entrance was to reappear, however, in the 'double apartment' of a later century.

The housing habits of the peasantry mirrored those of their feudal lords, in a simplified way which helps us to decipher the intricate combinations that appeared in castles and fortified manor houses. Three patterns were common in the medieval Scandinavian country' side: to give them their Swedish names, there was the *skålmostuga,* the *ramloftstuga,* and the *morastuga.*

The single-story two-room house that appeared on farms in the thirteenth century was the *skålmostuga* (Fig. 40). The larger of the two rooms contained the entrance, recessed to shelter the doorway from the weather. This room had a big brick fireplace for cooking and heating. The *skålmostuga* developed in imitation of the upper' class two-room houses although these had more than one story. At the same time there was the parallel development of the South Scandinavian house, an aggregation of two or three separate units.

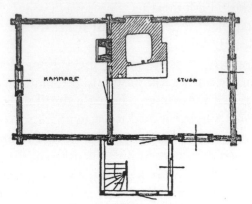

FIG. 40. Skålmostuga.

FIG. 41. Ramloftstuga.　　　　FIG. 42. Morastuga.

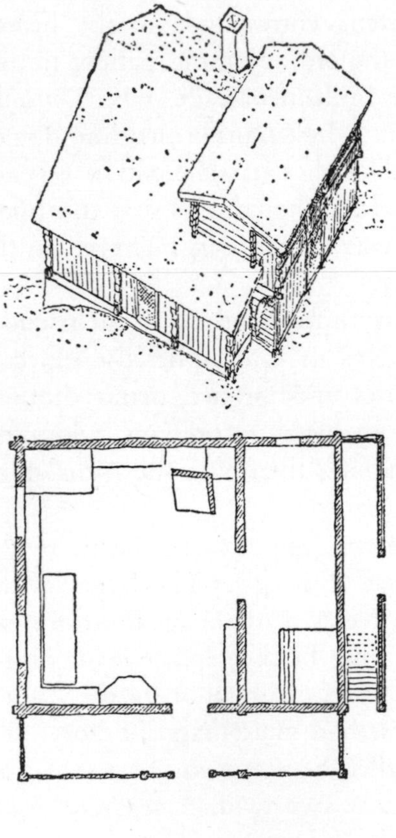

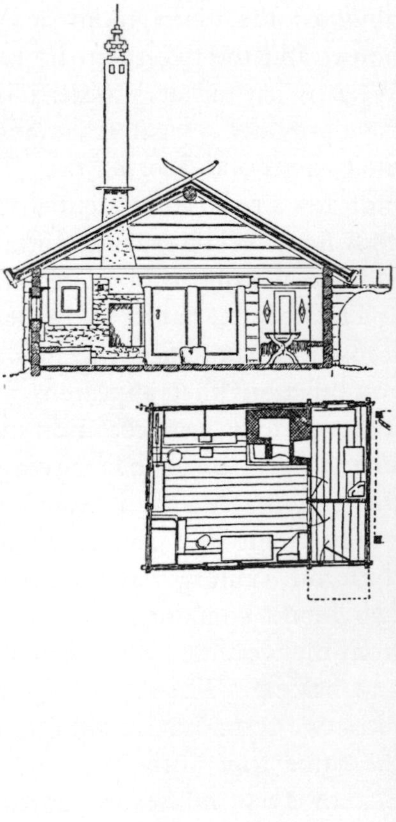

During the Middle Ages there grew up the method of putting these within uniform walls under one roof, and this was the *ramloftstuga* (Fig. 41). The entrance went into the larger room which was con-nected with an inner two-story part of the house through two doors, the inner part corresponding with the old gallery house, even to having the staircase on the outside, leading up to a gallery. The gallery, however, instead of overhanging the entrance passage that went right through the South Scandinavian house, was placed on the back of the *ramloftstuga*.

Another alternative was the *morastuga* (Fig. 42), in which the entrance led into what had been one of the inner rooms instead of directly into the room with the main fireplace; that is, there was a separate entry space in addition to the main room and another inner room. The *ramloftstuga* had been a union of the single-storied and the two-storied portions of the South Scandinavian house; the *morastuga* was this plan without the upper story. The *skålmostuga* used the basic Continental two-room plan on one story, with the entrance leading into the larger room.

Tradition divided the living-room into two parts in these farm-houses. The women's place was by the fire, and the men's side with the seat of honour was furthest from the entrance. In the *morastuga*, a beam in the ceiling went right across the living-room from the fireplace, marking a boundary beyond which beggars and poor people might not set foot unless specially permitted to do so. On Gotland a brick arch served the same purpose.

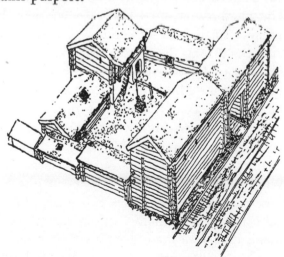

FIG. 43.
Medieval merchant's house.

Such Swedish house types, carried to the New World in the seventeenth century, are said to have introduced what was later to become that great American political symbol, the log cabin.

Medieval Market Towns

During the Middle Ages the earlier 'buying fields' and market villages throughout the countryside grew into towns. They have been called agrarian market towns, partly because they served as trading centres for the surrounding country, and partly because the merchant households composing them were organized in much the same way as the farms were. Such towns arose at road junctions in agricultural land and have the irregular shapes of spontaneous expansion.

The household of the merchant (Fig. 43) was, like that of the farmer, a domestic establishment of patriarchal structure. Livestock were kept for household requirements, and their owner had the right to pasture them on the commons surrounding the town. The special function of this house was the provision of warehousing and shop space. The site was planned in the following manner, with the buildings along the sides of an open yard. During the Middle Ages the residential part was situated across the yard on the inner side; first it was a South Scandinavian house, later a house of the two-rooms-to-a-floor type. Facing the street were warehouses—gallery houses with the galleries towards the yard. The façade towards the street was a closed one with only a few openings and no proper windows. The gate between street and yard was kept locked at night. If the site was small, the warehouses were built at right angles to one another. Along the sides of the yard were stables and cow-sheds, while behind the dwelling house was a private garden. Towards the end of the Middle Ages the residential part was moved over to the ground floor of the building on the street (see Chapter XII).

Originally, then, life was concentrated in the yard. It was here that transactions were carried out and the stables were ready to house the horses and carriages of visiting farmers. The craftsman's premises were planned in exactly the same way, the only modifications being those required by his trade—ropewalks, for instance. The arrangement of every householder's property was basically the same in these towns, except for the few who were too poor to have property, who lived in smaller circumstances. Examples of towns that began as agrarian market centres are Uppsala, Linköping, Vadstena, Söder-köping, and Ribe.

A regional pattern within such towns developed early. The centre was the market-place, near the church and sometimes the castle. The foremost merchants lived along the main streets, noisy and space-demanding workshops were pushed out of the centre towards the outskirts of the town, and the smaller, less important craftsmen found

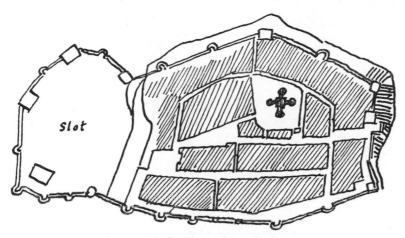

FIG. 44. Kalundborg, the medieval town.

their sites in less prosperous areas. The whole was surrounded by a fortified wall or perhaps only a wood fence. This form of town organization was kept alive in Scandinavia right up to the nine-teenth century and was only slowly dissolved by the different func-tions of the industrialized town. Kalundborg (Fig. 44) was a concentrated example of the old fortified pattern.

In South Scandinavia the structure of the agrarian town was the same, but the tendency of the South Scandinavian house plan and the half-timber technique was to link the outbuildings more closely to the main house, so that the plan was more compact. The next change in appearance would come with the ornamental brick gable, but something new was needed to bring it, and that was long-distance trade.

The Hanse towns that grew up during the thirteenth century were differently organized, which was quite natural since they were based on long-distance trade, and traders from Lübeck formed a great part of their populations. The houses of Stockholm and Copenhagen represented a variety of building traditions. A cardinal example of an international trading centre, where groups of foreigners were settled even before the days of the Hanseatic League, was Visby on Gotland (Pl. 20*a*), that strategic island in the Baltic.

Since at least the twelfth century merchants on Gotland had car-ried on trade between Novgorod and western Europe. They estab-lished warehousing and docking facilities in sheltered places and creeks mainly on the west coast of the island. The spot where the

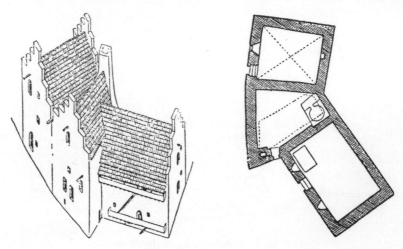

FIG. 45. Häggska house, Visby.

still inhabited town of Visby stands seems to have been especially favoured, and even before the twelfth century Germans came and settled, eventually forming their own merchant companies to com-pete with the various Scandinavian companies already established there. In the thirteenth century all these companies were united, and the town of Visby was the result. Independent of the surrounding countryside, the town was encircled by a wall two miles long, equipped with defensive towers and turrets and later enlarged by further ramparts set off by moats. Even the waterfront was protected by a wall, with here and there an arched opening in it to allow access to the docks—the Kruttornet, an old keep built in the eleventh cen-tury, was not regarded as strong enough to hold the harbour by itself.

Visby grew up around the harbour, where its earliest visible core dates from the twelfth or possibly the beginning of the thirteenth century. The foreigners who came to trade built their enclaves, each with its own church, outside this core. Pastures and commons were included in the area surrounded by the town wall.

The rise of Visby as a Hanseatic power in the Baltic continued during the thirteenth and early fourteenth centuries. But in 1361 the town surrendered to the Danish king Valdemar Atterdag and his powerful army, out to halt the Hanseatic monopoly of the trade routes to Russia. A hastily assembled peasant army was beaten just outside the town wall. A breach in this wall still shows the way Valdemar and his army made their entry, according to the best

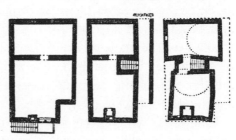

FIG. 46.
Stockholm merchant's house.

medieval tradition. He robbed Visby of all its riches, but the spoils so easily got were as easily lost, for the ships loaded with Visby riches now rest at the bottom of the Baltic. Yet the decline of Visby had started before Valdemar looted it, for the Baltic merchants depended on it less and less as more skilful navigation carried them past Gotland. The opening of the Elbe-Münde canal in the 1390's marked its end as a great port.

Trade left its mark on household planning in Visby. Large ware-houses occupied most of the sites, and the actual dwellings were either in 'tower houses' behind them or sometimes alongside them in the street. Since the centre of Visby was very crowded, there were no yards as on the mainland. The warehouses were gallery houses of stone with cross-vaulted ceilings. An example of a tower house built up to the street line is the Häggska house (Fig. 45), which indicates a growing likeness to Continental houses in having an ornamented gable towards the street. The dwelling part of it was equipped with a large oven for cooking and heating on the ground floor, and was not unlike a Saxon house, without the unsegregated livestock.

Extensive archaeological investigations in Stockholm have proved that the medieval town, Gamla Sta'n or Old Town, to a large extent consisted of a later type of house (Fig. 46) than the one so common at Visby. This was built on the two-room system and also included compartmented warehouses or workshops apart from the residential rooms. Each house had one gable facing the street. A similar house exists on Præstegade, Kalundborg, built of bricks and with storage space on the top floor.

Of medieval civic institutions there is little left to see today. The town hall of Næstved in Denmark—a remarkably well-preserved town—is the oldest remaining in Scandinavia. It was built in 1430 and in a later addition received a very elaborately decorated steep gable facing the street, a gable ornamented with the sort of recesses and blind circles so common on the churches. The town hall of Visby was like many others of the time, the upper story on the pattern of the feudal banquet hall, the ground floor surrounded by open arcades. Near the harbour the various companies had halls and storehouses.

Churches, which were just as much manifestations of corporate effort as guildhalls, were especially numerous at Visby, partly because of the wealth of the town and partly because the residents of each foreign quarter built their own church. St. Maria was the German church, St. Clemens may have been the church of the Danes, and it is supposed that St. Olof was the Swedish church; there were many more. Town churches were being built in all the mercantile towns at this period. The hall type of church was preferred by these townsmen with their strong sense of community, where no one was better than his neighbour, no one sat in a more distinguished part of the church than another, and the roof was the same height over everyone. The influence of this conception appears in cathedrals such as Västerås and Strängnäs, which were both in prosperous towns. Churches in the trading towns around the southern Baltic were usually built of brick with stepped gables embellished with pointed blind panels.

Many Danish and South Swedish towns still show that the stone houses with decorated gables turned towards the street were something new and that many burghers still kept to the old half-timber technique. We can turn again to Næstved, to the Apostlahused (the Apostle House) on Riddergade, 1589, and find an example which has derived its name from the twelve disciples carved on the façade as decorations. Market towns were conservative in their taste and this house has no steep gable turned to the street, but more and more they did. Usually it was a question, not of the function of the house, but of space, since crowded towns had much narrower building lots and houses had to turn their short ends towards the street. As will be shown, later the Danes made a synthesis of both types.

The visual character of these towns can still be imagined in Skåne and Denmark, where warehouse ranges along the streets are still preserved here and there. These and the brick houses with their decorated gables, together with town halls which often had impressive towers, all give evidence of the dawning self-esteem of the burgesses and embody the symbolic framework of the town.

The wooden towns of Sweden, because of the old-fashioned character of the all-timber technique, had a more severe and closed appearance. The streets were lined with massive wooden walls in the corner-joint technique which gave little opportunity for ornamental features. Decoration was restricted to the balusters on the galleries facing the yard. But whatever was lost to the street in private display, the householders made up for it in communal fashion in their church towers. At Uppsala, Västerås, and Strängnäs (Pl. 13) and elsewhere it was the townsmen themselves who financed the heightening of the west towers of their churches and cathedrals. The towers at Roskilde (Pl. 12) and Assens show a similar tendency in Denmark.

Contrary to the earlier medieval trend towards attenuation, these fifteenth-century towers had a rather massive character, some of which has since been lost by restorations and rebuildings. The plans are square, the openings quite small and regular. The solidity is marked rather than eased by plain sunk reliefs in the brick in the shape of quatrefoils, little blind arcades, and so on, stressing horizontal division rather than verticality. At Uppsala there were once blank recesses in the shape of coats of arms, clearly proclaiming the secular natures of the sponsors. The spirit in these self-contained church towers was hardly medieval. It foretold the assertive architecture of a new age.

Part Three

THE NATIONALIST KINGS

)lofsborg, Finland (p. 113).

(a) Glimmingehus (p. 103).

(b) Malmöhus (

Pl. 38. Castles in Skåne.

Pl. 39. Hesselagergård, Denmark (p. 106).

(*a*) 'South Scandinavian' House, Setesdalen Valley (p. 21).

(*b*) Rosendal manor-house, Hardanger Fiord (p. 111).

Pl. 40. Types of houses, Norway.

(a) Torup (p. 107).

(b) Skarhult (p. 111).

Pl. 41. Manor-houses, Skåne.

(a) Decorated gable (p. 120).

(b) Entrance (p. 120).

Pl. 42. Royal Vadstena, Sweden.

(a) Gripsholm (p. 115).

(b) Kalmar, the well (p. 122).

Pl. 43. Royal castles, Sweden.

(*a*) Rydboholm, panelling.

(*b*) Gripsholm, ceiling.

Pl. 44. Painted decoration, Sweden (p. 117).

Pl. 45. Kalmar, King Eric's State Chamber (p. 118).

(a) Rosenholm, Denmark (p. 108).

(b) Ulstrup, Denmark (p. 108)

Pl. 46.

(a) Rosenborg, Copenhagen (p. 110).

(b) Kronborg, Helsingør, hall of state (p. 109).

47. Royal castles, Denmark.

Pl. 49. Frederiksborg, Denmark (p. 109).

Pl. 50. House (left centre) on Stengade, Helsingør, Denmark (p. 124).

Pl. 51. House on Østeraagade, Aalborg, Denmark (p. 124).

Pl. 53. The Old Town, Stockholm (p. 125).

Pl. 54. Hillebola *bruk*, Sweden (p. 174).

IX

THE NEW KINGDOMS, 1500-1640

In Europe the dividing line between the Middle Ages and modern times is often put at about 1400, when the Renaissance was beginning in Italy. 'Modern times' on the Continent can be divided into three periods: the time before the Reformation when national traits in art were emerging; the period of the Reformation and Counter Reforma-tion; and finally that of the absolute monarchies, which came to an end with the Industrial Revolution. It is not possible to write the history of art for each separate nation in Europe during this era, for by this time the arts were becoming more international, produced by differing types of culture or societies rather than by national trends.

In the sixteenth century, when the peripheral parts of Europe were coming into closer contact with Italy and Burgundy and the Nether-lands, it goes without saying that the arts of the peripheral countries were largely being imported from outside. It is, of course, quite impossible to say that any country is self-supporting in this respect. So it would be misplaced loyalty to worry too much over what was Scandinavian and what was non-Scandinavian in the architecture of this period. Yet the sorting out of sources is interesting for the light it throws on those who chose them and on the use native architects then made of them. Buildings by Simon de la Vallée in Sweden do not become less valuable because he was born in France, or Swedish patrons seem less perceptive because they invited him; the same was true of Holbein's portraits of the English court. The importing of artists is not like the military invasion of a defenceless country, and artists are not chosen by blindfolded patrons—nor did Swedish and Danish artists undertake journeys abroad haphazardly. It was always a question of selection.

The coming of modern times, heralded in Italy by the Renaissance, was delayed in Scandinavia just as, later on, the Industrial Revolu-tion appeared almost a century after its emergence in England. The change from medieval to modern times was much slower than in

H 97

Italy, where one could speak of a change between one generation and the next. The term Renaissance will be little used in this book: as a conception in the history of culture, it must really be limited to Italy. When the term was transformed to France and the Netherlands it lost its true meaning—there being little or no classical background to be reborn—and became instead a borrowed stylistic idea. Eventually the term embraced so much that it covered everything that was not Gothic. So I shall attempt to characterize buildings, architecturally and socially, without resort to stereotyped stylistic analysis.

When modern times were beginning in Scandinavia around 1500, agriculture was just as dominant in Denmark and Sweden as it had ever been. The export of timber and tar from Norway and Sweden was another economic factor. During the late sixteenth and early seventeenth centuries Swedish mining began with the help of Walloons from the Low Countries. Louis de Geer, who was invited to come from Holland, was really the father of the mining industry in central Sweden and became a highly successful industrialist on a social level with the old aristocratic families. His numerous arms factories equipped the Swedish army under Gustavus Adolphus for the Thirty Years War. Besides the export of timber and iron, extensive export of copper from Falu Koppargruva provided an important basis for the expansion of Swedish power during the seventeenth century. The toll levied at the Sound played a similar part in the economy of Denmark. Many wars were fought over this toll.

The organization of agriculture went on for more than a century much as it had during the Middle Ages. It was not until the Storskifte law of 1757—forced by a severe deficit of agricultural products from the loss of the Baltic provinces at the beginning of the eighteenth century—and the Enskifte law of 1803–1807, that the Swedish farmer got his land within one boundary line. Production then went up, but the pattern of the old agricultural villages disintegrated. Enskifte, by the way, was introduced in Skåne by Rutger Maclean of Scottish origin.

Towards the end of the Middle Ages important social reconstruction and revaluation took place in Europe in an upheaval created by new economic conditions, especially in the early-industrialized textile centres of northern Italy and Flanders. The capitalist appeared on the stage. This meant that the old feudal organization of society lost its significance; economically, the feudal lords were quite inferior to the new capitalists. Furthermore, the industrialist, and to some extent his employees as well, had another attitude towards life. The belief in the next world became unsettled by the growing interest in the human being in this world. Far-reaching trade carried capitalism and new ideas with it. One feudal lord after another lost the solid ground beneath his feet and was replaced by estate-owning lords, owners perhaps of various means of production, either bought or got by robbery. Through landowners like this the national states emerged, for the struggle to national sovereignty was financed by the capitalists.

All this political, social, and economic reconstruction, to start with, touched the peripheral parts of northern Europe as distant rumbles from a storm centre. The only real centres of production and commerce in Scandinavia were Copenhagen and Stockholm. The timber industry, by its very nature, was not centralized, and mining did not really become an industry until the seventeenth century. The Hanseatic trading powers, moreover, had their centre at Lübeck outside Scandinavia. But the European upheavals echoed there. The art of printing, for one thing, came to the Scandinavian countries by way of Lübeck before 1500.

When in the middle of the fourteenth century Valdemar Atterdag became the king of Denmark he did not found his power on giving away parts of his own country to feudal lords as his predecessors had, but sold one of his possessions, Estonia, to the wealthy Teutonic Order, who in this way acted as the king's financier. When he divided the power over the Danish Church between himself and the Pope, he took Philip the Fair of France as his prototype. Margaret, Queen of the Kalmar Union, did what she could to imitate the sovereigns on the Continent and forbade her own aristocracy to build fortified houses, a prohibition that was observed fairly faithfully for a little while. This ambition to form a strong monarchy in Denmark did not get very far. The feudal prerogatives of the nobles on their country estates were not broken until the time of absolute monarchy in the middle of the seventeenth century. They then assumed a new sort of power as royal advisers in the capital city.

The fact that a strong monarchy did not appear in Sweden until the accession of Gustavus Vasa in 1523 does not mean that the royal idea did not exist before in Sweden. Earlier rulers did all they could to crush the Church and the feudal lords, but their economic resources, for one thing, were much more limited than those of their opponents. Borrowing money from the Hanse was a new idea invented by Gustavus Vasa, who was enabled by this loan to realize the Reformation of the Church in Sweden in 1527. The fact that he later made common cause against the Hanse with the successor of his worst enemy, Christian III of Denmark, was just part of the strategy of his day. The Reformation in Denmark occurred in a similar manner ten years later, in 1537, when Christian III drew in the ecclesiastical properties under the Crown.

Politically this meant that modern times dawned in Scandinavia in the early sixteenth century. But architecture, in the fifteenth-century church towers and town halls of the merchant towns, had already expressed the new spirit. Royal efforts to strengthen the ruling power in both Sweden and Denmark during the fifteenth century had had an almost entirely negative effect architecturally. Slowly the power of the Church was undermined and its role as a commissioner of buildings grew steadily less. The claimants to royal power were still too weak to commission any themselves, and a vacuum ensued, so that—outside the world of the merchants, who stoutly went their own way—important buildings under construction became fewer and fewer towards the middle of the fifteenth century.

However, in both countries, after a centralized royal power was firmly established in the next century, the king became the most important patron of architecture, and with him his councillors and officers of the partially subdued aristocracy. During the sixteenth century and at the beginning of the seventeenth, Danish nobles and especially those of Skåne were more independent than their counter-parts of Sweden. Politically this was due to the declaration that Frederick II was forced to make, when he succeeded to the throne in 1558, establishing the 'power-balancing' position of the Danish aristocracy.

Having put themselves firmly on the throne, both kings started building or rebuilding fortified strongholds at strategic points. Defensive measures were more important than gracious living at first. In Sweden it was not until Gustavus Vasa's sons were ruling the country that residential quarters became more important than battle-ments and bastions in the planning of a castle. At first the Swedes found it difficult to combine successfully all the different structures composing a castle. Danish castle design was more advanced.

Having gone his own way as much as possible while the ruling classes were jockeying for position, the citizen in his market town during this period of royal ascendancy increased his own power, if not his progressiveness, as a patron of architecture. His surroundings of dwellings and warehouses and guildhalls were strongly rooted in medieval tradition even when influenced by aristocratic fashion, and this conservatism was especially strong in the planning of houses which only very slowly developed an independent character of their own. The design of farmhouses changed even more slowly. The only true progress in merchant-class house planning took place in the international trading centres such as Copenhagen and Stockholm.

X

DENMARK, WITH SKÅNE
AND NORWAY

THE Reformation in Denmark in 1537 was a purely political affair. The reign of the last Catholic king, Christian II, ended with his exile and civil war. The victorious Christian III had to pay for success with vast fiefs both in Denmark and Norway, but in the end it was the Church and the monasteries that had to pay. The result was a dividing of power between the king and the nobility. The Danish nobles, being more independent of their king than the lords of Sweden, more often took the initiative in architectural matters. But it was now up to the king to consolidate his political position. To this end several strategic fortifications went up along the coast of the Sound.

The aristocracy meanwhile built themselves castles, a new sort of castle unfurling a spirit of national and worldly self-esteem. For defensive reasons they still abided by certain medieval traditions of fortification, but the demand for a residence that was roomy on the inside and impressive on the outside dominated the planning. The new way of life in these Danish castles demanded new symbolic expression which did not exist in the older castles that represented feudalism. Political and mercantile alliances with Holland did not entirely account for the fact that, at first, it was the Dutch style that inspired the builders. Their patrons' appraisal of the Dutch style must be regarded as admiration for the Dutch way of life. This implied the approach to a new economic organization, that is, to capitalism—a long step from the feudal organization of society.

The aristocracy of Skåne in southern Sweden, still a part of Denmark, showed a particularly independent attitude towards their Danish king, and it was not only to guard the Sound that the largest royal castle built by Christian III was at Malmö. In their independence the noble lords of Skåne developed their own local and conservative tradition of castle design; and a certain tension

102

existed there between them and royal Malmö. Through the Peace of Roskilde in 1658 Skåne became a part of Sweden, which caused an interval in the building programme there, for economic conditions immediately changed. It was not until the eighteenth century that Swedish building traditions were introduced in Skåne.

The new spirit in Danish architecture was in full bloom by the end of the reign of Frederick II (1558–88), but the new style has been given the name of 'Christian IV's Renaissance', which is not quite fair to Frederick. The name, however, was meant to convey the personal contributions made by Christian IV at his drawing table and his position as one of the leading cultural personalities of Europe. This architecture is characterized by a use of fragments of classical detail, pilasters, cornices, volutes, etc., especially on the high gables. The king's accomplishments as architect and town planner are described below (p. 110). Inigo Jones, early in his career, is said to have visited the court of Christian IV (whose brother-in-law was James I of England) although with what effect on his own or the Danish king's work is not recorded.

Fortified Castles and Manor-Houses

One consequence of the prohibition against fortified houses issued by Queen Margaret was that the continuity between the fortresses of the Middle Ages and the new castles built near the end of the fifteenth century and after was less apparent than in other countries. For example, the fourteenth-century keep or Kärna at Hälsingborg (Fig. 37) built by Erik of Pomerania and designed, like the contemporaneous Krogen at Helsingør, to defend the entrance to the Baltic, consisted of a high residential tower intended to serve as a royal residence in time of warfare. It was surrounded by a high quadrangular wall and had but one room on each floor—like the earlier Gaasetornet at Vordingborg castle in Denmark—except that the upper stories had certain small rooms in the wall. During the hundred years, roughly, passing between the erection of this keep and Glimmingehus in eastern Skåne, house plans in Europe had had time to change.

Glimmingehus (Pl. 38a, Fig. 47), begun in 1499 by the Danish admiral, Jacob Ulfstand, is to be regarded as an extended residential tower: the plan is rectangular, four stories high. The ground floor consists of kitchen and other household departments, while the

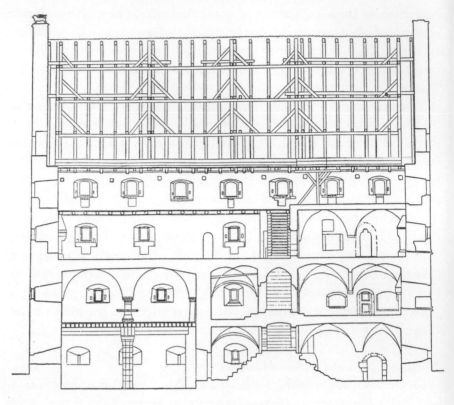

FIG. 47. Glimmingehus.

next floor contains an ante-room, a hall, and a combined living-
and-bedroom and a closet. The floor above that has a simpler plan,
and the top floor was a firing loft for gunners which could also be
used as a hall. All rooms on the living floor and the smaller rooms
above are vaulted. In the main hall there is an octagonal table set
into and surrounding the central column, which together with
benches fixed to the walls constituted the furniture. In the basement
was a big open fireplace for cooking. Hot air was let through
channels in the castle walls—a very early and remarkable central-
heating system not used before.

Glimmingehus was a typical water-castle guarded by broad moats,
and equipped with loop-holes, portcullis, machicolations, and windows that were small and few in its plain, solid walls. It was partly
medieval and partly modern. The plan of the main living floor was,
so to speak, on its way to becoming a regular double apartment (see
below), with two rooms on either side of the central staircase. The

withdrawing room on the next floor has ornamental reliefs that indicate its occasional ceremonial use; the plan was more traditional here.

This castle was built by an aristocrat. Admiral Ulfstand, who had lived on Gotland before 1499, was one of the mightiest men in Denmark. His castle bears full evidence to the self-assurance that was so characteristic of the man, and it dominates the countryside as he did himself at one time. Each end wall was built up as a stepped parapet concealing the eaves, in a simplified version of the stepped gables so common on fifteenth-century houses and churches all over northern Europe. The man who built and decorated Glim-mingehus was Adam van Düren, who had earlier been occupied with sculpture at the Carmelite monastery at Helsingør. Similar but more conservative establishments are to be found at Örup and Bollerup in Skåne, and at Rygaard on Fyn.

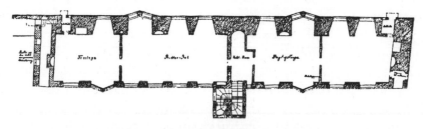

FIG. 48. Malmöhus, the royal apartments.

Between Glimmingehus and the building of Christian III's Malmöhus (Pl. 38b, Fig. 48) lies a generation, but an eventful one. The planning of the residence and the defensive dispositions show considerable changes. When Malmöhus was begun in 1536, it was planned to consist of a rectangular residence and corner towers linked to it by a high wall, a plan firmly anchored in the medieval concept of passive defence. During construction, however, new ideas were introduced and it is likely that new builders had been taken on. The bonding of the brick, for one thing, was changed part-way up from a medieval to a more modern type. Malmöhus, which was designed to be the Danish king's foremost stronghold, still stands as a rectangular building in three stories plus a firing loft, flanked by low cannon towers placed apart from the residence. But the royal apartment, distinguished by the row of larger windows, was laid out as a double apartment (see also p. 114 and Fig. 53) containing four symmetrically placed rooms, two on each side of the ante-room leading to a staircase tower. The floor below is divided into two almost identical parts, one containing the rooms of the commandant of the castle. On the ground floor are two large cantonment halls.

Malmöhus is part of the background of the so-called 'Christian IV's Renaissance' and stands today as a typical example of a new architecture without any medieval features. The gables are stepped and the long parapet towards the sea is punctuated by stepped dormers. The horizontal emphasis is increased by a string-course underlining the main story on the façades. The architect was probably Marten Bussaert from Holland.

A similarly symmetrical plan was used at Hesselagergård (Pl. 39) built for Jens Friis about 1550, a rectangular house having two small attached corner towers without much defensive function. The gables are unusual. Three large blank arches which entirely conceal the roof form a motif resembling some Early Renaissance façade in northern Italy, with a certain French flavour as well, but executed here with a youthfully unsure hand. The gun towers at Hesselagergård are octagonal but other forms appeared. Nackebølle, built in 1559, has quadrangular towers while Egeskov has round ones. As at Malmöhus these and many other Danish castles also have a staircase tower—one result of a wish for improved amenities derived from a similar trend in France where comfort was more highly regarded.

This sort of rectangular block was not to become the ideal house plan for the nobles of Skåne, who came to prefer the plan surrounding a courtyard, with two diagonally placed towers to guard all four sides. The first castle to be laid out in this manner in Scandinavia was Steinviksholm in Norway, which was built about 1520. Svaneholm in Skåne and Spøttrup in Denmark prove that the development towards the four-ranged type took place by degrees: at the beginning the yard was simply walled in on one side, but around the middle of the sixteenth century four ranges were found useful for defensive protection, and castles being built at this time were four-ranged from the beginning. One of the earliest examples was Eriksholm, now Trolleholm, of 1538 but since rebuilt after ruin in the seventeenth century.

The best-preserved examples of castles in Skåne now are Torup (1545; Pl. 41a, Fig. 49) and the larger Vittskövle (1553). These are regularly quadrangular in layout. Two of the ranges were purely residential, the east and the north, and the larger of these may have been occupied only during the summer. That these two ranges were chosen is natural since their big windows faced the sun and the yard where there was no need to think of defence—the windows on the outside were very small. Parts of the other two ranges contained household departments. A somewhat unusual feature of both castles was a small arcade on the ground floor facing the yard.

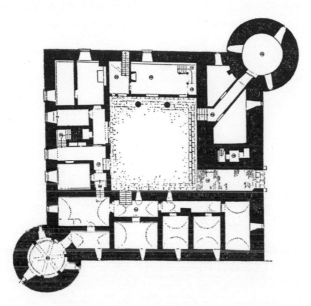

FIG. 49. Torup.

The façades at both Vittskövle and Torup are quite intact, simple and unsymmetrical, the placement of windows unrelated from one floor to another, and only the stepped gables ornamented with mouldings and arcaded strips. As yet there was no amalgamation between towers and house-ranges, one of the towers at Torup intersecting a gable so that the façade is cut in half. This was one of the old-fashioned features characteristic of medieval Skåne when it was somewhat isolated from the main streams of both Danish and Swedish building traditions. This type of castle with diagonal towers spread to Sweden; Mörby in Uppland, of the mid-sixteenth century and now a ruin, was a typical example.

The medieval features in these Skåne castles are prominent when compared to such as Vadstena in Sweden (to be described with the 'later Vasa castles') or Rosenholm (Pl. 46a, Fig. 50) on Jylland, both also built during the middle of the sixteenth century. At Rosenholm, originally consisting of one gateway range and one parallel residential range linked to it by walls, the new French architecture was being adopted as it appeared in Du Cerceau's Verneuil, where the corners of the ranges were developed into accentuated pavilions and the middle was emphasized by the gateway. Ulstrup (Pl. 46b) is another example of this influence. The desire to create such a plan at Rosen-holm was so strong that the unsymmetrical functions of the first range, the left side of which was used for storage, were partly hidden.

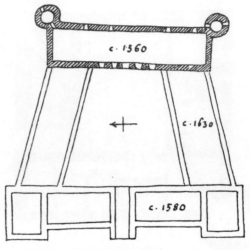

FIG. 50. Rosenholm.

But the elevations at Rosenholm were not French, with steeper roofs and pronounced pavilion gables, where the transition from one story to the next was carried out with a mixture of stepped gables and pedi-ments. The division of the stories is clearly marked by thin mould-ings. A few years later, Egeskov, consisting of two parallel ranges linked together, was constructed on an artificial island in Denmark.

The Triumph of Frederick II and Christian IV

The toll at the Sound continued to play an enormously important part in the finances of Denmark. Like his predecessors, Frederick II wished to symbolize Denmark's power at the inlet of the Baltic, and this he did in the 1570's by thoroughly rebuilding Kronborg at Helsingør (Pl. 47b, 48). The architects were Flemish master masons, Hans van Paeschen and Anthonis van Opbergen. In the creation of a truly Renaissance palace they were able to work the more freely because the defences were moved away from the castle itself. These consisted of bastions built in 1575, but they were not the earliest of their kind in Denmark. Frederick I had in the 1520's built two round gun towers outside Sönderborg Castle and his successor Christian III continued in the next two decades this building activity, with Tønderhus, Ribershus, and Landskrona among many others. These bastions were consequences of the introduction of artillery and the pattern followed was that of Italian fortification officers. Much later, the pattern was to be that of the French Vauban.

Kronborg became a fourranged building with corner towers and was the largest castle in the whole of Scandinavia. The gables and upper window frames are decidedly curvilinear in the more Dutch spirit, and all earlier rigorous elements had been, as it were, dissolved. Thin stringcourses stress the division between stories in a decorative way but in the gables volutes in sandstone link them together. Towers are polygonal with lanternlike tops, entirely in the Dutch picturesque style. This contact with Holland is quite natural as at this time the Dutch had succeeded the Hanse merchants as the foremost trading people in northern Europe. The Scandinavian countries had numerous alliances with Holland, on whose ships goods of vital importance were imported. What is remarkable, however, is the fact that what was imported for use at Kronborg had been in the Low Countries a style belonging entirely to the burghers. It was a striking contrast that it should be used in Denmark by the sovereign. What happened, then, was that the content of a form in one country, when transferred to another, became entirely different. With the vast size of Kronborg this kind of architecture received princely dimensions.

Frederick II also built the castle of Frederiksborg (Pl. 49) at Hillerød, between Copenhagen and Helsingør, but his son Christian IV considered it much too modest and in 1602 appointed two brothers from Holland, Hans and Lourens Steenwinckel, to rebuild it. This stands on three small islands and with the remains of Frederick's palace forms an intricate pattern of ranges, towers, and moats. The threeranged royal residence, with entrance, staircase, and corner towers, was symmetrically divided into two sections, one for the summer and one for the wintertime.

There were also within the walls an audience chamber and a splendid church—a threeaisled church which with its interior walls and ceiling rivals many European buildings. Christian IV himself made many of the plans and the builders worked under his direc- tion. In Frederiksborg the Dutch style in Denmark reached full bloom. The picturesque sandstone ornaments form an animated contrast to the red brick walls, and the green copper-covered roof and bulb-shaped cupolas and lanterns make a dazzling visual im- pression. In 1618 the huge entrance tower was added to the building on the central island; it is known that Hans Steenwinckel the younger assisted in the work, probably to the royal design, on a theme familiar in Holland.

Christian IV's main interest lay in Copenhagen. With the pleasure palace Rosenborg, 1606–17 (Pl. 47a), and the Exchange, 1619–30, both built mainly after plans drawn by the king, as well as the Arsenal for the navy and Regensen, the University and its church, Trinitatis, he left a distinctive impression on the capital. The Exchange (Pl. 52) is especially impressive, consisting of a long two-storied building of brick and sandstone with numerous richly decorated gables and a highly imaginative lantern tower whose spire is a twisted whorl of dragons' tails twined together. The king had visited his sister, Queen Anne, in London in 1606; he is said to have observed everything, with great curiosity and little apparent admiration, including the Royal Exchange, no doubt with the mental note that Copenhagen should have a better one.

Christian also acted as town planner in Copenhagen. He drew the plans for the octagonal square which was to be the centre of New Copenhagen, in which the palace of Rosenborg was to be a focal point. The plan was not carried out, however, until it was taken over and adapted by Eigtved for the Amalienborg layout in the eighteenth century (Chapter XIV). Christian's plans were inspired by the mathematicians and fortification engineers of Palma Nuova and other Italian 'ideal' towns, Eigtved rather by French royal planners. Another building erected by the king was the so-called Runde Taarn, or Round Tower, of 1642, in style a medieval echo from northern Italy, originally designed as an observatory and noted today for its picturesqueness. It is also the tower of the Trinitatis Church.

During the reign of Frederick II the Danish aristocracy had obtained a great number of fiefs in Norway. At the beginning of the seventeenth century under Christian IV, that country was even more firmly tied to Denmark, and so the capital of Norway, Christiania

(now Oslo), developed rapidly as an administrative centre and architecture in the 'Christian IV style' is to be found there. In the capital
the castle of Akershus was finished in this manner; its appearance
has since been changed, however. At Rosendal (Pl. 40*b*) by the
Hardanger Fiord—a manor-house with central core and two smaller
wings—the ornamented porch is in this style, and there is a similar
doorway on a church at Bergen.

Town building was carried on in many parts of Christian's kingdom. Christianstad, or Kristianstad, in Skåne was founded as a
stronghold against Sweden and in Blekinge Christianopel was built.
Christianstad was planned with a rectangular network of streets and
symmetrical blocks within fortified walls. Its Trinity church, or
Trefaldighetskyrkan, probably by the younger Steenwinckel about
1617, is a remarkable example of the curly-gabled style.

The style even spread to the castles in Skåne. The architect of
Kronborg, Opbergen, was responsible for Skarhult Castle (Pl. 41*b*)
in 1575, giving it curved gables instead of stepped ones. The plan
of Skarhult showed the transition from the four-ranged plan to the
new compositional principle of one main building with two smaller
wings. Still more picturesque gables were used by Hans Steenwinckel the elder on Svenstorp, built 1596–99, which lacked all
defensive attachments and was thus entirely freed from medieval
features: it was a pleasure palace. Rosendal in Skåne, the first
example of the three-ranged castle, was a final, subdued expression of
this architectural tendency. On Løvenborg in Denmark, of 1630,
the lanterns of the corner towers were modelled on those of Frederiksborg.

A remarkable achievement is Christian IV's burial chapel at
Roskilde Cathedral, built 1614–41. It is more strict and classic
than his other buildings, with an austere yet somewhat mannerist
combination of strict orders of columns symmetrically arranged
with many features from earlier architecture.

XI

SWEDEN, WITH FINLAND

Fortified Castles and Manor-Houses

THE fourteenth-century castle at Kalmar in south-eastern Sweden was a fortress based on the principle of passive defence, guarding the strategic sound, Kalmarsund. It consisted originally of a circular citadel around which a larger establishment had grown up, encircled by a wall. There were also residential quarters and estate offices. (It was to receive considerable remodelling and a collection of outstanding decorative features in the sixteenth century, to be described with the later Vasa castles.) The towers were designed to protect the wall, and if that were breached the citadel was to serve as a last place of refuge. There were, as well, the usual accoutrements of defence: trenches, loop-holes, palisades, and so on.

During the latter fourteenth century the leader of the Council, Bo Johnsson Grip (d. 1386), founded Raseborg in Finland (Fig. 51). Here were all the elements of Kalmar: the circular keep, encircling wall with towers, and fortified dwelling house. The massive central tower is the most important part of the establishment, protecting all

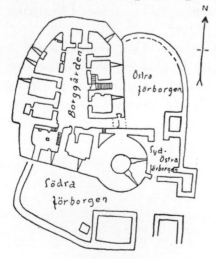

FIG. 51. Raseborg.

four courtyards. The residence is a two-room house, the rooms not directly connected, as in the gallery house.

One of the first Scandinavian castles of modern times was Olofs-borg (Olavinlinna) in Finland, built as a defensive fortress on the Russian border by Erik Axelsson Thott in 1477 (Pl. 37, Fig. 52). Now some vital differences in plan are noticeable. The encircling walls are discarded and the towers are here parts of the castle itself—

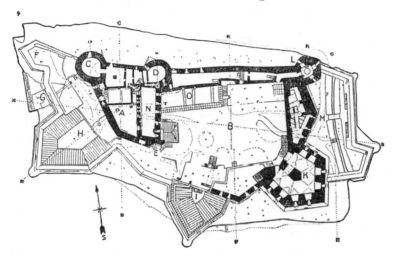

FIG. 52. Olofsborg.

it had originally three corner towers—or, in other words, the entire space inside the wall could be taken up by the castle itself. The central tower is also discarded. There is no tower over the entrance, which has been moved to the west side where it is protected by the north-west tower. These alterations mean in reality that the most powerful parts of the castle, the towers, are now on the periphery in more aggressive positions and this was done to take advantage of the greater efficiency of firearms, which from the towers could sweep the walls. The same pattern was followed in other Scandinavian countries.

With such a plan the residence could be made larger. The main dwelling is on the north side and south of it, along the east side, a hall was built. Principally this follows the plan of the feudal manor-house during medieval times on the Continent. However, Olofsborg belongs to the type of castle that carried within its walls the embryo of the most common house plan of the new era, the pair house or double apartment (Fig. 53).

I   113

The development towards this type of house was roughly the following. The feudal two-room house, which contained one living-room and one bedroom to a floor, proved to be insufficient towards the end of the Middle Ages. This was especially true when the number of troops stationed at feudal castles was considerably increased by the introduction of mercenary troops. The master of the house and his family then retreated from their former apartment to the upper story of the house, which had been the reception apartment and had identically the same layout, the two-room plan.

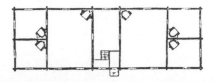

FIG. 53.
Embryo of double-apartment plan.

Simultaneously, habits changed and there was a tendency to remove the daily life to the more private inner room, the bedroom. The restriction in space meant a certain lowering of the standard of living, and consequently the original plan was added to, in reverse as if reflected in a mirror, by building on the opposite side of the stairs the same two rooms, living-room and bedroom. The original apartment deserted by the family was degraded into accommodation for the troops. Communications between the family apartment and the new addition were always arranged in such a manner that the most private rooms, the bedrooms, were placed nearest each other. Between them was the staircase and entrance lobby. This is the basic outline, then, of the double apartment, the principles of which are by no means changed by the addition of numerous other private rooms to the bedrooms. This type has its logical end in Vaux-le-Vicomte and Versailles; it cannot be carried farther. It is impossible to point to any one origin for a plan that evolved in a gradual process.

The double apartment differs from the medieval two-room house in so far as it consists of two mainly identical halves serving principally the same purposes. In the courts the lord used one half and his wife the other; on the farms one side was used for everyday life and the other by guests at feasts and celebrations. The two-room house provided for different functions for its two or more rooms. Glimminge-hus, built in 1499, can be said to consist, in a medieval manner, of a vertical double apartment with one half on top of another instead of beside the other. That the staircase leads up to a central space between the bedroom and living-room does not in itself constitute a double apartment. The new arrangement was followed four decades later at Malmöhus, as we have seen.

The Castles of Gustavus Vasa

The first castle built by Gustavus Vasa was Gripsholm (Pl. 43a, Fig. 54) on Lake Mälaren about thirty-five miles from Stockholm, planned by Heinrich von Cöllen, a German architect invited to the Swedish court. The foundation year was 1537, one year after the

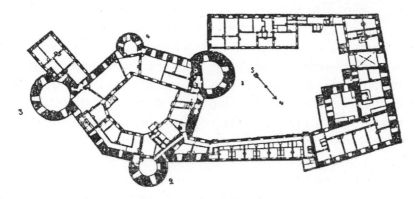

FIG. 54. Gripsholm.

Danish king's Malmöhus. Originally Gripsholm consisted of a hexagonal building with four towers. The royal apartments were in the north ranges and the hexagon was completed by a high wall on the opposite sides. The so-called Grip Tower and the Theatre Tower were the largest, mounting the heavy fortress artillery, while the other two towers were more traditional in character and served as ordinary old-fashioned defence towers. The defensive arrange-ments included, for the protection of the moats north of the castle, parts of the old fortress built by Bo Jonsson Grip, the fourteenth-century founder of Raseborg. The two cannon towers are equipped with low loop-holes, a more modern feature.

The royal residence in Gripsholm, compared to the castles then being built by the Danish sovereign, was rather primitive. The centre was in the Grip Tower, containing the king's cabinet or private council chamber, with an ante-room outside it. The hall of state, in the west range, and the queen's apartments with her drawing-room in the east range were placed at the two extremities of the resi-dence, each with a staircase and entrance of its own. This shows a clear desire to create an old-fashioned double apartment with the private rooms as close to the centre as possible. They could also be reached through a small staircase direct from the courtyard. But, as an inheritance from the Middle Ages, the symmetry is not carried out, and to the main residence described above were added a large number of small rooms in the stories above and underneath, connected with one another by staircases in the wall.

When the Duke of Södermanland, youngest son of Gustavus Vasa and later Charles IX (1604–11) but already in fact leader of the country, moved to Gripsholm in 1572, he found his father's residence out of date. He therefore built a new one opposite, where before there had been only the wall. Demands on the plan had become more complicated and they were met with more logic and lucidity. In the new house two apartments were laid out. The lower one was parted into two halves on the pattern of the old royal apartment, one half for the duke and the other for the duchess. The two parts were joined through the private rooms and also through the king's guard-room and the queen's drawing-room. Upstairs a similar double apartment was provided for guests and festivities and for the hall of state. Parts of this residence are still intact and can be seen in their original condition. Hertig Karls Kammare, or Duke Charles's Chamber, in the prison tower, with its wood panelling and some of the duchess's rooms with painted walls deserve special mention.

The arrangement of rooms is very much the same as that in the range built thirty-five years before, but the difference is clearly noticeable in that rooms were not merely added where there was space for them but were laid out one after the other in a definite succession. The old castle in Stockholm, extended several times and destroyed by fire in 1697, was planned for Gustavus Vasa in very much the same manner as Gripsholm.

In 1545, eight years after the foundation of Gripsholm, Gustavus Vasa started another castle, Vadstena on Lake Vättern in south-central Sweden (Pl. 42, Fig. 55). His architect, the Pomeranian fortification officer Joachim Bulgerin, struck a new note right away. The four tower-like bastions, which were kept low, were separated from the castle and it was therefore possible to create a more homogeneous palace than at Gripsholm. The cannon towers were connected with the house by passages and with each other by impressive ramparts, instead of the earlier type of plain wall. The centre of the castle is emphasized by an entrance tower and its ends by staircase towers. Originally the tower roofs were higher than that of the main building, so that they were once much more conspicuous on the skyline.

The apartments were laid out symmetrically on either side of the entrance tower which contained unemphasized main staircases. The ground floor contained accommodation for troops and for officers, and the royal apartment was on the upper floor. It contained a large hall of state, but when John III added one floor to the castle (see p. 119) this apartment was much altered. The cannon towers were of an entirely military character and contained no household apartments.

The exteriors of these early Vasa castles were little decorated. Such ornamental features as there were consisted of plain mouldings, medallions, and blank arcades. Interiors were, on the contrary, very richly decorated with wood panelling, plaster or wood ceilings, and frescoed walls. Little is left for us to see, but there are still decorations at the king's estate Rydboholm (Pl. 44*a*) in Uppland to show fairly accurately what this work must have been like; it was probably all done by immigrant artists, most of it by Dutchmen under the influence of Italy. At Gripsholm there remain carved wooden ceilings dated 1543 painted with portraits surrounded by symmetrical floral ornament (Pl. 44*b*). Similar ornament, sometimes realistic, sometimes grotesque, appears in the wooden panels at Rydboholm. An entirely new world was being introduced almost at once within the art of decorative painting in Scandinavia. It is wrong to judge the older Vasa castles from the rather severe exteriors that are left to us; the rich decoration inside completed the picture.

The austere façades are easily understood, however, if seen against the background of Gustavus Vasa himself. At the beginning of his reign, his political position was unsure, surrounded by antagonists to fight down. Conditions within the country continued to be unsettled and the king had to fight a number of revolts in different parts of Sweden. During the whole of his reign he was occupied in setting Sweden on its feet, so to speak, and in introducing the machinery of modern western government: central administration, the organiza- tion of the army and navy, and so on. He had time for little else, but then he succeeded in what he did. The austerity of his castles did not mean that the king was hostile to culture. Through two of his three marriages personal relations were established with Continental courts. His eldest son, Eric XIV, went so far as to propose marriage to Queen Elizabeth of England. In many other ways, bonds with European culture were sought. Numerous Germans were called to the Swedish court to supervise the new administration; there was no other alternative than to invite foreigners in this effort to organize the country. The power of the Roman Church was ended. Medieval traits in the mental or worldly way of life of Gustavus Vasa were nowhere to be seen, as we can tell from his architecture. It must be remembered that he had to start from the beginning. His sons could reap the harvest.

The Later Vasa Castles

Gustavus Vasa's main interest in castle-building had been concerned with impressive defence arrangements; his three sons could concentrate instead upon the residential amenities.

The eldest of the three sons, Eric XIV (ruled 1560–68), continued his interest in keeping in touch with foreign countries, to which end he continued the building of a fleet on the Dutch pattern and instituted the titles of 'count' and 'baron' for his diplomats. He brought two artists named Urban Schultz and Marcus Wolfram to Kalmar, where they started the decorative work that culminated in the so-called King Eric's State Chamber, of about 1560 (Pl. 45).

The wainscot panelling in this room consists of pairs of columns enclosing shallow niches and flanking intarsia panels of castle scenes; above, a continuous hunting scene, in a combination of painting and stucco relief, interlarded with strapwork, runs along the upper parts of the walls below a heavily moulded ceiling. The profiles of the ceiling mouldings are considerably deeper than at Gripsholm. Scenes in fresco combined with stucco had first been introduced north of the Alps at Fontainebleau only a generation before, and this was a very cosmopolitan room for its date. The castle in Stockholm was also refurbished for Eric XIV.

Eric's younger brother John, who ruled the country between 1568 and 1592, had a more extensive building programme. During his reign a great number of foreign architects came to Sweden from different countries. To a certain extent these could be called the king's colleagues, as he once said that most of all he wanted to occupy himself with architecture. Besides Wilhelm or Willem Boy, a Dutch master who had been active in Gustavus Vasa's time, his most prominent architects were four brothers of the Italian architect family of Pahr from Milan and the Dutchman Arendt de Roy and his successor Hans Fleming. The last two were occupied with the re-building of Vadstena Castle, to which an upper story was being added, while the brothers Pahr were sent to Kalmar, Uppsala, and Borgholm. Wilhelm Boy supervised the work at Stockholm Castle.

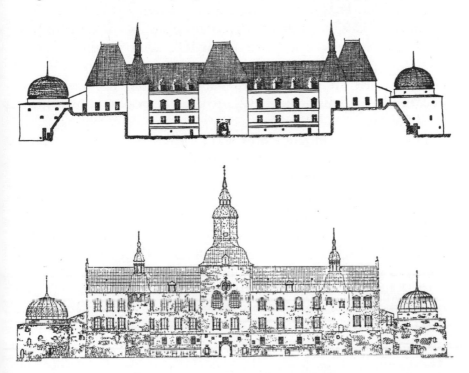

FIG. 55. Vadstena, first and second elevations.

At Vadstena a third royal apartment was added in the new top story, and a large chapel was created out of what had been the upper part of the entrance tower, with vast rooms placed symmetrically on either side of it (Fig. 55). There was of course an entirely new roof, and the old artillery bastions were later given new roofs, so that the entire character of the castle today is mainly that given by John III. The chapel had Gothic vaults and two long windows on each side. At first these windows were to be like the rest of the windows on that floor, each surmounted by a small pediment, but during construction they were enlarged and vaults were built.

When the roof was completed, the remodelled gables were decorated (although not finished until 1598 after a fire) with paired pilasters, volutes, and statues in niches (Pl. 42a) in accordance with the design drawn up by Wilhelm Boy for Stockholm Castle. These Vadstena gables have distinctly Dutch features, yet are much more austere than contemporary Danish decorations.

The symmetrical planning of the different building elements at Vadstena was French in character from the time it was first built in Gustavus Vasa's time, resembling certain plans by Du Cerceau, and this character was not lost with John III's additions, but mingled with the Dutch features on the splendid gables. The doorway (Pl. 42b) has an unmistakably Italian flavour and was in fact designed by an Italian, Pietro della Rocca, who called himself Pierre de la Roche.

This import of different motifs was typical of the Vasa era because no strong local tradition of design was then in existence. It is quite possible that engravings and books by French and Italian and Dutch architects and decorators were contributing to the Swedish repertory during this period. At Vadstena, the disparate details would be more notable than the total effect were it not for the extremely impressive bulky symmetry of its silhouette, with the curves of the central tower repeated in the cupolas of the flanking round towers.

Of John III's other castles, Borgholm and Uppsala are the two most important. Borgholm, on the island side of Kalmar Sound, stands today as a ruin, and Uppsala remains only in a rather mutilated condition. In contrast to Vadstena, these two castles were from the beginning consistently planned, for they were designed by Italians. At Borgholm, there was no earlier building to take into consideration—an old citadel on the site could be disregarded—and Uppsala Castle, which had been begun by Gustavus Vasa in a manner resembling that of Vadstena, was ravaged by fire so that the new builders had a free hand. It must be remembered, moreover, that Arendt de Roy had started work at Vadstena before John became king, so that there he was tied to a certain programme. The ruined state of Borgholm, and the fact that Uppsala Castle was never finished as intended, necessitates caution in discussing them; and there are parts of Uppsala Castle that have not yet been excavated.

Both castles seem to have been laid out as symmetrical buildings with four circular towers at the corners. These were linked on one side by the main building, which contained the hall of state and residential quarters on either side of a central chapel. At Uppsala this main building had covered arcades facing the courtyard and a similar arrangement was planned for the east range, but this was not built until the beginning of the seventeenth century and then in a different manner. A narrow building was intended for the third side, while the fourth was intended to consist of a short wall. At Borgholm this wall was put opposite the main building to make the whole plan symmetrical. At Uppsala it is believed that the wall was to have occupied the west side (facing the present Botanical Gardens); in later times a terraced garden was laid out there in a baroque style.

FIG. 56. Uppsala Castle.

A view in *Suecia Antiqua et Hodierna,* a collection of engravings (1661–1723) of Swedish buildings from drawings by the architect Eric Dahlberg, shows what Uppsala Castle looked like during the seventeenth century (Fig. 56). The corner towers were decorated with a sort of bold rustication adapted from the Italian, as for instance on Wüstrow Castle in Germany and in some of the sixteenth-century work at Kalmar. The east wing is treated in a unified way with the windows in all three stories framed by one discreetly profiled moulding. The centre of the south range is accentuated by the three large round-headed windows of the chapel, reminiscent of the early Florentine Renaissance. Parts of the original stuccoing can still be seen in the south door.

The differences between Vadstena and Uppsala are considerable. There is little French character about the latter, except for the corner towers, while the former shows many French elements. But the relation of these to the main building is quite new, and the castle is no longer divided into a number of loosely connected elements. The architects also struck a new note when they tried to integrate the two main stories by carrying down the vertical lines of the large chapel windows. The arches thus created were slender and flat, but the motif expresses a desire to work with fewer elements dominating the many minor elements.

Among the ornamental features of all these castles must be noticed the doors. In 1558 Boy's outer doorway to Stockholm Castle was made, and in about 1570 the Kalmar doors and its famous well were created by the Pahr brothers. Like the entrance at Vadstena, these doors have a Roman air, with a modified triumphal arch motif whose classicism is strict. In the later doors at Kalmar, carved by Roland Mackle, there is a stronger vertical stress and the flanking columns are doubled. It was not surprising, in the Scandinavian climate of ideas, that the more fantastic designs for doors then being produced by French and Italian 'mannerists' were ignored, and purer Renaissance themes were adopted.

The famous hexagonal well (Pl. 43b) in the courtyard at Kalmar has a very classical flavour. The high base is decorated with flat heraldic cartouches bearing Swedish coats of arms. The Tuscan columns carrying six little temple gables are fairly temperate, but the crowning lantern is carried out in a playful fantastic style and finished off with a lively dolphin.

Decorated doors similar to those on Swedish castles were common in royal Danish castles. At Kronborg the design of these is more advanced and other sources, mainly Dutch and French, have given inspiration. A famous feature is the marble gallery at Frederiksborg which shows a fine rhythm with niches and openings crowned by statues. It was more up to date than some of the doors, which shows that it was designed by H. Steenwinckel the younger who was less traditional than the king himself and who adopted new trends from Europe.

XII

BURGHERS' HOUSES

TOWARDS the end of the fifteenth century the North European type of town house penetrated into Scandinavia and appeared alongside the old type of house, described in Chapter VIII, that had been derived from the medieval farmhouse and adapted to mercantile life by the addition of warehouse or shop. The new kind of house differed from the old in that it was not built around a yard on all four sides. It consisted of two houses, the one on the street and the one across the yard.

During the fifteenth century the residence on the Continent had been moved from the house at the back to the front house, where it occupied the upper floor, while the ground floor was still used for storage. This was the case especially in France and Italy; the habit of living on the *piano nobile* is therefore an old one in these countries. The development in northern Germany was somewhat different. The main space on the ground floor was turned into a large hall which served as the everyday living-room, and originally as work-shop, business premises, etc. as well.

When the fireplace was placed in this hall it became a still more central room, and placing the bedrooms close to the fireplace side of it became a natural thing to do. This development probably has a certain connection with the Low Saxon house formerly prevailing in the Netherlands, wherein the different functions of a household were assembled in one single space, more or less effectively partitioned off from each other. Ceremonial occasions were either provided for in the old house across the yard or, more frequently, in the part of the hall which faced the yard.

Since the fortifications of medieval towns were seldom moved as the population increased, the old towns often became overcrowded. The size of each man's site decreased and then the yards were built upon. As houses were rebuilt they turned their gables towards the streets and extended their length towards the back. The yards and

123

the buildings in them grew smaller and smaller until in many cases the yards disappeared altogether. The fashion of turning the gable of the house towards the street became, before the end of the Middle Ages, the special trade-mark of such a house, and the high orna-mented gable became the symbol of the well-to-do citizen. Then in towns where there was room for it, this gave birth to the practice of building a gable-like façade on a house that had its long side facing the street—a phenomenon quite common in the more sparsely built-up trading towns in Scandinavia. The Danes call this type of house a false gable-house (Pl. 70a). Later the gable was to take on the look of a classical pediment when superimposed on a long front in this way. Sometimes it was a case of developing the dormers into gables. By maintaining the succession of gables along the streets the town-picture was not spoilt—the symbolic setting was the same.

An early house remains at Vadstena, where parts are still preserved in the house of Mården Skinnare. In spite of the extensive site avail-able the house was placed with its gable facing the street. The ground floor was occupied by a cellar and other household depart-ments, while the floor above had the two-room plan, and there was a two-story oriel facing the street. Nothing is known about the looks of the gable.

Most of the houses like this, however, are to be found within Danish boundaries, where the evolution was richer and where the tradition of building in stone and brick prevented destruction by fire. The oldest burgher house in Denmark is to be seen at 76 Stengade in Helsingør (Pl. 50). It has a stepped gable crowned by a little pediment, and divisions between stories are indicated by thin sand-stone mouldings. The windows have sandstone frames and shallow pediments containing little carved heads. The door is at one side, which was an old-fashioned feature. It is believed that this house (erected 1579) and another on the Strandgade in the same town were both built by a stone-mason who was active in the construction of Kronborg Castle.

The architecture prevailing two generations later is shown in a tall brick house at Aalborg, 9 Østeraagade, built 1623-24 (Pl. 51). It has its long side facing the street and the roof is equipped with three gables, richly decorated with imaginative sandstone strapwork which also appears in more concentrated fashion above the windows. There is a boldly projecting oriel, and the doorway next to it is abundantly decorated with sculptured reliefs. The contrast with the house at Helsingør is striking.

This is of course the ornamental style of Christian IV's 'Renaissance'. It spread to Stockholm, where the burghers' houses came to be just like the Danish ones. Only fragments are left of this neighbourhood, unfortunately. The Schantz House and its neighbour the Seyfridz House in the Gamla Sta'n, or Old Town (Pl. 53) are examples of this building tradition in Stockholm. The Schantz House is a particularly good example of the late Christian IV style —late because the ornament on door and gable is heavier than on the Danish houses mentioned above. Houses of this type along Skeppsbron and around the Stortorget in Stockholm gave it an air of tradesmen's domesticity in strong contrast to the stateliness of the Royal Palace.

This type of house developed in Denmark more rapidly than in Sweden. It was encouraged by the kings and as early as 1520 Christian II commanded the citizens of Copenhagen to use half-timbering or bricks to give their houses more permanence than primitively built ones. He also ordered the builders to let the gables face the street. During the sixteenth century and the next, however, the half-timber technique came to be regarded with aversion by the government because timber in these times became very scarce in Denmark. This, of course, did not discourage disobedient and traditional-minded South Scandinavians from sticking to the half-timber technique so familiar to skilled craftsmen.

Under the influence of the ornament on the wealthy burghers' houses, the ancient technique showed great imagination not only in the timber work of the gables and façades but also in different bondings of the brick. Farm buildings were built in much the same technique, but with some variations of the timber work according to the size of the barns and sheds. Denmark and Skåne can still show wonderful examples.

Part Four

THE AGE OF ABSOLUTE MONARCHY

Illustriß. et Excellentiß. Comitis DñiMAGNI GABRIELIS DE LA GARDIE
Magni Cancellary, Palatium Holmenſe qua parte templum Sˑ Iacobi ſpectat

(*a*) Makalös, Stockholm (p. 135).

(*b*) Old Amalienborg, Copenhagen (p. 137).

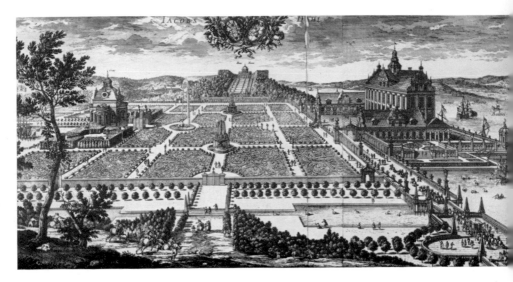

(a) Ulriksdal (Jacobsdal), Sweden (p. 155).

(b) Charlottenborg, Copenhagen (p. 14

Pl. 56.

PALATIUM COMITISSÆ EBBÆ BRAHE
in suburbio meridionali Stockholm

(*a*) De Geer House, Stockholm (p. 149).

(*b*) Vordingsborg, Denmark (p. 155).

Pl. 57.

Pl. 58. Riddarhuset, Stockholm (p. 150).

(a) Opera House, Copenhagen (p. 151).

(b) Oxenstierna Palace, Stockholm (p. 136).

Pl. 59.

(*a*) Drottningholm (p. 157).

(*b*) Eriksberg (p. 158).

Pl. 60. Country palaces, Sweden.

(a) Christianssaede, Denmark (p. 158).

(b) Steninge, Sweden, garden lodges (p. 159).

Pl. 61. Country houses.

(*a*) The east range (p. 138).

(*b*) Tessin's plan for the surrounding area (pp. 137, 168).

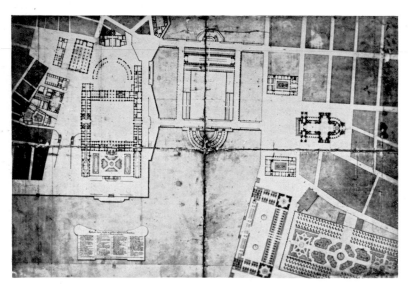

Pl. 62. Royal Palace, Stockholm.

63. Royal Palace, Stockholm, south range (p. 138).

Pl. 64. Frederiksberg, Denmark (p. 143).

Fredensborg (p. 143).

(*b*) Clausholm (p. 158).

65. Country houses, Denmark.

(a) Ledreborg (p. 160).

(b) Lerchenborg (p. 161).

Pl. 66. Country houses, Denmark.

(*a*) Christiansborg, riding ground (p. 147).

(*b*) Hermitage, Dyrehaven (p. 147).

67. Royal residences, Denmark.

(*a*) Royal Palace, Amalienborg (p. 147).

(*b*) Danneskiold-Laurvigens Palace (p. 148).

Pl. 68. Royal town planning, Copenhagen.

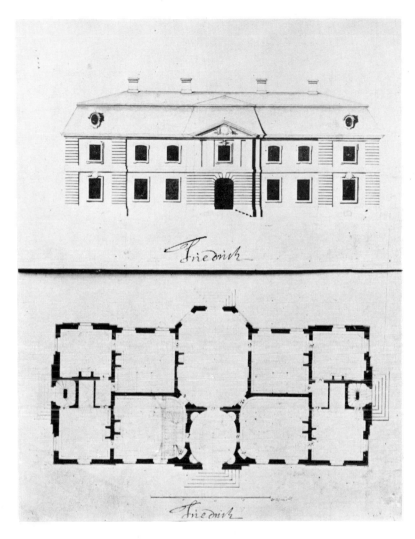

Pl. 69. Svartsjö, Sweden, architect's drawing (p. 160).

(b) No. 65, Nyhavn (p. 152).

(a) No. 9, Nyhavn (p. 124).

Pl. 71. East India Company, Gothenburg, Sweden (p. 152).

Pl. 73. Damsgård, Bergen, Norway (p. 161).

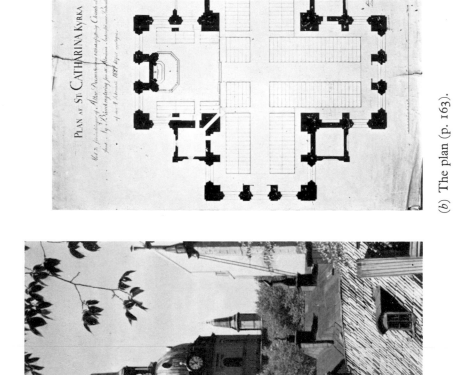

(a) The tower (p. 164).

(b) The plan (p. 163).

Pl. 74. St. Katarina, Stockholm.

(b) Laxå parish church, Sweden (p. 166).

(a) Frelserkirke, Copenhagen (p. 163).

Pl. 75.

(*a*) Kalmar Cathedral (p. 164).

(*b*) Mausoleum, Floda (p. 167).

Pl. 76.

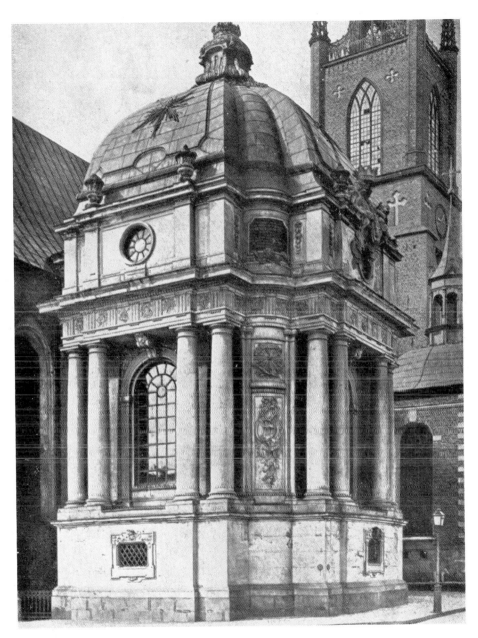

Pl. 77. Caroline Mausoleum, Stockholm (p. 167).

Pl. 78. Royal Palace, Stockholm, the chapel (p. 139).

Marble Church (Frederikskirke), Copenhagen (p. 168).

Pl. 80. Kongsberg parish church, Norway (p. 167).

XIII

POWER AND GLORY, NORTHERN STYLE

THE philosophical system on which sixteenth-century sovereigns had based their rule reached its logical development in the seventeenth century in France with the trend to absolute monarchy. The theory behind the seventeenth-century state was absolute in character and did not take into consideration the individual nature or nationality of a ruling sovereign. The other monarchs of Europe felt that they must copy Louis XIV so far as their resources would let them. The character of European court life was French, only the degree of its splendour varied according to national finances. In the Catholic countries political absolutism maintained an uneasy alliance with religious absolutism and its foremost instrument, the Jesuits. It was argued that the war of the Spanish succession and the unrest after the Reformation showed the need for absolutism.

In Denmark and Sweden an absolutist ideology had been in the back of royal minds for some time. In 1660 Frederick III of Denmark took advantage of the deranged finances and unsettled conditions resulting from the Thirty Years War to take over power and declare the crown hereditary; and absolutism remained in Denmark for ninety years. Another factor here was that the burgesses of Copenhagen benefited by the recent troubles with Sweden, for thanks to their heroic defence at the siege by the Swedes in 1658 they were able to secure a great many privileges. In Sweden the first absolute king was Charles XI, whose reign opened with the remarkable Reduction, when numerous manor-houses and castles belonging to the nobility were drawn in under the Crown.

It does not matter too much which man became the first absolute monarch in Scandinavia, because tendencies in this direction had appeared much earlier. What Charles XI meant to Sweden in the latter seventeenth century, the nobles of the Council, and especially the Oxenstierna family, had meant after the death of Gustavus

Adolphus in 1632, when the Council constituted a regency. The so-called Period of Liberty in the eighteenth century cannot be attributed to dissolution of these autonomous powers; while the reduced importance of the monarchy during this time was one result of protests launched by the philosophers of the Age of Enlightenment against the ideology of absolute monarchy, the strongest party politically still managed despotically whenever possible. But an occasional *coup d'état,* such as the one organized by Gustavus III at the end of the eighteenth century, and the personality of the first Bernadotte on the Swedish throne, showed that the powers of a strong monarchy were not yet exhausted.

In Louis XIV's France, art and architecture were nurtured through royal academies to glorify the superiority of the sovereign over all other human beings. In painting and sculpture the allegory was adopted, surrounding the monarch in portraits and historical scenes with an aura of inaccessibility. Architecture aimed at the same thing by giving royal buildings a magnificent scale and by placing them and their settings on an axial system, so that the entire vicinity was dominated completely. Extensive ranges of columns, and the precise accentuation of block-like volumes, performed the same emotional and glorifying functions as the allegories in the paintings.

Religious art and architecture under Rome's Counter Reformation had an absolutist quality as well. In the Protestant Scandinavian countries an analogous absolute religion was never established. Ecclesiastical building programmes, however, not only did not cease, but a remarkable thing occurred in that the Protestant Church adopted the interior and exterior architecture of the Catholic Church, especially when the building of a church was commissioned by royalty or by a similarly autocratic body.

The impressive expansion of the Swedish and Danish nobility during the seventeenth century was not entirely dependent on the vast and prosperous estates in their possession. Something else was necessary to transform them from country lords of the manor, regarding the world from their castellated farmhouses. This was partly accomplished by appointments to key positions in the king's government, as officers or administrators, and partly by the thorough education many young noblemen received on their now almost obligatory grand tour of Europe. This expanded a self-esteem that was already visible in their castles—a self-esteem that was not, however, bombastic but contained a certain amount of self-criticism. When in the year 1644 the coronation of Queen Christina took place, no foreign guests were invited in order to keep Swedish poverty a secret.

Their duties as the king's advisers brought the nobility regularly from their estates to the two capitals of the North, cutting their old bonds with the country for part of each year. This added life in the city meant a dual pattern of living, for the new administrative aristoc-racy in Stockholm and Copenhagen created a town environment that was quite different from their provincial mode of life. This happened for the first time in Stockholm, where the Oxenstierna palace was built in 1650, the first example of a purely 'Roman' architecture in Scandinavia. And so there was being created that civilized phenomenon, similarly evolving in England, of the respon-sible nobleman who lived his life both in town and in the country.

The absolute conduct of life by kings and nobility did not contra-dict the human ideal of the Renaissance, but was a logical conse-quence of it. Another was the emancipation of the burgher merchants; for example, Louis de Geer, the Dutchman who became the first modern industrialist in Sweden: his contributions to the mining industry there cannot be overestimated. Through him and others like him the capitalistic individual ideal of the Renaissance was transmuted into a modern idiom. The spirit of those men is symbo-lized in the numerous trading companies founded in Scandinavia after the Continental pattern during the seventeenth century. The sphere of these companies and the people creating them was entirely different from that of king and nobility. For purely personal reasons, through Louis de Geer and his family's architects in Holland, this new industrialist class in Sweden was strongly influenced by the Palladian style as practised in Holland. The dominant note in the merchants' domain was community and not, as in the royal domain, superiority.

XIV

PALACES IN STOCKHOLM
AND COPENHAGEN

THE architecture of seventeenth-century Scandinavia became more richly various than it had been. Even though royal building activity decreased in Sweden after 1600, the nobility took the initiative and built much more than they ever had before. There was a similar interval in the royal building programme in Denmark because of her many unfortunate wars. The erection of noble palaces there was delayed for about a generation, but once emerged these burst into riches.

To Sweden the Thirty Years War meant not only that she acquired possessions on the Continent, which can be regarded as doors opening up towards Europe, but the nobility of Sweden also laid the foundations for great wealth during their campaigns, and their habit of going abroad for studies can be said to have been started by these campaigns all over Europe. During all this travelling about their eyes were opened to the possibilities of European architecture. Comparisons with their own way of building at home must have made it appear somewhat pale, and northern eagerness to introduce new ideas from the Continent grew keener than ever before. In the building of country houses and castles Sweden occupied a leading position in Scandinavia during this century, while the architecture of the Danish capital continued for many years to be superior to that of Stockholm. In Scandinavia as a whole, a splendid variety of architectural styles was employed.

In Sweden Caspar Panten, a Dutchman, and Hans Christler, a German, were vigorously making the most of the Danish style of Christian IV, especially with pilasters, volutes, and cornices on the gables, while adding new elements such as window frames of rusticated sandstone. Towers and lanterns were used much as they had been in Denmark, and the result was a style of architecture with a stress on the picturesque. This style flourished in Sweden during the first thirty years of the seventeenth century, with the flourish most dominant on the gables.

After a few decades, however, the picture became more compli-cated. Different styles then appeared alongside each other in both capitals: the so-called Dutch Palladian style from Amsterdam and The Hague, the old French classical style as developed by Lescot at the Louvre and by Du Cerceau at Verneuil, and finally that of the churches and palaces of Rome.

The most important architects in Sweden at this time were Simon de la Vallée, engineer and builder from France, who was appointed Royal Architect in 1639, two years after his arrival in Sweden. He educated his own son, Jean de la Vallée, and also Nicodemus Tessin the elder, who was of Flemish origin; both of the latter also studied abroad in the middle of the seventeenth century. Towards the end of the century the son of Nicodemus Tessin went abroad, primarily to study the Rome of Bernini. In the 1640's the Dutch architect Justus Vingboons paid Sweden a rather short visit, and later on there was the Swedish architect Eric Dahlberg.

In Denmark the most important architects working in the middle of the century were Albert Matthiessen, Thomas Walgensteen, and Hans Steenwinckel the younger. The first baroque architect was the Norwegian Lambert van Haven, and there was Wilhelm Friedrich von Platen, both educated in Italy. During the second quarter of the eighteenth century when Carl Hårleman was active in Sweden, E. D. Häusser from Germany and Nikolaj Eigtved together with Laurids Thurah, both Danes, dominated Copenhagen.

Scandinavian architects studying abroad acquired the various European styles. Oddly enough, none of them showed any tendency to keep to one specific style: they became all-round practitioners, skilled in French and Italian and Dutch Palladian design. Only in details were there purely personal variations. There was as yet little development within Scandinavia during this time towards a tradition of her own, except in the design of great country houses. The various styles which came on the scene at about the same time appeared independently and hardly influenced each other at all. New develop-ments usually occurred only when an architect had just returned from abroad.

There is one more fact that should be mentioned in this connec-tion. When the Scandinavian architects went abroad to study, they did not look for the most recent styles to take back with them. Tessin the elder, visiting France in the 1640's, noted for future use many features which had appeared in French architecture towards the end of the previous century, and later, when he studied Roman *palazzi,* he chose the older types. The same can be said of his son when studying the work of Bernini. It was the calm, emotionally cool side of Bernini that inspired Tessin the younger, not the dramatic side of that great genius. Only Dutch architecture was carried over in its most contemporary form, but that was achieved through a visit paid by one of the most distinguished Dutch architects of his time. Circumstances in Denmark were the same, and had been in the time of Christian IV.

The explanation for this undertone of conservatism in Scandinavian seventeenth-century architecture, which was sometimes fifty years out of date from the Continental angle, must have lain in the personal natures of architects and their clients. So much was being taken over at once, they were not quite ready to go all the way and adopt the latest fashion. This traditionalism was an old and familiar feature of Nordic architecture, particularly in Sweden.

As most of the seventeenth-century architects used a variety of styles in their work, it is quite impossible to understand the architectural character of palaces and churches by concentrating on the careers of their architects without reference to the functions of the buildings or of those who commissioned them. For a mansion in the country, French architecture was the source of inspiration—as well as the French way of life as it was led in the *châteaux* of the Loire valley. If a palace in town was on order, inspiration was sought in Italy, because the Romans were the oldest citizens of the world; while an industrialist like De Geer preferred the classicism of Holland. The same patron and the same architect might on the same day discuss a *château* for the country and a *palazzo* for town. As for the merchants, they still built their town houses in a continuation of the Christian IV style far into the eighteenth century. The nobility of Stockholm in their assembly house subscribed to the purer Dutch Palladian style imported by the more up-to-date merchant princes. One almost concludes that the choice of an architect was secondary —the stylistic category of a building being already decided by the programme it was to fulfil.

Influence from France, which to some extent had left its marks on earlier Danish and Swedish buildings, was reintroduced into Sweden by Simon de la Vallée after his arrival in 1637. A few years later Vingboons arrived in Stockholm from Holland. Roman palace architecture could make its appearance only after 1649, when Jean de la Vallée returned from his studies abroad. In Denmark improvements on the style of Christian IV were necessarily in abeyance until after the king's death in 1648, and consequently nothing new appeared until Frederick III succeeded him on the throne, but even then the buildings commissioned were few, little more than Sophie Amalienborg (below). The main interest lay in building the fortified town of Fredericia.

Mention might be made at this point of the peculiarly Scandinavian and especially Swedish roof-form known in Sweden as the *säteri* ('chalet-style') roof, which has two slopes usually interrupted by a short vertical portion (Pl. 58, 60, 61, 66a, 67, 69, 71, 75b). No doubt it initially grew from the curving roof and tower forms of northern Europe. A striking and early example of the curved *säteri* roof, on the Riddarhuset in Stockholm, will be described in the next chapter.

In Stockholm the architectural situation was tentative before 1650, when the Oxenstierna Palace introduced the Roman *palazzo* style. Its Danish counterpart was not begun until 1672: Charlottenborg, the pleasure palace of Christian V's half-brother Gyldenløve in Copenhagen. Noble patrons new to the commissioning of town houses could not accept the picturesque style beloved by the burgesses, nor was it seemly to them to introduce the French *château* tradition of their own country houses; in fact, they did not know where to look. The first result, an eclecticism (Pl. 55), was not long in coming: the Makalös Palace in Stockholm, of 1630-39, and in Copenhagen much later—and so less of a mixture—the queen's Amalienborg, of 1667-73 (both since destroyed).

Makalös (literally 'Matchless'—or, indeed, Nonesuch like Henry VIII's fabled palace) was destroyed by fire in 1825. It was designed in 1630 by Christler, who probably came from Nürnberg, for Jacob de la Gardie, the general who had marched into Moscow and by so doing procured for Sweden domination over the Gulf of Finland, cutting off Russia from the Baltic until the next century. His palace in Stockholm must be seen against the background of his military reputation and the position he held in the public estimation there.

This mansion (Pl. 55a) stood by the water, Norrström, facing the Royal Palace—without doubt the foremost site in the city. It was rectangular in design, the corners emphasized by four projecting pavilions, and had covered ground-floor arcades on the two long sides, while the upper stories were stepped back in a sort of extended roof with no less than three levels of dormers. Here were architectural features from almost every part of Europe. The ground plan was French with its corner pavilions, and the water front became a Venetian arcade; the roof was South German in elevation and decoration; the window-frames were North-west German or Dutch in character; the balustrades were Roman, and the corner lanterns were heightened versions of those on Boy's old palace across the water. It is as if the builder wanted to put together everything that had been in vogue in Europe the century before, attempting with a sort of naïve mimicry something absolutely matchless.

It should be remarked here for chronological sense that the Riddarhuset was soon after tentatively begun in Stockholm; while it is to be discussed under civic buildings in the next chapter, it has all the scale and elegance of a private palace. It did not, however, receive definitive shape until the mid-1650's.

About 1650, Jean de la Vallée, who had just returned from Rome, got his opportunity to show what he had learned: he was asked by Axel Oxenstierna (who had ruled Sweden before Queen Christina came of age) to design a palace for him in Gamla Sta'n, the Old Town in Stockholm. The result is a nobly Roman façade-architecture (Pl. 59b), with such advanced details as illusionary perspective in the window-frames.

Everything about this palace is clearly early Roman baroque. The ground floor is treated as a quietly rusticated basement. Out of those grow the two main stories with interjacent mezzanine, the windows cut with sophisticated precision on the flatness of the unrusticated wall, which is only sparely decorated with a row of garlands. The centre of the façade is left quite unaccentuated. Tessin the elder, a colleague of Jean de la Vallée, obtained much the same results in his Riksbanken (Bank of Sweden) completed some ten years later, with differences only in details. It is significant that the Swedish architects did not 'dare' to copy the alternating rhythm of pediments on the façade of San Gallo's Palazzo Farnese in Rome, although Tessin copied the door.

Another kind of Roman architecture was brought to Scandinavia when Queen Sophie Amalia of Denmark, Frederick III's queen, decided in 1667 to build her own palace, Sophie Amalienborg (Pl. 55*b*), finished in 1673 and destroyed by fire in 1689 (its name being later given to the palaces and town planning undertaken there in the eighteenth century). It was a pleasure palace on the outskirts of Copenhagen, and so models were sought among the Italian villas; examples such as Guiliano San Gallo's Poggio a Caiano in Florence and Grimaldi's Villa Doria Pamphili in Rome have been mentioned in this connection. But, as was the case with Charlotten-borg on Kongens Nytorv, the result was a somewhat tentative Italian style. The architect was possibly Albertus Matthiessen.

Tessin and Royal Stockholm

If the tide of architecture within Scandinavia had earlier run from Denmark to Sweden, it turned in the opposite direction towards the end of the seventeenth century and so continued for some time after. The man who brought about the change was Nicodemus Tessin the younger (1654–1728), a dominating personality who did not hesi-tate to compete with the giants of his time in one of the competitions for the design of the Louvre. He was a child of the Roman baroque. His great work was the Royal Palace in Stockholm (Pl. 62, 63), for which plans were begun early in the 1690's. A far-reaching plan became possible in 1697 when the old palace was fire-ravaged, and the whole tremendous design occupied him until 1704.

Inspired by the Rome of Sixtus V and by the Paris and Versailles of Louis XIV, Tessin planned the palace to be the centre-piece in an extensive scheme that would remould the whole of northern Stock-holm (Pl. 62*b*). Only parts of his scheme were realized: the Palace, the rebuilt Storkyrka, or Great Church, the Norrbro, or North Bridge, and parts of the great square, Norrmalmstorg (now Gustav Adolfstorg). The rest of the money was used instead to finance the wars of Charles XII (ruled 1697–1718).

One of the projects not carried out was an impressive design for a royal burial church or Gravkyrka to face the palace from the square across the bridge; it would have been in part a descendant of S. Agnese in Rome, as well as cousin to Wren's St. Paul's with its dome and towers and Latin-cross plan. Others included arsenals by the water at Kungsträdgården opposite the Royal Palace, government offices and private mansions west and south of the palace, and stables and bazaars at Norrbro. However, what was completed was remarkable enough. The Royal Palace became the largest in Scandinavia, and the planning of Norrmalm as sketched by Tessin became the foundation for its appearance far into the nineteenth century. It was not until the present redevelopment of Lower Norrmalm was started that the idea of a north axial stress was finally abandoned.

The idea of a palace as a four-ranged establishment surrounding a courtyard came from Italy, but the grouping here of different ranges, wings, and details to form an entity was the particular achievement of Tessin himself. The perfect proportions of the almost square courtyard were carefully 'worked up' in numerous sketches. On the east (Pl. 62a) there are two rather low wings projecting on each side of a small garden, Logården, while on the west the two curved wings for the Main Guard form an introduction to the principal building and a transition from surrounding buildings with the Storkyrka. The north range is the oldest—it was started before the fire in 1697— and is the least ornate. The basement story is high with ramps in front. The main façade was treated as a unit and the only accent is that created by the door with its columns and the balcony above it. The other façades have projecting central bays accentuated by colossal colonnades of different designs and by gateways in the style of triumphal arches; the inner courtyard is similar but less emphatic. The adherence to Italian prototypes is at times very accurate and many comparisons in detail could be made with *palazzi* such as the Sciarra, Odeschalchi, and others.

Among the numerous residential apartments that were furnished by Tessin and his followers, Charles XI's Gallery in the north wing (dedicated to the reigning monarch's father) is the most consequential. The emotional effect of the enfilade of rooms grows as one proceeds from the inner private rooms towards the gradually larger ones. A similar intensification of feeling arises between the outer and inner courtyards: the former is open and light, the latter more close and secluded.

The centre of the south façade (Pl. 63) has the most vigorous design of all. A profound solemnity and a heroizing atmosphere are created by colossal Corinthian columns, the entablature projecting over each and surmounted by trophies and statues which posture in front of the windowless attic, all in sharp contrast to the regular elevation on either side. Here is the entrance to the vestibule between the hall of state and the chapel. Inside the vestibule the grandiose effects are somewhat modified; the tone is still heroic, here empha-sized by the sculpture, but the oval form of the room and the curves of the symmetrical staircases give it a quieter character. Because of the severity of the great inner doorway the atmosphere is certainly not intimate, but the great air of triumph is held within human scale and the tempered sweep of the twin staircases is not overwhelming.

The chapel of the Royal Palace was rebuilt in the eighteenth cen-tury by Carl Hårleman according to Tessin's directions. In it the heroic heaviness of the south façade gives way to a more other-worldly dignity, of different rhythms of columns and pilasters inter-laced with a smaller order against the walls, and containing within a great triumphal chancel arch a sculptured retable (by L'Archeveque, Pl. 78), framed in a flourish of broken pediment.

It goes without saying that the influence of Stockholm's royal building in Scandinavia was great. Even before designing its eleva-tions Tessin had made sketches and a large wooden model for a new (unexecuted) royal palace in Copenhagen, in which the palace of Stockholm was foreshadowed (see p. 143).

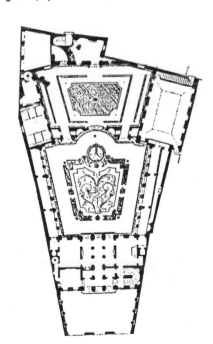

FIG. 57.
Tessin's own house and garden
near the Royal Palace.

Among Tessin's buildings his own mansion (Fig. 57) in Stock-holm south of the Royal Palace holds a unique position of great consequence in spite of its small scale. The garden is a superb example of baroque illusionary perspective, its unparallel sides and adroitly placed garden buildings making it seem much larger and more monumental than it actually is.

So far as Stockholm was concerned, the Roman styles adapted by Tessin continued to be mandatory until neoclassicism steered archi-tecture into new courses, for example, in the Ruutska Palace by C. F. Adelcrantz, 1755 (now Vattenfallsstyrelsens House), and the Opera House built by the same architect in 1777-82 in Gustav Adolf's Square, and the Exchange built 1767-76 by E. Palmstedt (Pl. 81, and see Chapter XX).

Royal Copenhagen

The architectural frame for absolute monarchy in Stockholm, introduced by Charles XI's succession to the throne, had been put in the hands of Nicodemus Tessin the younger. Apart from a few additional churches built on royal initiative (see Chapter XVII) the building programme in Stockholm was then complete. Abso-lutism was running out and the death of Charles XII in 1718 brought great changes. But before that day the nobility had already put its hallmark on the city.

Events in Copenhagen, however, followed an entirely different course. The reasons were partly political—an interval in the build-ing activity occurred during the mid-seventeenth century due to Denmark's unfortunate role in the Thirty Years War and her loss of vast territories to Sweden. Another political reason—and economic as well—was that the power of the Danish nobility was greatly reduced at the introduction of absolutism, so that they could not as in Stockholm rival the king as patrons of architecture. The Danish king was now more dominant, and when the nobility started building their programme became part of their king's. However, the most important factor was that the country had a different cultural back-ground from Sweden—richer and more varied. Add to this that the starting point for absolute architecture and cultural achievements in general was the life work of Christian IV, who was far ahead of his contemporaries in Sweden; the capital by the Sound therefore had a richer appearance than the capital at Lake Mälaren.

The urge to build, which was almost an obsession with Christian IV, was based on the wish to give his capital the same glorious appearance as that of other European cultural centres. Simul- taneously the extension of Copenhagen was energetically dealt with, an extension made necessary by an enormous increase of its popula- tion. All this was taking place when town building in Europe was at its peak; towards the end of the sixteenth century Sixtus V had started the replanning and revival of Rome, the last years of that century saw the birth of Palma Nuova, the ideal city, the Place des Vosges in Paris was created at the beginning of the seventeenth cen- tury and the city was extended to the west, the Palais de Luxembourg and Palais Royale were built, the town of Richelieu was founded, and the first squares appeared in London; towns were built and extended all over Europe, and Copenhagen was to become the Scandinavian showpiece.

The first steps towards the extension of Copenhagen were to equip the old town with ramparts and bastions, completed in 1624, the establishing of Christianshavn on Amager Island—a strongly forti- fied naval base protecting both the harbour and the south side of the city—and the rebuilding of St. Ann's redoubt north of the city. By linking this to the city wall by means of new ramparts (the present Østervoldgade, literally East Wall Street) the significant step out of the old medieval city could be taken without risk, for the new town was thus carefully guarded from the start.

The centre of New Copenhagen was planned by the king to con- sist of an octagonal square with radiating streets. This was not carried out according to plan, however, a gridiron street pattern being used instead, partly to conform to the shore line. The possibilities of the octagon remained in the minds of Copenhageners, however, and it was later realized in a changed form. In the king's lifetime only a few one-storied houses, the Nyboder, were built (1631–41) for naval crews in New Copenhagen.

With his numerous public buildings Christian IV changed his capital from a medieval town to an up-to-date city which could com- pete with the flourishing Dutch merchant towns. With his city plans he set the pattern for generations to come. He was so advanced that his son and grandson were unable to grasp the potentialities of his plans, which only slowly were developed into realities. It was not until 1662 that the new streets were drawn, Bredgade, Adelsgade, and others after a plan by Henrik Rüse, to connect the new town with Copenhagen proper.

During the reign of Frederick III, 1648–70, little was built, although a few alterations of older castles are worth mentioning, especially the marble room at Rosenborg, apart from the beginning of the queen's Sophie Amalienborg in the last year of his reign (see above, p. 137). Under Christian V, 1670–99, the country recovered from its wars and rebuilding started to show results. Danish architects began to catch up with the styles of the rest of Europe, and 'Renaissance' became baroque. The need for a modern royal residence was great and in the 1670's the problem was tackled when the king commissioned plans for a residence on the Slotts-holme, where Absalon's castle once stood. It was not solved, however, until much later, and two kings were to succeed Christian V before the royal castle was finally built. Instead the king's half-brother Ulrik Frederick Gyldenløve—the illegitimate son of Frederick III and the foremost power in Denmark—built himself a private palace, Charlottenborg, on Kongens Nytorv, a new and fashionable square between old and new Copenhagen (Pl. 56b). In its building history this conspicuous palace illustrates an interesting evolution, the transition from 'Renaissance' to baroque. According to the first design the palace was to consist of a main building with a pediment and four smooth pilasters flanked by towers crowned with cupolas. During the course of erection the towers became projecting parts of the main building, and the pediment disappeared in exchange for a balustrade. Roman details were added to a French conception—the plan shows a large hall in the middle and one bedroom in each of the projecting ends. The patron had just returned from his Grand Tour and he was anxious to introduce the latest novelties. But what is more remarkable, a synthesis of a square, a palace, and its garden was made for the first time in Scandinavia: behind the palace was a private Dutch garden, in front of it Kongens Nytorv (King's New Square) with the equestrian statue of Christian V. The Roman ideals introduced here were more firmly established by a plan for a royal residence that Nicodemus Tessin the younger submitted to Christian V.

Due to the destruction of Sophie Amalienborg in 1689 the king was without a residence, but the earlier discussed plans for a palace on the Slottsholme had been abandoned for a while. Tessin, in competition with Lambert van Haven, planned a four-ranged Roman castle, for which the wooden model was handed over to the king in 1697. Although never carried out, his designs were of great interest to Danish architects. The reason why this project was never realized is uncertain; it might have been the king's death two years after the arrival of the model, or the outbreak of war between Denmark and Sweden in 1700. A fact that might have had some importance was that the new king Frederick IV wanted to turn his back on Copenhagen, for he loved the countryside. One of his first buildings was Frederiksberg Castle just outside Copenhagen (Pl. 64, not to be confused with Frederiksborg). Plans were drawn by H. Scheel and Tessin while the king was still a crown prince. In its original state the castle was too small and it was later extended. It consisted of a three-storied main building with projections both in front and at the back. Like Gyldenløve the king had seen Versailles during his Grand Tour and was greatly impressed not only by the enormous palace but also by Marly le Roi, the *maison de plaisance* of Louis XIV. It is believed that Frederick IV was well acquainted with the architecture of his time. At Frederiksberg many different prototypes have been pointed out as having influenced him. In form the palace is Roman with a plan in accordance with that at Charlottenborg, that is to say with a large hall in the middle and bedrooms at both ends. This shows that a Danish tradition was being created. The extensive park at Frederiksberg was modelled on that of Versailles, but this layout was altered in the early nineteenth century for Frederick VI and became English in character. The palace, too, is much changed: a semicircular extension, which entirely reshapes the pure Tessin façade, was built in 1734 after designs by Häusser and Thurah.

Frederick also built himself a pleasure palace to celebrate the peace after the long and extensive Nordic War in 1720. It was called Fredensborg and was situated well out of Copenhagen. This return to nature was nothing exceptional in Europe in these days. As early as the Renaissance the Florentine merchants, like the ancient Romans in Horace's day, had built themselves country villas as a kind of compensating environment entirely free from the strenuous life of the city. The villa type was formed for years to come through examples like the Villa d'Este at Tivoli and by Andrea Palladio's villas in the Veneto. The connections between such villas and

Fredensborg, which have frequently been pointed out, are perhaps not too striking; many generations of architects had given their contributions to the original principles and when Palladian architec-ture appeared on Nordic soil sometimes only remnants of its pattern survived. Fredensborg was built by Tessin as a domed building with a tall, galleried hall under the dome.

The basic principle of the Villa d'Este was the unification of man with nature. The villa was placed on high ground with a magnifi-cent view, and a co-ordination between the house and nature was arranged by symmetrical stairs, terraced gardens, and artificial cas-cades. This combination of house and nature was enhanced by Palladio with his extended loggias embracing the garden terraces. But in his villas the plan was partly a function of other needs, those of humanism.

The ideal of humanism was the free human being; a human being who had mastered the sciences and with their help substituted know-ledge for medieval faith, harmony and self-assurance for fear. Humanism characterized Renaissance Rome and few cultural values received such worthy expressions as the creations of the artists nourished there—Raphael, Michelangelo, Bramante. When Rome surrendered to Charles V in 1527, humanism was too strong to die and spread instead to all the cities of Europe where it was often fostered by academies. Such an academy existed in Vicenza, and the atmosphere of this academy is strongly felt in Palladio's architecture. The feeling of space in these villas was similar to that which Raphael created in his 'School of Athens' in the Vatican; the space is in both cases unlimited for free men. Palladio's symmetrical and axial creations were consequently not meant for ceremonial purposes but for learned lectures and discussions, an environment like that of ancient Greece.

With these humanist academies, official or private, humanism spread all over Europe and as the royal ideal of Louis XIV and his *milieu* was imitated, humanist architecture appeared in many places. But it hardly ever appeared unchanged; this depended on how fully humanism was grasped (the differences between the Whitehall Banqueting House and Marly le Roi are many but the similarities outnumber them). Perhaps its first appearance in Scandinavia had been in the astronomer Tyge Brahe's private palace (Fig. 58) erected near the end of the sixteenth century, Uranienborg on Hven in the

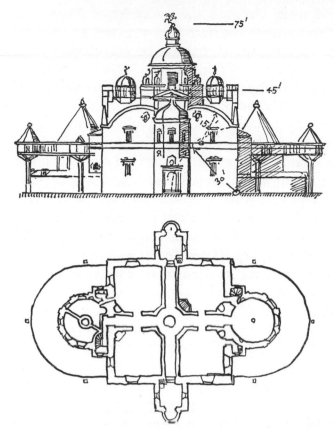

FIG. 58. Uranienborg.

Sound. Although the symmetrical plan is clearly visible, what
would have been originally the cupola-covered hall became here in
the North only corridors, and the exterior shows how strained and
painful the encounter with southern culture could be. In general,
the colonnades and the pediments of Palladio's villas became the
hallmark of humanism, symbolizing a correct order, harmony, and
knowledge. At Uranienborg nothing was yet visible of this clarity.
As time went on, however, this harmonious architecture of humanism
was to be particularly nursed and valued by the new burghers of the
seventeenth century, that is, the sons of the merchants of Copenhagen
and Stockholm who had embraced the style of Christian IV's
'Renaissance'.

At Fredensborg the lofty central room and the outside gallery
facing the courtyard became the most important parts of the buildings. The central hall was carried up much higher than the other

L   145

rooms, and so in Denmark the principles of Marly were applied further. (Fredensborg has since been changed by the addition of a mezzanine floor and pavilions, and by altered chimneys; it stands today as a compromise of different styles.) Both at Frederiksberg and Fredensborg, however strong the foreign influences, the northern architects created something of their own. The two castles were characterized by an elegance, a grace, fully worthy of a royal *milieu*.

Frederick IV did not limit his building to these two palaces which were rather distant from his capital city and his subjects in Copenhagen. In him Denmark had found a king who was able to take up the theme where Christian IV had left it. Among many administrative buildings which can be mentioned are the Generali‑tetet, the headquarters of the armed forces (1706), and the Kansliet, the Chancellery (1715). These buildings are marked by massive‑ness and gravity, in the strongest contrast to the two country estates. The architects, W. F. von Platen and J. C. Ernst, have achieved a baroque unity and rhythm. The heavy, elaborate decorations of these buildings began the pattern which would later recur at Christians‑borg, and Copenhagen had now acquired its royal absolute dimen‑sion.

The architects commissioned by Frederick IV were not the last 'Franco‑Italian' generation. The French tradition survived in Den‑mark until the Frenchman Nicolas‑Henri Jardin arrived in Copen‑hagen in the middle of the eighteenth century and as Director of the Royal Academy made this a French subsidiary establishment. But through clearly personal interests of the new royal patron, Christian VI (ruled 1730–46), interest was focused mainly on Germany, where the king had many relatives and friends. In princely competi‑tion with these he decided to give his capital a worthy royal residence, Christiansborg.

The evolution of the plans for this palace are very intricate. The idea of building a palace with four wings round a square may have been an inheritance from Lambert van Haven's and Tessin's plans, but it is recorded that an unknown foreigner, probably German, was consulted. He gave the building its elaborate South German character, and its exuberant pilasters aiming at a highly emotional effect. E. D. Häusser, the German who had been the king's teacher of domestic and military architecture, was commissioned to execute the building programme according to these designs but was later pushed aside for

Nicolai Eigtved, who designed the bridge and entrance pavilions, and Laurids de Thurah, who designed the interior decorations and the Riding Grounds. Today only the Riding Grounds (Pl. 67a) remain to remind us of the once impressive palace (for Hansen's re-building, see p. 192). The stables and domestic apartments and indoor riding ring formed a yard, a kind of entrance court to the palace, where an imaginative tone was struck by covered arcades, segments of elliptical colonnades, and stately gateways. There is a pleasant variety of clear-cut shallow surfaces, on which the architect has handled the lights and shadows with precision—such a building is gay in spite of its dignity. The older static style had now sur-rendered to a more dynamic style that was full of movement instead of the classical calm of Frederiksberg.

The terminal building of this kind of Danish architecture was the 'Hermitage', Christian VI's elaborate little hunting box at Dyrehaven (or the Deer Park) just north of Copenhagen (Pl. 67b). The archi-tect, Laurids Thurah, placed the building on a high basement so that it dominates the surrounding landscape. The functions of this *maison de plaisance* were simple: the entire centre of the main apart-ment is occupied by the king's dining-room. The façade of the main floor is magnificence on a small scale by an architect who had mastered all the elements of the later baroque style. The projecting ends under segmental gables form together with the recessed central part under its balustrade a triple rhythm which recurs in details such as windows and their flanking pilasters, the sculptured niches, and the crisp garlands in relief. This degree of late-baroque complexity was never attained further north than Copenhagen. When the Swedish king Adolf Fredrik gave to his queen on her birthday the little pleasure palace, Kina (i.e., 'China') Slott at Drottningholm in the 1760's, the architects Cronstedt and Adelcrantz used an exotic style, a modified rococo with a touch of *chinoiserie,* that playful mode for garden structures to which authority may have been lent by the publications of the Swedish-born English architect Chambers.

Frederick V, 1746–66, was the last of the great royal patrons of architecture in Scandinavia, and far from the least important. The creation of the Place Royale of Copenhagen, the Amalienborg, took place during his era. This was sited north of the old Copen-hagen and here the old idea of an octagonal plaza was realized (see p. 110). In the middle of it Saly's equestrian statue of Frederick V was raised in 1768. The layout of the Frederiksstaden, or Amalien-borg quarter, was planned by Marcus Tuscher and begun in 1749; that is, it was in the main stream of eighteenth-century city planning that produced Nancy and Bath.

Eigtved had originally planned the octagonal plaza surrounded by buildings of similar design and continuously identical height, but Tuscher split it up into four palaces, each flanked by two small pavilions, giving the whole a more articulated effect. This does not mean that Eigtved was put aside, for in reality he executed the major part of the four palaces. The remarkable thing about this piece of city planning is that the king and his architects designed the whole area from the very beginning so that the neighbouring streets would be furnished with houses of similar design, that is, it was master planning on a comprehensive scale which in Stockholm was not carried out until the end of the eighteenth century around Gustav Adolfs Square, where the equestrian statue of Gustavus Adolphus stands.

The four most exclusive palaces of Amalienborg faced the octagon itself, for the court aristocracy. The finest is Moltke's palace, the present royal residence (Pl. 68a). Here are clearly visible traditions from Charlottenborg; the façade has an accentuated centre contain-ing the elliptical main room, as well as newer international elements such as colonnades, pilasters, and so on. At ground-floor level the proportions and articulation of the elevations were to be repeated in the remarkable proportions of Eigtved's design for the Marble Church (see Chapter XVII).

This became the architecture of the ceremonial pattern of life, a completely urban counterpart to Christiansborg, because related to the plan of the city and not set off by itself, yet as elaborate in character, with conspicuous façades and grandiloquent interiors. This decora-tive language was borrowed from Versailles. A similar architecture appears in the two palaces, Berstorff's and Dehn's, situated at the intersection of Frederiksgade and Bredgade, at a very important point in the transition from the octagon to the Marble Church. These repeat the language of the palaces on the plaza, but have higher roofs, to prepare for the loftier dimensions of the church. The Danneskiold-Laurvigens Palace (Pl. 68b) is nearby on Store Kongensgade. Eigtved also designed the Frederik Hospital, further north, which still has a similar triple rhythm in spite of Thurah's rebuilding of the pavilions.

XV

TOWN BUILDINGS IN AN ARISTOCRATIC AGE

THE houses built for themselves by the merchant citizens of Copen-hagen and Stockholm continued to be variations on the style of Christian IV. During the latter part of the seventeenth century the so-called false-gable house was developed, the abundant decorations in sandstone disappeared, and the proportions of the gable became more like those of the classical 'temple' gable. The old high isosceles triangle based on the entire width of the house had had one practical advantage: any number of windows could be set in it, for which dormers now had to be made. The old house always had a living-room facing the street, with bedrooms behind it and above it in the gable, if this space was not used for storage in which case there would be a crane projecting from the gable.

This type of house had put down such roots in Scandinavia that it had become indigenous there. However, towards the end of the century the new wave of Dutch influence, taken to Sweden by Louis de Geer and to Denmark by other Dutchmen about the same time, began to have its effect with the rise of a new kind of city dweller. These were different from the local business men in that the new men had a more international point of view: these were cosmopolitan capitalists on a larger scale. It was quite natural that when this new type of man appeared as a patron of architecture, he chose the new Dutch architecture even if he happened to be Danish or Swedish born, since northern capitalism had its first great impetus in Holland. It was both socially and commercially sophisticated to know what was going on there.

The first house to be built in Stockholm in the new style was Louis de Geer's own house (Pl. 57a, now known as Ebba Brahe's), built in 1646 and probably designed by a member of the Vingboons family. This mansion was pure Dutch Palladian, altogether in the style of the Mauritshuis, which had been built in The Hague the

149

decade before. The most outstanding example in Scandinavia, however, is the Nobles' Assembly in Stockholm—the Riddarhuset (Pl. 58), literally Knights' House or House of Lords, on contemporary engravings grandiloquently called Palatium Ordinis Equestris.

A few years after his arrival in Sweden, Simon de la Vallée was commissioned to work out plans for such a building wherein the members of the nobility would meet officially with each other and with the Riksdag. In 1642 the architect drafted two designs. One showed a main building in three stories with basement, extending lower wings (Fig. 59) both in front and at the back; these wings also connected with each other by means of still lower ranges that formed two courtyards. The second plan was a less extensive copy of the first mainly at the expense of the 'back yard'. Relationships to the Palais de Luxembourg, where the architect's father was working under Salomon de Brosse, were numerous both in plan and elevation. Simon de la Vallée died in the same year that the designs were prepared, and a new architect was appointed to carry on the work, possibly already started.

The new man was Heinrich Wilhelm, from Hamburg. Both he and Nicodemus Tessin the elder wanted to make changes in the plans and diminish the busy colossal French order of rusticated pilasters designed by Simon de la Vallée. Nothing was done, however; the nobles seemed to regard the building of their communal house with a certain lack of enthusiasm. They and their leader, Axel Oxenstierna, understandably did not find it natural to ape the elaborate tastes of Marie de Medici—with her they had nothing in common. What they were looking for was an expression of the new humanistic ideals they had acquired on their travels, ideals which meant a new way of living, and consequently new forms in their architecture. It was Axel Oxenstierna who, in his capacity as Chancellor, had invited the foremost humanist of his time, Descartes, to the Swedish court to educate the young Queen Christina.

In 1653 the enterprise began again when Joost Vingboons was brought over from Holland by the personal initiative of Oxenstierna's ambassador to that country. He was assigned to this undertaking for three years only, but he was able to change the appearance of the building completely, for it was he who was responsible for the elevations. The huge pilasters were made smooth according to Palladian practice, a pediment was added in the centre, and at the level of the

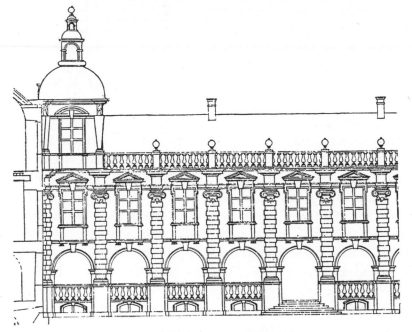

FIG. 59. Riddarhuset, part of first design.

capitals an attic was inserted. The change from the earlier designs was striking. This façade has precision and clarity, with the play between the walls and the crisp ornament above and below the windows and the impressive order of pilasters. This is clear humanism.

After the departure of Vingboons in 1656, the work was finished by Jean de la Vallée, the son of the first architect. The shape of the roof and the windows in the attic are his work. Little as this may seem, it is important, for here we find the first full curved develop-ment in Sweden of the so-called *säteri* roof (see p. 135), consisting here of two curved parts separated by a short vertical part, as fore-shadowed in the pavilion roofs of his father's design.

Erik Dahlberg's Town Hall at Jönköping and the old Town Hall in Copenhagen both belong to this category of seventeenth-century architecture. Lützow's palace on Stormgade in Copenhagen, designed in the 1660's, is a dignified and larger example of this style. Dutch classicism appeared as well on the Opera House (Pl. 59a) in that city of 1702.

Hybrids between the Dutch Palladian style and the false-gable type of house soon became a common sight in the mercantile towns.

In Copenhagen, in Nyhavn, there is number 65 (Pl. 70b), which had deeply moulded 'pediments' on gable and dormers with greatly elongated pilaster strips. Pilasters were to become the most common ornamental feature on the foremost burgher houses; some had rusticated pilaster strips instead, but the simplest had none at all. Emphasis on sheer volume became more the custom as the eighteenth century wore on.

This sort of architecture also developed in the countryside, mainly for a new kind of country dweller who was closely related to the rising burgher class in the cities. Such was Nysø, built about 1673 by a Dane of this new class. Another fine example in Denmark is Sorgenfri, rebuilt by Thurah in 1745 as a country estate for the royal family.

The Amalienborg quarter in Copenhagen is characterized by its homogeneous appearance. Amaliengade, or Amalie Street, was planned for the new burghers from master designs by Eigtved. The façades, varying from five to nine windows in width, are given horizontal stress by a prominent string-course corresponding to the top of the ground floor of the neighbouring palaces. Above the slightly projecting centre is here a pediment, there a balustrade; or the centre may be recessed instead, very slightly, as a reversal of the old Danish triple rhythm.

The East India Company building at Gothenburg (Pl. 71), designed by Carl Hårleman about 1740, belongs to this family of architecture. The projecting centre outlined by rusticated pilaster strips forms the Palladian dimension of the building, the composing of the centre of the façade as a unit with domestic dimensions. A well-developed rhythm exists especially in the ground floor, repeated in the next floor more gently. Because of its size the East India Company leaves its distant relatives—the burghers' private houses—far behind. A contemporaneous translation of the style from stone into wood can be seen at Trondheim, where the Stiftsgården (Pl. 72), built 1774-78, with its studiously applied rhythm of little pediments over the windows, is a fine example of provincial Palladian as it was interpreted in Norway.

XVI

COUNTRY LIFE

TOWARDS the end of the sixteenth century the Scandinavian aristocracy had grown eager to build residences on their estates or replace the
old with new ones. Architecturally the transition to new types of
houses was at first rather slow. The Danish Rosenholm, which has
been dealt with above (p. 180, Pl. 46a), showed many old-fashioned,
French trends such as towers and projections vaguely reminiscent of
pavilions and the like. Such details can also be found at Ulstrup
(Pl. 46b) built at the end of the sixteenth century, although the design
is stricter, especially on the gables, where decorations are limited to
linear and horizontal strips. Although new tactics characterized
warfare with powerful guns, Ulstrup still had small defensive turrets
which flank the pavilion-like ends of the building—clearly vestiges
of the past with little or no practical meaning. Apart from this a
strong will to create symmetrical buildings is evident. Nørlund in
Denmark can be mentioned. But this tendency is not always visible
now, since later changes and additions have often altered the original
effect of symmetry. When dealing with smaller achievements one
must remember that lack of wealth hindered the realization of theories.
For this reason Katholm in Denmark is rather irregular in plan as
well as elevation.

Between 1622 and 1626 Vibyholm Castle (Fig. 60) in Södermanland, Sweden, was built for Charles IX's widow, Queen Christina.
The architect was the Dutchman Caspar Panten, who had earlier
worked on the rebuilding of Stockholm's castle. This architect, who
to a certain extent had been a pupil of his fellow-countryman Lieven
de Key (architect of the Leyden Town Hall and the Slaughter House
at Haarlem), was the first to introduce into Sweden a Palladian plan,
adding some of the spirit that ruled at Chambord in France. In this
case only the central portion of the house was planned in a Palladian
way. Vibyholm consisted of three parts, a central core and two side
wings. The central part was taken up by a large vestibule and an

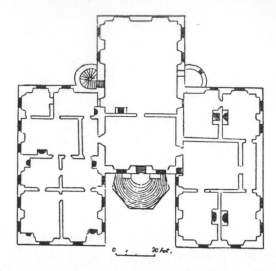

FIG. 60. Vibyholm.

extensive banqueting hall. The left wing is supposed to have contained the private rooms of the queen. The right wing was designed
for her guests and it was divided into two apartments with an ante-
room between them that was entered from the main hall.

The first floor, not the ground floor, contained the main apartment
at Vibyholm; in the severe Nordic climate, there was less choice than
in Italy. In plan the two wings did not symmetrically repeat each
other. This lack of complete symmetry could be called an old-
fashioned feature, but it is better explained by the fact that the two
parts had different functions: one was the everyday part, the other was
put aside for guests. The Palladian features are thus limited to the
planning of the middle block, which was designed in a strongly
formal and ceremonial spirit.

In the central core, however, there are some essential divergences
from Palladio's own type of plan as it appears, for instance, in the
Villa Trissino, a villa with a wholly symmetrical plan and particularly small residential quarters, which were inserted in the upper
story—a mezzanine story on a small scale. When the Palladian
villa was copied all over Europe, both plan and elevation were often
somewhat misunderstood. Apart from this partially Palladian influence, the French castles of the Loire valley also must have meant
much to the Scandinavian aristocracy. Such vast achievements as
Chambord with its magnificent double stairs in the very centre of the

castle could not of course be imitated too closely, as the Scandinavian patrons lacked money for such enterprises, but the intricate plans and elaborate exteriors of the *châteaux* made a long-lasting impression. Nevertheless, the exterior, which was badly damaged by fire in the eighteenth century, was entirely Dutch. The architect achieved an abundantly rich surface by freely using such elements as volutes, pilasters, and other ornamental features in sandstone, which in contrast to the smooth red brick walls create an impression of glittering festivity.

FIG. 61. Fiholm.

The second architect who was working in Sweden at the beginning of the seventeenth century was the earlier mentioned Hans Christler from Germany. In 1639 he designed a country palace called Jacobsdal (Pl. 56a) for Jacob de la Gardie. The name was later changed to Ulriksdal, and the exterior has been greatly changed since the days of Hans Christler. In many ways it was similar to Panten's Vibyholm, but a remarkable difference lies in the fact that Jacobsdal consisted of a main building with two projecting, separate, and subordinate wings. The main building also dominated the elaborately laid-out garden in the front planned by the garden architect Hans G. Kraus. In the gables Christler used the same elements as Panten, but the façade of the main building was given a purer Palladian character by a colossal order of pilasters of the Composite order. As a whole this palace was more purely baroque in character, particularly in its setting of the extensive terraced garden with walls, balustrades, and triumphal arches.

In 1671 a similar palace was built in Denmark for the brother of King Christian V. It was called Vordingsborg (Pl. 57b) and was designed by Lambert van Haven, who drew designs strongly related to the Dutch type of country houses. In Holland these houses had been built by the new intelligentsia—the industrial patricians—and the rather late date of erection here proves what a firm anchorage this way of building had in Denmark, while the development in Sweden by that time had travelled along other paths. The palace, which also included a Dutch park, was pulled down about 1750.

The French architect Simon de la Vallée, who came to Sweden in 1637, devoted his first years in Sweden to the Oxenstierna family and especially to their leader, Axel Oxenstierna. For this family he built Tidö in Västmanland, Fiholm in Södermanland (Fig. 61), which was never finished, Rosersberg in Uppland—this was built

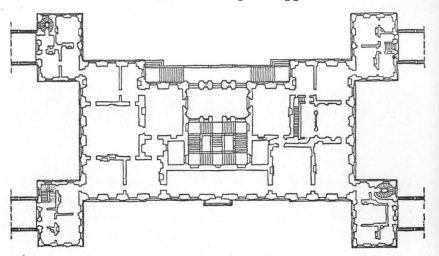

FIG. 62. Drottningholm.

for Gabriel Bengtsson Oxenstierna—and Jäder church in Söder-manland. With Simon de la Vallée the French style vaguely fore-shadowed in the plan for Jacobsdal obtained its firm hold on the design of the Swedish country estates and manor-houses which it was not to lose for almost two centuries.

Clearly French in character is the grand composition of the un-finished Fiholm. The establishment was planned to consist of one main building with two projecting smaller wings forming a court-yard. In front of these, four parallel ranges were to have been placed containing the estate offices and forming outer courtyards; two of these ranges were the only buildings to be erected. On the other side of the main building a French parterred garden was planned with quadrangular plantations and a monumental double staircase lead-ing up to the house. At Tidö and Fiholm the sculptural decorations were carried out by other men, not by the planning architect, and therefore there are few complete examples of his work during his

156

few years in Sweden. But Simon de la Vallée had given these houses their special form, and this spirit persisted.

Nicodemus Tessin the elder received his most important commission when in the 1660's the Dowager Queen Hedvig Eleonora decided to build a country palace, Drottningholm. The commission went to Tessin because since 1649 he had been the Royal Architect. The desire to create a symmetrical plan according to the French pattern is clearly visible (Fig. 62). A monumental entrance hall with

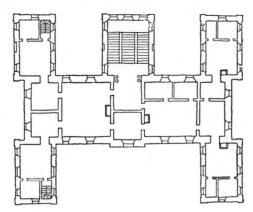

Fig. 63. Mälsåker.

a staircase occupies the centre of the palace and three immense doors lead into it. On one side in the main apartment is the banqueting hall and on the other the queen's state bedroom. To both the banqueting hall and the bedroom are added numerous smaller rooms, anterooms, servants' rooms, etc. The private residential parts are placed in projecting pavilionlike buildings in each of the four corners of the palace, which together with connected buildings form courtyards. A ceremonial hall of state is not to be found in the centre of the palace; but there is a gallery which, like the staircase, serves as a link between the two halves of the palace. Compared to contemporary building traditions in France this is a conservative feature at Drottningholm, but it must be remembered that it was a queen and not an absolute king who was building this palace: to imitate too closely Louis XIV's Versailles that was then being built might have appeared somewhat challenging as well as expensive. But the main factor was the cultural lag—the oldfashioned plan was preferred in the North.

The exterior was given a magnificent appearance (Pl. 60a).

Impressive doorways linked the inner rooms to the staircase hall on the water front. The sculptural decoration of the interior staircase was by Nicholas Millich, and there are extensive gardens and a surrounding park that give the dowager queen's palace a splendid setting. The pavilions, it will be noticed, have the *säteri* roof. The walls were treated in a relatively subdued manner, with flattened pilasters, arches, and mouldings that do not diminish the play between the volumes of the main block and the wings.

The Danish castle Clausholm (Pl. 65*b*) was built some years later than Drottningholm and showed the evolution that took place in the latter half of the seventeenth century. The wings of the castle embrace a large courtyard. One can here find resemblances to the Dutch architecture erected for the capitalistic patricians, mainly in the pediment of the main building, but the French tendencies are perhaps more strongly felt. The symmetry is clear and the treatment of the walls unelaborate; thus only the porch is lightly decorated, and the volumes of the blocks consequently even more apparent. This is baroque: the different sections are integrated and all old-fashioned reminiscences such as pavilions, towers, and dividing walls between garden and house have disappeared. One vast motif dominates: the main building with its pediment rests as a co-ordinating volume and the lower wings are subordinated to this theme as are courtyard and garden. It is restful and yet full of power.

In Mälsåker Castle in Södermanland, Sweden, of about 1660, the elder Tessin created a reduced edition of Drottningholm (Fig. 63). The same can be said of Sjöö in Uppland, but at Skokloster, the erection of which also occupied Jean de la Vallée, the patron, Karl Gustaf Wrangel, apparently did not give Tessin a very free hand. Eriksberg Castle in Södermanland with a magnificent baroque garden is one of the best-preserved examples (Pl. 60*b*). The *säteri* roof is one of the finest in Sweden.

A similar French character can be seen in Christianssaede in Denmark (Pl. 61*a*), built in 1690 for one of the king's councillors, Jens Juel. Plans by Nicodemus Tessin the younger were the basis when construction was started, but during erection they were entirely revised by an unknown architect. The Dutch spirit, which earlier prevailed in most Danish manor-houses, was completely abandoned for the benefit of such details as the Roman balustrade, French dormers, and the Nordic *säteri* roof.

Steensballegård occupies a middle position. It was built approxi-
mately at the same time as Christianssaede, and for a member of a
very old aristocratic family. The links with the old traditional country
castles consequently remained clearly visible, especially in the firm
austerity of the decorations. The wings are later additions.

The symmetrical plan foreshadowed in Drottningholm got its
final logical expression in Steninge, a manor-house built by Nicodemus Tessin the younger in 1694-98 for Karl Gyllenstierna. The

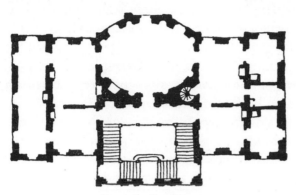

FIG. 64. Steninge.

plan (Fig. 64) is best described as a simplified version of Vaux-le-
Vicomte, where the simplification consists in a reduction of the
number of rooms and the corner parts being drawn into the building.
The big staircase is placed as a monumental part of the building
immediately inside the entrance from the yard, and the middle of the
house consists of a large drawing-room in close connection with the
garden. On either side of this room there are residential suites
connected with both the drawing-room and the staircase.

The exterior of Steninge (Pl. 61b) is the least French of all Tessin's
country houses. Contributing to this is the fact that the ground floor
with its rusticated ornament was treated as a base for the upper story.
Because of the balustrade over the central part the *säteri* roof, which is
low, is not so apparent as usual. The plan, however, is entirely
French.

In Sturefors manor-house in Östergötland, designed by the same
architect, the projecting central part is crowned by a pediment and
the *säteri* roof has here its most usual elevation, strict and rectilinear.
The establishment consists of only one block with only a slightly
accentuated centre. This style of architecture, the main characteristics

of which are the smooth, often quite undecorated, ranges—whereby the volumes of the buildings appear with emphasized clarity—formed a tradition in Sweden and was spread all over Scandinavia. One example was Gunderslevsholm in Denmark. As Carl Hårle-man (1700–53) and Jean Eric Rehn (1717–93) adopted it, it persisted in Swedish manor-house architecture far into the eighteenth century. Among the buildings by Hårleman are Svartsjö in Upp-land (a replacement of an older castle built in the sixteenth century by Wilhelm Boy, which had included a circular courtyard with interesting arcades of Franco-Italian character). Svartsjö was rebuilt 1735–39 (Pl. 69, design endorsed by the owner, Frederick I). Åkerö, built in 1776, is another example. With the building of Övedskloster, finished in 1776, the type is represented also in Skåne. Jean Eric Rehn built Gimo in Uppland and Erstavik in Söderman-land, among many others from the 1760's. At about this time a predominant habit of living on the ground floor which had been adopted with the French plans ceased to be practised, and the resi-dential apartments were once more moved up to the floor above.

Carl Fredrik Adelcrantz (1716–93) is another architect among the many who designed manor-houses according to the type introduced by Tessin. To represent his work there can be mentioned Skedevi in Östergötland, built in the 1780's. In this building the once strict plan is, however, somewhat broken up by various corridors.

Generally speaking, this type of manor-house with a more or less accentuated middle part and a rectilinear *säteri* roof was spread all over Sweden, thanks to many unknown architects. It is so common that one can find such a manor-house in almost every township. During the eighteenth century the size was somewhat reduced—the reason for this was sometimes a question of money, sometimes a desire to create more intimate and comfortable residences—but the appearance and the spirit remained the same.

Towards the middle of the eighteenth century this type of undeco-rated and rather 'uncomplicated' architecture was abandoned in Denmark. Ledreborg (Pl. 66a) of 1740 is a two-storied building with the centre of the façade illustrated emphasized by plain pilaster strips and surmounted by a segmental pediment while either end is crowned by a balustrade; the other façade is a variation on these themes. This is a lively composition in which the main building is framed by lodges and wings, lamp standards and pools in a cunningly shaped open space to supplement the rhythm of the façade, and the whole is carried to a fantastic climax in the garden, one of the most famous in all Scandinavia. A similar façade can be seen at Lerchen-borg (Pl. 66*b*) which was built at the same time. These buildings mean a complete victory for the French taste in Denmark, empha-sized not least in the gardens and their terraces, and earlier heralded at Clausholm, among many others.

Finally, the more secluded and intimate French style appeared in Scandinavia in the pleasure palaces, such as Frederiksdal in Den-mark and Kina Slott at Drottningholm in Sweden. To this group of buildings also belongs the Hermitage near Copenhagen. In fact the royal residences of this kind naturally set the pattern for the aristocracy.

A blend of this small-scale French style and the baroque is found in the small manor-house Damsgård (Pl. 73) at Bergen in Norway, where the ornamental details are abundant within the severe and strict composition of the building as a whole. This was a rebuilding of 1770.

In Norway and Finland the two centuries dealt with here did not make any remarkable additions to architectural history. Norway under Denmark and Finland under Swedish rule were both regarded by their mother countries as rather peripheral colonies of little interest and they were without local gentry who could have fostered an archi-tectural spirit. Two manor-houses in Finland are worth mentioning, however: Louhisaari and Sarvilahti, both built in the seventeenth century and inspired by Swedish building traditions.

XVII

CHURCHES FOR THE NEW RELIGION

To say that with the Reformation church-building activity abruptly stopped, is valid only with some modification. After the cathedrals and parish churches, and later the town churches, were finished the needs for places of worship were covered for the time being; the building programme was accomplished, until new communities should arise. The Reformation was naturally a shock to many and to church builders in particular. But soon a new type of programme emerged and churches were built once more, if less numerously. This new programme came, in fact, with the Reformation because the Lutheran and Calvinistic man could not, of course, accept the old type of church any more than he could accept the old religion. To him the old churches filled with mysticism and ecstasy were obsolete. The foundation for a new type of church was the religious discussion that went on in all European countries in the sixteenth and seventeenth centuries within the framework of the Reformation, the Counter Reformation, and religious wars.

An example of this new type of church in Scandinavia has earlier been given with Christian IV's church at Kristianstad in Skåne (p. 111). Another example, and a somewhat earlier one, would be St. Jacob's or Jacobs Kyrka in Stockholm. The interior of this many times rebuilt church, founded near the end of the sixteenth century, shows a desire, among all the somewhat Gothic details, to create a new kind of space, a bright and clearly defined space, rational in conception, in the place of what could be called the old Catholic spirit.

This repudiation of mysticism and ecstasy had been carried much further in Italy. Rational Florence, whence new ideas swept all over Europe, saw the revival of the domed church when Brunelleschi presented his design for the cathedral cupola in 1418. It was not made by the architect Brunelleschi but by the mathematician Brunelleschi. New churches were soon being constructed at a great rate all over Italy, churches in which the sermon and the liturgy did not dominate the design, for there now began the theoretical discussion of the central church plan—a square, a Greek cross, a circle, covered by a dome—seeking to realize the ideal church entirely based on geometrical and mathematical laws. The terminus of this discussion—where the mathematical laws by which great masses were manipulated received a mighty infusion of drama—was the complex plan and elevation of St. Peter's in Rome as it was designed by Michelangelo.

The same rationalistic way of thinking was the basis for the centralized church of the seventeenth century in Scandinavia, and it is therefore quite natural that the Catholic church plan was conveyed to the Nordic countries. But in appearance the façades are modified versions of the Italian, which can be explained by the fact that the Lutheran church did not possess the same emotional foundation as did the Roman Catholic church. In the churches with the Latin cross plan, especially Tessin's design for the burial church on Norrmalmstorg in Stockholm (discussed below, p. 168), however, the problems were not the same and emotion still outweighed theory.

This importance of the mathematical laws is well illustrated in St. Katarina in Stockholm (1656, Pl. 74) and the Frelserkirke in Copenhagen (1682, Pl. 75a, Fig. 65). The two architects, Jean de la Vallée in Sweden and Lambert van Haven in Denmark, have used almost identical plans. This can be described as a square with projecting rectangles on each side, one of which forms a vestibule. Four piers carry the superstructure. In the Frelserkirke the long side of the rectangle is equal to the distance between the middle piers, which equals half of the side of the square. The short ends of the rectangles are one-fourth of the side of the square and this last measurement reappears for self-evident reasons in the square corner-chapels, the inner angles of which are formed by the middle piers. The plan can be regarded as a very simplified version of Michelangelo's plan for St. Peter's, achieved by 'subtracting' the emotional elements from Michelangelo's design and by completely avoiding its more complex articulation.

An identical plan was used for the Stockholm church, which was built on royal initiative, but with a very different effect on the exterior elevation. The two churches in fact look quite dissimilar. If one disregards the Frelserkirke's spiral tower (designed by Thurah), that church was treated as if there were but one interior space, for the two rooflines of the main axes of the church are unbroken and the four secondary spaces are not accentuated. The architect of St. Katarina, on the other hand, has made a clear distinction between the central space and the four separately roofed arms of the cross; and the four secondary spaces, the chapels, have their own little cupolas. It can thus be maintained that St. Katarina is closer to the Italian prototype. The divergences from the theoretical ideals in the Frelserkirke are founded on religious reasons and such divergences can also be found in St. Katarina, where cross-vaults were used instead of barrel vaults.

Quite apart from the fact that the Frelserkirke has no dome, but a high west tower which takes away the impression of a centralized church altogether, the two seventeenth-century elevations differ entirely. St. Katarina has four pedimented façades from which four hipped roofs slant towards the block-like core under the octagonal drum. Around the drum rise four little corner towers, and the tall dome gives the church a special splendour. The Frelserkirke has a less elaborate appearance on the exterior. The façades are more restful and look as if they formed a base for the west tower. It is an exterior closely related to those of Dutch reformed churches.

It may be remarked, parenthetically, that the seemingly identical medieval centralized plan of St. Lars on Visby—a plan perhaps originally derived from Kiev—cannot be called a forerunner of the Frelserkirke-St. Katarina plan because, for one thing, when these latter churches were designed St. Lars itself was unknown (its ruins were entirely covered by trees and bushes until discovered by archaeologists in the last century). In any case, such centuries-old forms do not seem to have provided patterns for the completely new state of mind of the baroque age.

This type of centralized church, based on a central square and halves of it, never obtained a firm footing in Scandinavia. The cathedral at Kalmar, Sweden (Pl. 76a, Fig. 66), by Nicodemus Tessin the elder constitutes a remarkable modification of this plan in the way that the church is stretched out, so to speak; in both the east and west end a rectangle has been added, which is equal to half of the middle square, and a semicircular apse. But this is a cathedral requiring additional space for its bishop, and so once more the functions of the service have decided the shape of the church.

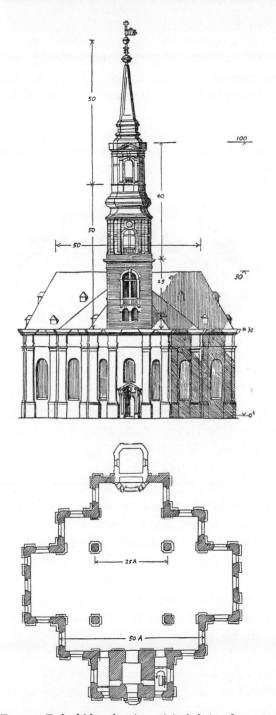

FIG. 65. Frelserkirke, showing original design for tower.

165

The intention was originally to crown the cathedral with a grand central dome. By so doing the impression of the two entrance façades —the long sides—would have been strengthened, and the church given the character of a centralized church. The two façades have at any rate a strongly accentuated middle part, created by the move, ment up towards the pediment in the upper story, where a simplified triumphal arch motif is formed. It is significant of Swedish church architecture that this example of the 1660's is much more subdued in its design than its models in Italy.

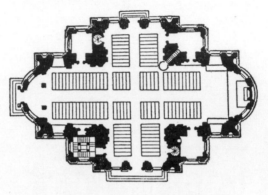

FIG. 66. Kalmar Cathedral.

The plan of St. Katarina was adapted by Eric Dahlberg in two buildings of the latter seventeenth century, the wooden church at Laxå (Pl. 75b) and the church at Karlshamn. In both these cases the plan was based on a Greek cross, at Laxå somewhat modified by oblique passages between the arms of the cross. One of the simplifica tions—probably undertaken because of the small scale—is that each church has a lantern over the crossing instead of a dome. The façades are suggestive of those of the Frelserkirke in Copenhagen. A purely national feature is the *säteri* roof which is used on both churches.

Towards the seventeenth century there emerged in Finland a need for churches in the inland districts, for it was now that these parts of the country were being populated. The Swedish colonization had restricted itself to the south-east coastal districts and thus the Finns now colonized virgin soil. All churches in these inland parts were centralized churches; the Finns had undoubtedly derived these from Russia, where the centralized church had been firmly established since the days of Byzantium. The Finnish churches were all built of wood. The oldest, at Saloinen, was built in 1632 on a square plan. A similar church was built at Kunpele in 1686 with an added tower. More articulated forms are to be found at Elimähl, in a church of 1678, and at Kenruu, of 1758, where the plan is a Greek cross. All these churches have interior paintings.

Wood was also the material at Kongsberg church (Pl. 80) in Norway. The church is famous for its interior work. The altar, the pulpit, and the organ are built together as one vast decorative unit. The curvilinear forms give it a South German character and the abundant decorations in gold and white create an almost ecstatic quality.

Commissions to design mausoleums were fairly frequent during the era of royal power in Sweden. The most important of these is the mausoleum of the Caroline kings at the Riddarholmskyrka in Stockholm (Pl. 77). It was designed in 1671 by Tessin the elder in the shape of a Greek cross with minor transepts which on the exterior appear to be only strongly articulated mouldings of the main volume. The deep articulation continues all the way up from the base through the coupled Tuscan columns, the plainer attic, and the dome—the latter redesigned by Carl Hårleman in the 1740's. The corner transitions between one colonnaded façade and another are curves, which give a dynamic impression as of a kind of synthesis between the round of the dome and the Greek cross of the plan. At first Tessin had planned the building with a peristyle, which would have made the exterior static and not, as it appears today, filled with movement. It has the same effect, on a smaller scale, as the dome of a large Renaissance church on its drum, for the body of this building serves as a base to the dome. The dramatic effect of this remarkable example of baroque monumentality is enormous.

Compared to the Caroline Mausoleum the Lars Kagg mausoleum at Floda church in Södermanland (Pl. 76b), built by Eric Dahlberg in 1661, is almost restful in character. It was built on a Greek cross plan, but here the arms are slightly longer than at the Riddarholmskyrka. The pilasters are flat, the mouldings spare, and only the deep-cut pediment over each arm and a strip of florid ornament in each corner panel vary the surface. The crossing has a low dome surmounted by a small lantern. This is a different kind of architecture, less deeply profiled, more suggestive of the Palladian, and more in the style of the Frelserkirke or the reformed church in the same city. There is no ambiguity in plane as on the Caroline Mauso-leum; instead of dynamic tension we find a static harmony. In the brilliant whiteness of the interior, eight Virtues in niches flanked by Corinthian pilasters, and a ceiling decorated with allegorical symbols and floral ornament in stucco, executed by Carlo Carove, give a dazzling impression.

A mightier mausoleum, never executed, was the Gravkyrka designed by Tessin the younger for the Norrmalmstorg (Pl. 62b, and p. 137) in Stockholm. It was planned on a Latin cross: thereby a sense of movement along a nave was once again introduced into a Swedish church, a movement from the entrance towards the mighty dome. The church was intended to be the burial church of the Caroline kings, a Swedish Pantheon, and it was natural that the architectural setting should be as triumphal as possible. The south elevation as seen from its main approach, Norrbro, was the important thing, so important that the church was not to be oriented from west to east in the usual way. Tessin adopted a type of façade not un-common in the seventeenth century in Rome with two side towers, a non-antique feature introduced by Bramante in his design for St. Peter's in Rome and used by Francesco Borromini in the seventeenth century. But Tessin's drafts were much less emotionally dynamic than Borromini's church façades, and in the centre of a composition which can be characterized as belonging to the mid-seventeenth century, Tessin introduced an old-fashioned Palladian or Pantheon type of porch which completely opposes and restrains what was achieved in the vertical side towers and still more in the large ellipti-cal cupola. The eclectic features were to be less obvious on the interior, according to what can be gathered from Tessin's sketches. The movement towards the north would have been carried beyond the space under the cupola, to the extreme absidal end, where lights and shadows would have emphasized a dynamic climax in the complex and partly open north end.

A similar problem was presented in Copenhagen with the Frederikskirke or Marmorkirke, the Marble Church, the background of the short axis of the palace square of Amalienborg; the problem was the elevation of the dome and the façade. The discussion can be described as mirroring the architectural situation not only in Denmark in the middle of the eighteenth century but throughout Europe.

The Frederikskirke, or Marble Church, Copenhagen.
FIG. 67 (*right centre*), design by Eigtved, 1754. FIG. 68 (*left below*), design by Thurah, 1754.
FIG. 69 (*upper left*), design by Jardin, 1756.   Comparative scale not exact.

Eigtved's first design for the church was dated 1752 and showed a church with a soaring cupola on a rather high drum flanked by two side towers. The façade itself was very low compared to the towers and the cupola, and had in fact a horizontal stress. An almost mathematical sense of proportions and symmetry characterized the whole design.

This design was much criticized, as its porch was considered to be out of proportion to the overall magnificent scale and in a design drafted two years later the porch was enlarged. Once this problem was solved a still more important one could be approached, that of the access of daylight into the central part of the church, a problem which directly depended on the construction of the cupola. Eigtved, who was a child of the late baroque, preferred a soft, indirect light in his church. Thus he planned two domes, an outer and an inner one, which did not coincide (Fig. 67). The inner dome, lit by small openings in its shell and by a small lantern, was to be supported by coupled columns and buttressed by a four-storied ambulatory around the central space. Above this was to be an outer dome, on a very high drum pierced by arched openings, and the cupola crowned by a high lantern. Penetration of the outer structure by the inner structure was limited to the openings and the small lantern of the latter rising into the open drum of the former for light.

According to Thurah this was a false solution. In his design (Fig. 68), made in 1754, he clearly demonstrated his wish for inner and outer congruency. His dome was to be supported by four massive piers separated by four arched openings and the drum was buttressed as in Eigtved's plan by an ambulatory. This dome, having the same curve within and without, was much lower and so less important as a focal point for the view from the Amalienborg square.

The central problem of the discussion was clearly very much one of construction. Nothing was more natural than to consult a French architect, since it was in France, and especially in J. H. Mansart's dome for the Invalides in Paris, that the use of new and bold means of construction achieved a new light in the interior and an elevation then unrivalled in its character. It must therefore have been a great disappointment when Nicolas-Henri Jardin, in the first design he submitted in Copenhagen, planned a church completely Roman in character and with a cupola that was poorly related to the voluminous lower parts. In reply to the heated criticism he at last submitted a new design, which was approved by the king in 1756 and which has in the main given the church its present appearance as executed in the middle of the last century (Pl. 79).

The exterior of this church has much in common with Tessin's design for the Stockholm burial church but is much more har- monious, in fact greater architecture. In section there are three cupolas (Fig. 69), the innermost one supported by coupled columns in two stories forming an ambulatory. This dome has a central opening through which the decorations of the second cupola can be seen. The outer cupola is framed with timber, a typical French way of construction, making a lighter structure that could thus be made very high. Only minor details were changed later when the church was built. By the arrangement of the two inner domes a play of light and shadow was set up—a feature especially common in South German churches of this period. The dualism between inner and outer appearance was resolved in a visual ambiguity. Towards the street from the royal square the church today serves as a background with its projecting temple front a climax to the Amalienborg palaces. On the drum of the big dome columns alternate with windows, and this rhythm is carried up in the copper dome and its lantern. Stock- holm only received such a dome in 1868 when Jean de la Vallée's church Hedvig Eleonora on Östermalmstorg was finished.

XVIII

TOWN PLANNING

THE absolute monarch's desire to manifest his splendour in magnificent streets and monumental squares, so abundantly carried out in Rome and Paris during the seventeenth century, also expressed itself in Scandinavia, as we have seen in the purely French Amalienborg in Copenhagen with the king's equestrian statue in the square, and in Tessin the younger's plan for Stockholm around the new Royal Palace. Similar trends were expressed by the great gardens laid out around palaces and manor-houses: the most magnificent of these were the gardens at Drottningholm and Fredensborg.

At the same time and earlier, new town plans were created for many Swedish towns, often carried out after the towns had been ravaged by fire, a fairly frequent disaster in the Swedish wooden towns during the seventeenth and eighteenth centuries. The seventeenth-century town plan became the accepted prototype until far into the nineteenth century, when it was replaced as a model by plans worked out by the railway architect Adolf Wilhelm Edelswärd and by Albert Lindhagen (see below, p. 194).

One of the first new plans executed on this theme involved the west parts of the Old Town of Stockholm, ravaged by a fire in 1625. Stora Nygatan then became the main artery in a new precinct with rectangular blocks and regular streets. In 1640 Claes Fleming, the first governor-general of Stockholm, carried these schemes further to the north and south, on to Norrmalm and Södermalm. The straight streets Drottninggatan, Regeringsgatan, and Storgatan on Östermalm were Fleming's work, and regularity and beauty his motto. None of the original houses remain, however.

But perhaps a more magnificent and better picture of Swedish seventeenth-century town planning can be found at Karlskrona in Blekinge, founded in that century as a naval base and designed by Eric Dahlberg. The houses were placed on a partly fortified island with a few squares on the central part of the layout. From the south-east square three streets lead out towards the north-west. The street in the middle leads to the next square with church and town hall, the other two offer views towards other, less open, spaces. The squares with their public buildings are thus the centre of the town plan, and they are public squares, not commercialized market-places. The regular blocks of houses do not differ much from one to another. It is, however, to be noted that the squares at Karlskrona were no longer just ordinary spaces left empty as in the sixteenth century. The surrounding blocks, their shape and contents became dependent upon the form of the square.

A rather rare style of square is Stora Torget at Uppsala, planned in 1643 and laid out in 1702 after a great fire (Fig. 70). This is the civic centre of the town with the town hall, as a counterpart to the ecclesiastical centre at the cathedral, the merchant centre at the river, and the academic quarter west of the cathedral. From the middle of each side of the square four main streets radiate, not as more often from the corners of the square, and so this square is more closed in character than it would have been with the streets in the corners. The only two squares of this kind in Scandinavia are both in Sweden, that at Uppsala and the other one at Piteå in Norrland. The idea derives its origin from Palma Nuova and other Italian 'ideal city' plans.

Another theme was struck in Sweden's main harbour on the western sea, Gothenburg (Göteborg). The town was founded in 1619 on royal initiative, as Karlskrona was, but the Dutch merchants and their spirit prevailed here for a long time. Consequently no grand axial vistas towards churches or other royal monuments were

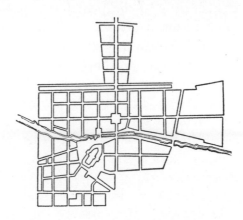

FIG. 70.
Uppsala, c. 1850, showing Stora Torget.

created, but a system of canals and streets was carried around the core of the town as these had spontaneously grown in Amsterdam and other Dutch cities.

In Copenhagen plans were worked out for the rebuilding of a devastated area in 1728, but the economic situation never allowed the plans to be executed. Thus only Kultorvet and Frederiksberggade are signs of this plan which was to have given Copenhagen more impressive streets and squares. One result of the fire was, however, that plans for new houses were drawn. These did not differ much from the old false-gable houses but their decorations were much less elaborate and limited to the gables only. All such houses thus became rather similar; windows, doors, gables, all measure roughly the same from one to another. Naturally stone was preferred by the city authorities to the half-timber technique, but conforming to this rule was far from general. What is more important, however, is that these designs for residential building always showed one house on the street and one in the back yard. This very old habit, then, was officially sanctioned at the beginning of the eighteenth century. It was to become a grim habit that did not cease to exist until the problem of the residential block was once again thought out in our own century under the influence of new ideas.

Most of the town plans described above were created on royal initiative. Another kind of community planning took place with the emergence of the Swedish *bruk* (Pl. 54), the little industrial villages in the mining and timber districts in central Sweden long before the industrial revolution. The initiative lay with the owner of the *bruk,* not the king, but the rectilinear and formal way of thinking so characteristic of the period also put its hallmark on the planning here. In the centre was a square in which stood the church and the owner's residence, and from it radiated streets along which were placed ordinary working-class houses. Sometimes only one side of the street was built upon, as at Åtvidaberg in Östergötland, while Söderfors in Uppland of the eighteenth century shows streets with both sides occupied by houses. The houses of such a *bruk* are usually rather small. All look the same and were planned so from the beginning, as all the inhabitants had the same social standard and occupation. This similarity gave to all the *bruk* a certain unity which is not less impressive than the housing conditions, for their time of a very high quality.

Part Five

DECLINING MONARCHY AND RISING MIDDLE CLASS

(*a*) Exchange and (*b*) Old Opera House, Stockholm (pp. 140, 185).

Pl. 81.

(*a*) Gustavus III's bedroom, Royal Palace, Stockholm (p. 186).

(*b*) Inventariekammaren, Karlskrona (p. 19

Pl. 82.

(a) Botanicum, Uppsala (p. 186).

(b) School, Härnösand (p. 189).

Pl. 83. Institutional architecture, Sweden.

Pl. 84. Chapel of Frederick V, Roskilde Cathedral, Denmark (p. 188).

Pl. 85.

(*a*) Architect's drawing
for chapel on Pl. 84.

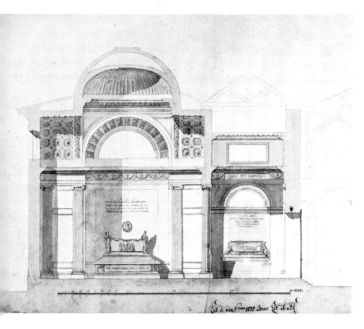

(*b*) Hämeenlinna
(Tavastehus) church,
Finland (p. 187).

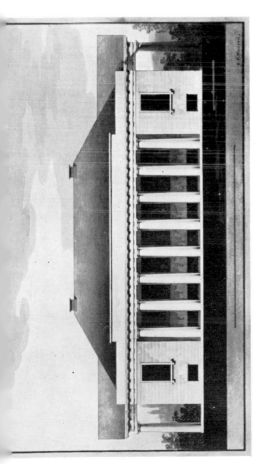

(a) Architect's drawing for chapel, Altona, Denmark (p. 190).

(b) Skeppsholmskyrkan, Stockholm (p. 192).

Pl. 87.

Pl. 88. Raad- og Domhus, Copenhagen (p. 188).

(a) Royal Palace, Oslo (p. 190).

(b) Exchange, Oslo (p. 191).

Pl. 89. Institutional architecture, Norway.

(*a*) Old Academy, Turku (p. 187).

(*b*) New Academy, Turku (p. 187).

Pl. 90. Institutional architecture, Finland.

(a) St. Nicolai (p. 191).

(b) Government buildings (p. 192).

Pl. 91. The Great Square, Helsinki.

(*a*) Nobles' Assembly, Helsinki (p. 198).

(*b*) Bern's Restaurant, Stockholm (p.

Pl. 92.

Pl. 93. 'The National', Copenhagen (p. 198).

Pl. 94. Exhibition of 1866, Stockholm (p. 211).

Pl. 95. Exhibition of 1897, Stockholm (pp. 182, 229).

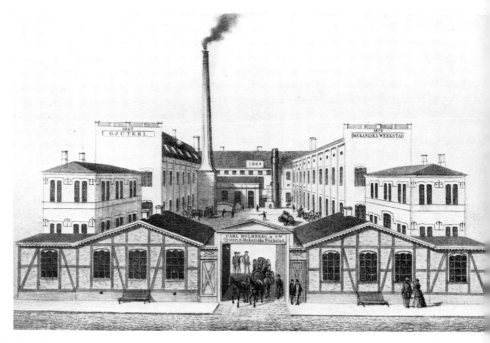

(a) Lund.

(b) Eskilstun

Pl. 96. Engineering works in Sweden, contemporary views (p. 213).

a) Kampenhof Mill, Udevalla, Sweden (p. 213).

(*b*) Fredericia Railway Station, Denmark (p. 211).

Pl. 97.

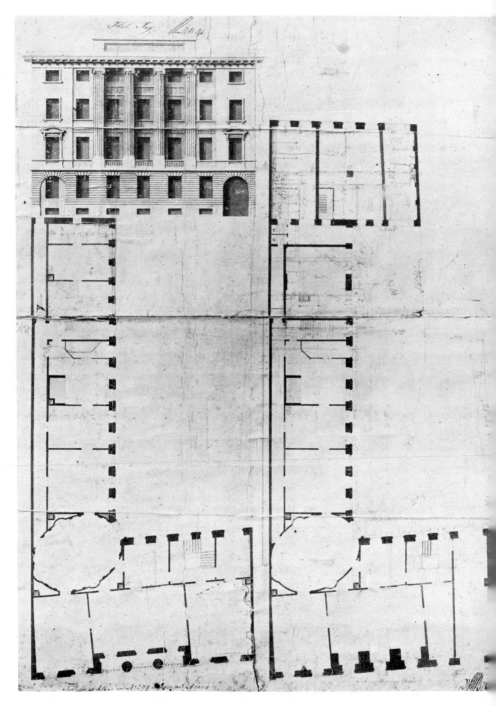

Pl. 98. Private house on Ved Stranden, Copenhagen, architect's drawings (p. 196).

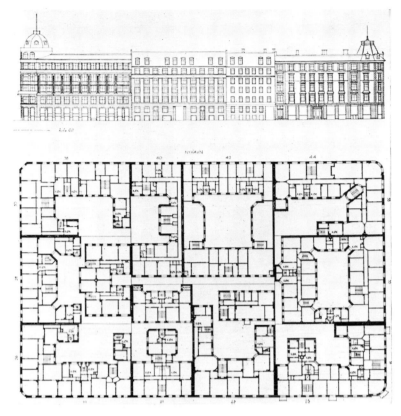

(a) Plans of blocks and façades on Nyhavn (pp. 196, 202).

(b) Blocks of flats, on Struenseegade (p. 218).

Pl. 99. Early flats, Copenhagen.

(*a*) Grundtvig Church, Copenhagen (p. 203).

(*b*) Museum, Faaborg, Denmark (p. 204).

Pl. 100.

XIX

ANTIQUE AND MEDIEVAL IDEALS

DURING the eighteenth century monarchal and aristocratic society dissolved and a new society was born. This was a result of the new economic organization of society: that is, industrialization. Among other things the French Revolution pointed out that an autonomous monarchy and a democracy could not exist side by side. Because of obstinate resistance from the old community, the emergence of the new society took place at intervals, with revolutions or other forms of social unrest far into our time. At first monarchal society was replaced by that of the bourgeoisie, which later gave way to democracy. The bourgeoisie was supported by a bureaucratic administration of the expanding State. Due to this expansion in all fields the bourgeoisie was firmly established all over the Western world. They became in fact so strongly rooted in society that some of the kings who were still tolerated during the nineteenth century became their foremost representatives: Louis Philippe in France and the rulers of the 'Oscarian Era' in Sweden and Norway.

However, the new bourgeoisie had not come to stay. They were soon replaced by a new class of society—the industrialists. In England this had happened in the middle of the eighteenth century, and it is doubtful if one can speak of this class as replacing the bourgeoisie there since they appeared almost simultaneously. On the Continent and in Scandinavia this happened up to a century later. Beside the emancipation of the industrialists, the industrialized community also saw the birth of the poor illiterate proletariat.

The first supporters of the new society, the bureaucrats, lacked their own norms and values, and this was true also of the industrialists. When the bureaucrats saw the society of the monarchal estate and its standards dissolving, they sought and found new and similar standards, first in classical architecture, and later in the Gothic style and soon in others. When the industrialists imitated the bureaucrats, they escaped as far as they could from their own environment of industry and the industrial towns. This rule had few exceptions; in England the industrialist settled in the country, on the Continent he moved to the new esplanades. And the proletarian was left to his normless fate. Or rather, he was left in the hands of the profit-hunting speculator, who found good profits in bad taste whether in consumer's goods or dwelling houses.

The consequences of this entirely revolutionary change in society were, from the point of view of architecture, just as revolutionary. The old domains, for which and in which architecture had emerged, were reshaped and replaced by new ones. Earlier the different domains of architecture had corresponded with the domains of the different patrons. The architecture of the nineteenth century must, however, be regarded as architecture created, not for certain outstand-ing yet typical individuals but for certain types of society. Those who 'paid' for a building were no longer the sole users of it. From the middle of the eighteenth century each human being existed in more than one sphere: the bureaucrat away from his office, at home in the new esplanades, or relaxing at the new resorts, or perhaps exerting himself as a member of a Free Church, etc. In this way a greater number of fields of life emerged, all demanding their specific forms of architecture, the function of which was to serve a particular field of life and its individual members.

The old monarchal society remained till the beginning of the last century. By Napoleon, who was imitated the world over, it was given an imperial character; with its terminus, Louis Philippe, also imitated everywhere, this arena of life coincided with that of the bourgeoisie. Its hallmark was a certain exclusive isolation from the rest of the world—that is, from those lower in society—an isolation which was both physical and mental. Comfort was the aim of the practical side of life and ostentation the aim of its cultural side.

When this way of life shed its monarchal-imperial trappings as it entered its bourgeois phase, these trappings were adopted by other patrons, the banks and department stores of capitalist society, and not least by the rational Church, the State, and county councils. In certain countries this field of life still exists. It has inherited the grand scale of empire, but its contents seem exhausted.

The third arena is that of the people. During the first phases of industrialism the poor proletariat had no status at all. Not until it became the object of the social policies of the community did a building programme in the modern sense—providing the rented house or flat—emerge. Attempts were made in the Germany of Bismarck, but for the first time in earnest at the time of the Weimar Republic; the problems they tackled in regard to the residential needs of an industrial community are still to a great extent valid. The forerunners were idealistic philanthropists, people interested in sanitation, and numerous municipal investigators. This belongs, however, to the last part of the book.

To these fields of life must be added a few others, which are new: the sphere of production, in factories and offices, and the sphere of compensation, that is, of recreation and entertainment. Finally there is the sphere of the 'free man'—one of the fields of life in which the detached house or villa emerged during the nineteenth century. Another field is that of the community, of the town which plans its own communal setting. But town planning is dependent on the structure of society at the time, and in Europe it runs the long course from the Rue de Rivoli of Napoleon via the boulevards of the bour-geoisie to the neighbourhood unit and supermarket of the modern society.

The dissolution of the aristocratic-monarchal community and the emergence of democratic society can of course be regarded as a deve-lopment from norm to individual. During the era of absolute monarchy the norm was personified by the monarch. With the opposition from the philosophers against this organization of society, his power was undermined to such an extent that few wished to see this personification any longer, and substitutes were sought else-where, for example in the garb of classical culture or of the Middle Ages, that is, in the new classicizing and medievalizing ideals that were being created—a new classicism, not that of the Renaissance, and a new medievalism. This search for norms outside one's own society must not be regarded merely as romanticism, for all classicist or medievalist enthusiasm cannot be entitled romanticism. The history of the ideology forming the foundation of the architecture of our times tells us something quite different.

Very soon, however, norms began to be sought not only in remote classical or Gothic styles, but in the medieval or other historical styles of one's own country, and an entire scale of new styles emerged. Out of pure sluggishness this so-called historicism went on right up to the 1920's in Scandinavia. Sometimes the architects found norms in more than one style, in more than one era, which were brought together in the same building. Examples of this can be found in the Town Hall (Raadhus) of Copenhagen and the City Hall (Stads-hus) of Stockholm. Much of this kind of eclectic architecture is second rate, and it can therefore be omitted from detailed discussion here.

The development from norm to individual has resulted in a con-tinued development towards the so-called middle class. By this course of things the old class-distinct community is becoming the classless community. The value of the individual has replaced that of the norm; but as this development is still going on, the shape of this kind of society has not yet been clearly defined, much less established.

The trend has gone on, however, sometimes accompanied by re-actionary revivals. In regard to art it has been said that when the norm is in power, art becomes idealistic; if, on the other hand, the individual rules, art becomes realistic. This two-poled scale is naturally divided into degrees. Needless to say, it is also valid con-cerning architecture. Therefore, the history of architecture during the last centuries must be among other things the account of a liberation from the norms.

Modern architecture, and especially the architecture of the nine-teenth century, is very often regarded as a mere façade architecture. Its true value cannot, however, be fully recognized if the plans and space-creating qualities are not accepted as part of the picture. Only then can architecture be recognized as something more than eclectic imitation of styles.

Architecture in this age will be dealt with, as earlier in the book, from the point of view of its functions. The fact must be remembered, however, that because of the frequently one-sided way of looking at architecture from the viewpoint of the façade, primary research work has so far contributed little to our understanding of Scandinavian nineteenth-century buildings. The problems have been approached in the wrong way. It was not until the emergence of functionalism —when architecture was given a social anchorage—that architectural historians once more regarded architecture as something more than a façade. Therefore our knowledge of the nineteenth century is still limited, a fact that has not become less accentuated by the great scorn with which some kinds of buildings from that era are discussed.

Before dealing with the actual monuments there are a few additional conditions to be dealt with, that is, the relation between the disposition of these chapters and that of earlier current ways of dealing with the architecture of this era from the point of view of historical styles. One way to approach this period of architecture would be to follow one category of buildings or one arena of activity at a time, from its emergence until today, or as long as it existed. Such a delineation would stand in the sharpest contrast to the current historians of style who instead make time the most important dimension, whereby, however, the pluralism is lost. Here a third disposition is chosen. It can be said to be a combination of the other two, that is to say, each field of architectural activity will be dealt with separately and in the order in which it appears. This disposition becomes quite natural if one bears in mind the fact that all the different fields are not active with the same force or impact all through the period. The first to appear is the monarchal field, which is so to speak inherited from the seventeenth and early eighteenth centuries. It dominates the scene for the first twenty years or so of the nineteenth century, whereafter it is replaced in its dominant position by the field of the bourgeoisie. *The Red Room* by the Swede August Strindberg, written in the 1880's, can be described as signalling the fall of the curtain for this community, and at the same time it supplied confirmation of its really happening. And so the problems of the industrial community—production and communication—become dominant.

One could borrow an image from mathematics and make a purely graphic description of the history of architecture during the last two hundred years. I am fully aware of the simplification this means. In a co-ordinate system the development from idealism to realism would be marked along the x-axis, the y-axis representing time. If the different monuments are put in, the result will be a number of parallel vertical fields, with the royal commissions close to the y-axis, the bourgeois buildings further to the right, and the buildings of the industrialized community furthest to the right. The resultant of the dominating creations will then appear as a slanting line at an angle of about forty-five degrees to the axes, for the most important royal buildings were created around the beginning of the century, the establishments of the bourgeoisie came about the middle of the century, and the industrial buildings last of all. This is what the historians of style have wrongly regarded as a development of styles, thereby forgetting that although a style dominates the picture for, say, twenty to thirty years, all the different kinds of architecture exist side by side. The dominance is explained by the structure of the society at the time.

The conception of nineteenth-century architecture as a development of styles has come into being mostly because of a one-sided analysis of the façades. This architecture is hardly ever as simple as it may seem from the outside; a façade in, for example, Neo-Renaissance style hardly ever conveys an interior of the same style. The museum Nordiska Muséet (Pl. 95, by the bridge) in Stockholm has a façade architecture that resembles that of Christian IV's 'Renaissance'. Its interior cannot be explained with the same concepts, for here instead is a large, light, and clearly defined hall serving different purposes from the façade—it is an exhibition hall. The symbolic values of the building as a whole could not be further from the Renaissance than they are.

There are, however, certain deviations from the slanting line of my hypothetical co-ordinate system. Time after time tendencies within the architecture emerge bringing architecture back to the old norm. The two most important deviations are the so-called 'national romanticism' of the end of the nineteenth century, which appeared in the other arts as well, and what is called the classicism of the twenties. About both it can be concluded that they were neither of them as significant as they have been said to be. It is more to the point that during the former period the scale of the buildings was more impressive than their numbers; and the classicism of the 1920's did not effect everything that was built. Classical buildings of this period are well outnumbered by other non-classical buildings.

The frequent returns to older and national patterns at the end of the nineteenth and beginning of the twentieth century were not going back to quite the same norms as in earlier historic styles. This is often explained as a reaction against the strong eclecticism, especially in interior architecture and decoration, which had emerged in Scandinavia in the middle of the latter half of the nineteenth century.

An anarchy of styles had appeared when Gottfried Semper in Germany renewed the discussion of styles. He tried a way out of the anarchy by means of deducing the programme from the basic function of the building. A church should be neo-Gothic—and this had been accepted long before Semper, as the Gothic style was the most 'religious' one; a bank building should be given the style of the Early Florentine Renaissance, since the bank in modern times first appeared in Florence, and so on. But after some time 'Semper-ism' declined as well, partly because its logic was perhaps somewhat too consistent, and more ornamented styles and 'false' materials started to imitate real ones. So eclecticism flourished once more. With the ensuing 'style fatigue' inspiration was sought in something new—in the histories of the fatherlands.

But this is only one aspect of the architecture of the last century, and an aspect that sometimes hides, from our point of view, what was really going on. The entire meaning of it cannot be found only by means of a stylistic discussion, however much the architects themselves discussed style and its significance.

I would emphasize that the architecture of the last century, and society as well, must be regarded not as one indivisible entity but as many, existing alongside each other. If, in order to exemplify this, one picks a façade from the 1880's on Bredgade in Copenhagen or a recreation hall, for instance the National in the same city (Pl. 93), the architecture of these buildings is the result of many forces. Should they be treated as examples of the bourgeois desire for a brilliant display of elaborate façades, according to current stylistic analysis? What results did new means of construction have? Should not the Bredgade building also be considered under its town planning aspects, or as the attempt (or lack of attempt) at solving the problem of the block of flats? Thus most architecture of the last century is more complex than that of earlier times, both in structure and in setting. Add to this that the nineteenth century was a dynamic and changing time. By isolating in this book the most important factors that forced architecture to become what it became, some abstractions have had to be made. But a sense of the totality must therefore not be lost.

This also gives the key to another problem, that of the borderline between bourgeois society and democratic society. The last mani-festations of the bourgeoisie can be said to be those municipal and governmental institutions with a formal ceremonial exterior, like some town halls which were intended to symbolize the supra-individual ideal of state, government, etc. Some of them were built as late as the 1920's in Scandinavia.

Modern society, on the other hand, had already begun to emerge in the middle of the last century, though often hidden behind elaborate façades. A new programme was created by the new economic organization of the society, industrial society. Because of the delayed departure of the old bourgeois society the time boundary was not fixed. The old society slowly grew into another, by the emergence of a new programme. The old society did not die suddenly but gave up ground slowly. The 'classicism' and romanticism of the 1920's were only the lagging manifestations of a relict society, and they are remarkably thin and uninteresting.

XX

THE ROYAL AND ARISTOCRATIC WAY OF LIFE

THE great interest with which Greek culture was cherished during the latter half of the eighteenth century in Europe came partly as a reaction against the old absolute monarchy. It introduced a classic culture from a newly discovered source: the ancient culture of democratic Greece. But this Greek architecture and sculpture did not, at least not to begin with, symbolize democracy but the heroic self-assured man who acted under inspiration from a higher power. The opposition to absolute monarchy had been led by the English moral philosophers, especially Locke, whose new ideal of the state was to overthrow the monarchies of Europe one after the other. In his state the ruling monarch had a right to govern the country only as long as he had the will of the people with him, that is, a democratic monarchy. It goes without saying that this new ideal and the new type of human beings supporting it could no longer feel at home with the baroque style in their architecture.

However, in Sweden it was an absolute monarch, Gustav III (1771–92), who became the intercessor for neoclassicism. He had acquired a personal interest in the classical cultures during extensive travels in Europe as crown prince, and now furthered his attempts to be an enlightened despot by imposing the new Grecian style from above—which was not the course of the neoclassic style in most other European countries.

The transition to neoclassicism in Sweden took place gradually and smoothly. On the Exchange in Stockholm by Eric Palmstedt (Pl. 81*a*), built 1767–76, the Roman building has a pediment that is somewhat Greek in character as an ornamental feature on the projecting central part, but the Greek ornaments are only very finely moulded and in low relief—they are but hinted at. The Opera House (Pl. 81*b*), designed 1775 by C. F. Adelcrantz and built a few years later, was slightly more Greek in character with a free-standing colonnade in front, but the sides were Palladian in design, and belonged to the baroque period. It is as if the neoclassic features were added at the last minute.

Therefore during the first of Gustav III's years on the throne it was only in interior design that the neoclassic appeared unalloyed, as in the theatre at Gripsholm Castle, built in 1781 by Palmstedt. L. J. Desprez, a French architect invited to Sweden, was the man to introduce the neoclassic in earnest. Palmstedt, who was still thinking too much in terms of the baroque, adopted the new features only by degrees. Together with Desprez, J. E. Rehn worked in the new architectural spirit.

Only a small part of all that these two architects planned with the king was ever built. Desprez's design for a royal palace at Haga, just outside Stockholm, showed the neoclassic in its purest form. It was designed as a rectangular Greek temple with a colossal eightcolumn temple front on one of the long sides. Because of the death of the king this neoGreek palace was never built. The same architect redrew the plans of Tempelman for a Botanicum, or Botanical Institution, at Uppsala (Pl. 83*a*), which was erected in 1788. The main façade with the Doric temple front is so wide in relation to the usual Doric proportions that it almost hides the building behind it. The difference between the main part of the building and the temple façade is in true neoclassic manner extremely evident. The temple front was added to the rest of the building as a projecting screen and gives great monumental value to the building as a whole. All walls are smooth. The façade was undoubtedly meant to serve as a background for the gardens that were laid out during the 1790's behind the castle; now these are broken through by a street.

In the Botanicum architecture had already started to leave the purely Greek dimensions behind. The scale of these Doric columns is such that they appear to convey other values than the Greek. There is something challenging in the character of such a building.

In the Bedroom of State of Gustav III in the Royal Palace in Stockholm (Pl. 82*a*), the quiet Greek character is altered by the splendour of precious materials. Here the triumph of the monarchy is symbolized. The interiors of Gustav III's apartment at Gripsholm are more temperate, partly because it was used as a hunting lodge and pleasure palace. The rooms in the Kavaljersflygeln or courtiers' wing display the same character although slightly adjusted to their less superior level.

In Finland there was a very easy transition between that kind of architecture which had appeared in the country estates and neoclassic design. The old Commandant house at Loviisa is rather to be considered as a small country estate moved into town; it is as if the commander did not like to turn his back on the countryside where he undoubtedly belonged. Swedish royal architecture of the eighteenth century was introduced through the personal initiative of Gustav III who ordered the building of the church of Tavastehus (Hämeenlinna, Pl. 85*b*) in 1798; it was designed by L. J. Desprez. The dome was intended, at the king's request, to resemble that of the Pantheon in Rome. Another example of neoclassic architecture is the Town Hall at Frederikshamn, a town on the coast of Finland with a remarkable plan of eight radiating streets. The building itself is three-storied with a central projection crowned by a pediment. A strange feature is the octagonal tower where the different stories are articulated with pilasters, niches, and blank panels, all in a very untraditional manner.

The official cultural buildings in Sweden, Gustav III's Opera and the Stock Exchange in Stockholm, were examples of the transition to neoclassicism. A similar change can be seen in the Old and New Academies at Åbo (Turku, Pl. 90), both built around 1800. The architects were C. C. Gjörwell (1766–1837) and C. Bassi (1772–1840), the latter born in Italy; both worked in Sweden as well as in Finland. Gjörwell used very few of the neoclassic decorative elements. His monumental Academy is very harmonious and the value of proportions is strongly emphasized. The walls are smooth and only in the central projection is the ground floor slightly rusticated and horizontal lines inserted between the stories. The pediment is undecorated; an unemphasized dentil moulding follows its contours. Bassi on the other hand aimed at a more imperial monumentality. A large colonnade stands in front of the central part of his building, which has a decorated frieze, and all volumes are pronounced.

The Danish kings took a similar personal interest in the neoclassic style, but for political reasons the Danish neoclassic architecture appeared in more diversified and original forms. The Danish sovereigns never claimed the concentration of power that the Swedish king did.

The first architect of the new style in Denmark was C. F. Harsdorff (1735–99), who was also the leader of the Danish Academy after

Jardin the creator of the Marble Church had been dismissed. Harsdorff had studied under Soufflot in Paris. His main work was the Royal Chapel at Roskilde Cathedral (Pl. 84; his drawing of 1763, Pl. 85a), begun in 1774, in which apart from Greek and Roman features there is even a 'Byzantine' dome. Perhaps the most remarkable feature is the source of daylight in this building, a very clear light entering through only one window, giving the interior and its architectural elements a particular distinctness—a complete change from the ambiguous diffusion of light so recently sought in the designs for the Marble Church. Among other buildings by him are the Colonnade at Amalienborg and the Hercules Pavilion at Kongens Have, the latter less Greek than his other works.

The true neoclassic was, however, adopted by C. F. Hansen (1756–1845). His two main creations, the Raad- og Domhus, 1803–15 (Pl. 88) and the church Vår Frue Kirke or the Church of Our Lady, 1810–29 (Pl. 86), both in Copenhagen, are the fore- most examples of neoclassicism in Scandinavia. In the church the architect dealt with a similar problem to that of the Roskilde chapel, the providing of light only from above. Here a synthesis between Roman and Greek was achieved: the arcade is Roman as is the barrel vault, but the decorations are mainly Greek. Still nothing is mixed but all is strictly articulated, arcades, colonnades, and coffered vault. The plan is very like a Roman temple with the statue of Christ in the rounded exedra. The church has been described as a classic environment for the statue of Christ by Thorvaldsen, and it must be regarded as being closely related to this statue.

In the Raad- og Domhus (combined Town Hall and Court House), the harmonies in the façade are brought to perfection. All parts of the façade, from the windows and the small side entrances to the large pediment, are in full harmony, as is the case with the smooth wall and the mouldings and columns in front of it. The contours are needle-sharp and as a consequence the building seems to stand almost in a vacuum—hence its idealizing character, above all passing of time. The result is self-confidence, but a well-balanced and harmonious confidence active at the same time in a moral sense, challenging those who regard it. It is something new in architecture, something that was only hinted at in the Botanicum at Uppsala.

Through Harsdorff and Hansen, Danish neoclassic architecture developed a remarkably high quality, for these architects were

much cleverer than their Swedish contemporaries. This style therefore received a reputation in Denmark which was of importance at
the time of the short classical revival during the 1920's and which
was more solidly based than neoclassicism in Sweden.

Education was during the eighteenth century a matter concerning
the clergy almost exclusively, especially in the case of further education in grammar schools. On the other hand, the Church was
closely connected with the king and was to serve him. Consequently the Gymnasium (secondary school) at Härnösand in Sweden
(Pl. 83b), built in the 1790's, was designed with a neoclassic plan
and façade, dominated by a pillared porch like a domed rotunda.
Contrary to the usual practice this school contained no dwellings
for the teachers, but it had a hall for the magistrates' court in the
upper story, while the classrooms were on the ground floor. The
isolation from the purely bourgeois residential parts of the town,
expressed by the façade of this school, is even more strongly accentuated by the fact that the school, together with the church, the
primary school, the residence of the governor of the county, and
other buildings of a similar official character, formed an entirely
separate part of the town with a park in its centre. This isolation
was persistent in many towns, where the 'traditional' cultural buildings did not constitute an integrated part of the rest of the town.

The buildings of the nobles in the countryside maintained on the
whole the Caroline plan and façade that had emerged in the
eighteenth century. To start with, it was sufficient to straighten the
roof and simplify the façades, and the demands of the new ideals
were satisfied. The old tradition was very strong, as can be seen
among many countryside estates like Frederiksgave or others in Denmark and the rest of Scandinavia. Especially on the buildings of the
peasantry the transition was easily made; the projecting ends of the
logs forming the inner walls were panelled in so that they formed
pilasters. When these were painted white they were to imitate the
Greek orders and that was all—not unlike the so-called 'carpenter's
Doric' in provincial areas of the early nineteenth-century United
States.

There were only slight alterations in plan during this period,
because it was still felt to be desirable to keep to the ceremonious
layout of the rooms with a large hall in the middle. In most cases,

however, the relationship between inside and outside became closer. The basement of the house was lowered, an example of this being Gunnebo outside Gothenburg in Sweden, built by Carlberg in 1786, or Godeffroy's country house at Altona by C. F. Hansen in the same year. As was the case with Hansen's Raad og Domhus in Copenhagen, no ramps or parterres surround such a house. At the entrance the small flight of steps is but a reminiscence of the enormous staircase and basement story of the baroque style. French windows open out to the terrace formed by the recessed façade behind the coupled Ionic or Doric columns. A non-domestic extreme example of the closed-in temple form is Hansen's chapel at Altona (Pl. 87a). In most manor-houses or rectories from this era, the neoclassic features are, however, less dominant than at Gunnebo or Altona. But the essential proportions of these houses and the lack of projecting wings, the building being as it were within one shell, is a repeatedly recurring feature. Such houses were built by a new kind of people—the houses were often summer residences. Through the aristocracy and civil servants this type of house soon moved into the towns; Geijersgården at Uppsala is a typical example. An especial importance was given to interior decoration, often the only part of the house where the neoclassic is clearly visible: as at Princens Palace, the interior of Christiansborg, or Christian VIII's palace in Copenhagen. The effect of the style of Gustav III's bedroom was as vivid in Sweden.

Pure neoclassicism in Scandinavia died young. In a French manner, as the so-called Empire style, it was adopted by Karl XIV Johan (Jean Bernadotte) and moulded to express the supremacy and triumphal power of the king and state, although it was not, as we shall see, baroque.

During the Swedish-Norwegian Union (1814–1905) Norway was much more independent than she had been earlier under the Danish rule. As a consequence Oslo (called Christiania until 1924) rose from its former status as just an ordinary provincial town; it became a city. During the reign of Karl XIV Johan a great number of administration offices were built in addition to the Royal Palace.

The Palace in Oslo (Pl. 89a) was designed by the Danish architect Linstow. It is a large building equipped with a classic portico crowned by an impressive pediment with pretensions to monumentality. It forms the background of Karl Johann Street and at the opposite end the Building of the Magistrates and the University were placed. These were designed by Grosch, as was the Exchange Building (Pl. 89b), begun 1826. He was here assisted by the German architect Schinkel. When building these colossal monuments, both patrons and architects had got somewhat beyond their depth. The work advanced slowly, and the Palace and the Exchange were not completed until 1848 and 1852 respectively. During construction certain restrictions had to be made in the building programme and the use of material.

The reign of Karl XIV Johan set up an extensive building programme in Sweden as well, producing administrative buildings, schools, and military establishments. At Uppsala, Carolina Rediviva—originally the University building—became a simplified, purer image of the palace in Oslo. In Stockholm the hospital Garnisonssjukhuset was built after plans by C. C. Gjörwell (1766–1837), and the barracks of the Horse Guards (now the Historical Museum), by the architect Fredrik Blom (1781–1851). For evident reasons the naval town of Karlskrona received numerous buildings during this time, among which the Inventariekammaren (Pl. 82b) by F. H. af Chapman and C. A. Ehrensvärd, and Mönster- och Modellsalen by Chapman, both of the 1780's, are worth mentioning.

Soon after the Russian occupation of Finland, after the peace treaty with Sweden in 1809, the capital was transferred to Helsinki from Turku. Helsinki was then a rather small town and had no buildings for the government and administration of the Grand Duchy. The task to create this civic centre fell upon the German-born C. L. Engel (1778–1834). The note that Engel struck was at once magnificent and consonant, no doubt, with Russian imperial dreams at the beginning of the nineteenth century; in fact a Russian imperial square was created which surpassed all Scandinavian dimensions and in the huge and massive monumentality of its buildings outdid anything so far seen in Scandinavia (Pl. 91).

At one end of the large market, the Great Square, is the Nicolai Church, a centralized church on a Greek cross plan and crowned by a dome (Pl. 91a). It is symmetrical with each of the four sides emphasized by a large Greek temple façade with Corinthian columns, a theme that reappears in the drum of the dome. The cupola itself has a semicircular section and thus finds its pattern in the Byzantine tradition, not the baroque cupolas of other European churches. The interior is more Italian in decoration, but its cross plan with four absidal ends keeps more to the Greco-Byzantine origin. The size of the church is enhanced by the broad banks of steps leading up to it so that it dominates the market and the two other monumental build-ings on the square, the University and the Senate (Pl. 91*b*), also designed by Engel. These buildings were handled in a similar way, both inside and outside, so that with the church they contribute a dominant theme to the large scale and integrated impression of the civic centre of Helsinki.

Engel had a huge production and among other buildings by his hand can be mentioned the University Library and the Observatory in Helsinki. He also built many monumental buildings in other Finnish towns. All these buildings in Scandinavia in the so-called Empire style speak a similar language. A corresponding effect was intended for the rebuilding of Christiansborg in Copenhagen by C. F. Hansen, 1810–26, but the architect tried to rescue something of its old character (p. 146) destroyed in the fire, so a compromise was made and the trend is visible only in details, such as pediments, gables, and so on.

The Empire style expressed the triumphal power of the king and the state in a self-assured manner and at the same time the fulfilment of duty towards supremacy, which to a certain degree can be said to be typical of the way of thinking at this period. But even if such ideals resemble those of the baroque era, they are really different. The grandness in scale is a similarity, but the smooth walls, sometimes accentuate only by window-frames of a pediment, are those of the neoclassic style. These buildings also have the needle-sharp effect in the contours and at the same time the plasticity which were hallmarks of that style. There is never a vibrating pictorial quality about such a building. The grandness of scale and severe monumentality are traits which thrust themselves upon the onlooker, since the buildings are always arranged as elements in a large axial system of streets or squares.

The church Skeppsholmskyrkan, in Stockholm (Pl. 87*b*), 1824–42 by Blom, occupies a transitional position between the new secular architecture of the Empire style and the old church architecture of the seventeenth century. The architect returned to the centralized church and gave it an octagonal plan on the exterior, but the octagon is transformed in the interior to a circle with a dome. The transition between the outer and inner forms takes place in an ambulatory, and the arcade on Ionic columns between the ambulatory and the central space forms, as it were, a drum for the dome at ground-floor level. The columns are echoed by Ionic pilasters on the outer wall of the ambulatory. On the exterior there exists a fine rhythm between the projecting porticoes and the windows, where the classical language used in the interior appears again.

Another centralized church plan from the Renaissance is to be seen at Uddevalla, built in 1811 by G. af Sillén on a Greek cross plan, while at Gothenburg the cathedral by C. W. Carlberg (built 1808–15) was planned as a Latin cross. In the latter it is only the porch on the west front that is purely Empire in character. The rest of the façade and other elements are more Roman.

XXI

THE BOURGEOIS WAY OF LIFE

TOWARDS the middle of the nineteenth century one of the first results of industrialization in Scandinavia was the emergence of the new bourgeoisie, in many aspects different from the earlier social classes in society and successor to the craftsman, the merchant, and the bureaucratic nobleman in capitals and provincial towns. The new bourgeoisie was well aware of this difference and tried to stress the fact. As had been the case earlier in England and on the Conti- nent, the wish to repudiate other classes in society expressed itself in their settling in new districts in the towns. This meant a social- ecological forming of regions, which helped to accentuate the dif- ferences in symbolic values of the different districts.

The precedent followed was that of the Paris of Eugène Haussmann and Napoleon III. The great increase of the population in that city, which came about thanks to the building of the railways, necessitated radical changes in the planning of the medieval town. The aim was to connect the railway stations and the central parts of the city by means of boulevards. At the same time the city was to be beautified, the so-called revolutionary centres were to be cleared, and better living conditions on the whole would be obtained. Even if only parts of this programme were achieved, the work of Haussmann involved a tremendous reorganization of the city. At the same time the phenomenon occurred that the western and eastern halves emerged with different social values; the west part is even today considered to be more distinguished.

In Stockholm these new characteristics were adopted in the city plan by Lindhagen in 1866: numerous new streets were built in the outskirts of the city—Ringvägen in the south, Karlavägen, Karlaplan, Sveavägen, etc. in the northern part. The plan was not, however, carried out in its full scale. Sveavägen was planned to be an axial street towards the Royal Palace, its main characteristic being its great width, and Karlaplan, which, in contrast to Sveavägen and the radiating circus for Kungsholmen, was on the whole carried out according to Lindhagen's plans, constitutes a repetition of Place de l'Étoile in Paris. The splendid, formal character of these streets is strongly emphasized. In Gothenburg Kungsportsavenyen was built, and most of the Scandinavian towns of importance commissioned magnificent new plans, most of which were only partly carried out in connection with the rapid development of industry and railways—sometimes only a railway station with an attached park was laid out. That the plans were on a grand scale is evident when one hears that they were usually drawn up to accommodate nearly ten times the number of existing inhabitants—a population that most of the towns have not reached yet.

The new streets received a decidedly bourgeois character when they were lined with large apartment houses or blocks of flats for the upper classes, in Stockholm mainly on Östermalm—or with imitations of these as was the case on Södermalm in Stockholm. The prototype for such blocks of flats came from Paris, where Haussmann had provided the general pattern.

The plans of these Swedish upper-class blocks of flats show in most cases a line of formal rooms facing the street and including a hall, one or more salons, a dining-room, and a study, sometimes also the bedroom. The kitchen and nursery—and in less magnificent flats also the dining-room—faced the yard. The foremost floor in the house was the first floor, that is, the *piano nobile* above the ground floor, and the 'value' grew less for each floor up successively. Sometimes the ground floor was set apart for shops.

The most dominant features in these houses are the isolation from other classes in society and the formal arrangement. There was also much stress on economic solidity, the hallmark of this new social class. To begin with, this was expressed by using precious materials as far as possible, marble in the staircases, façades preferably of stone, and expensive furniture. By and by, however, this tradition broke up and imitations began to appear. Plaster-work and marbling became frequent. This was often exaggerated when the bourgeoisie in a rather self-assuring manner wanted to show the abundance in which they lived or pretended to live, and such houses almost bulged with prodigal abundance. The façades became richly decorated and displayed a variety of ornamentation such as cornices, pilasters, columns, gables of different kinds and shapes, window-frames, and sculptural details of precious or imitated material.

The plans of blocks of flats in Copenhagen differed from those in Stockholm. In 1796 J. H. Quist had built himself a house on Ved Stranden which in its classic façade continued an old tradition and simultaneously set a pattern for the distribution of the various rooms (Pl. 98). Towards the street are three rooms in line and the 'side-house' or wing contains the domestic rooms. In the angle between this and the 'fore-house' is an oval dining-room, in form reminiscent of the rococo interior decoration of palaces. There is a corridor between this room and the 'back-house' where the kitchen is. Before the middle of the nineteenth century, façades were only simply decorated with small pediments or other profiles above the windows, but towards the 1850's these became more pronounced. Soon historicism flowered in the new streets and esplanades of distinction in Copenhagen. Renaissance, baroque, or even Gothic fragments appeared on the façades mainly above the windows. One of the most famous architects of blocks of flats in Copenhagen at this time was Milldahl. It was through this kind of architecture (see below, p. 202) that the so-called 'façade street' emerged; a well-known example is Bredgade in Copenhagen, another in Frederiksborgsgade. Karl Johann Street in Oslo and Nya Esplanaden in Helsinki, built about 1880, play the same role. The most famous architect for the bourgeoisie in Finland was T. Höijer.

The new bourgeois districts, then, symbolized these four related values: exclusive isolation, conventional formality, economic solidity, and expanding self-assertion. The bourgeois community, moreover, not only built residences along the boulevards but also institutions such as schools, colleges, banks, and naturally facilities for recreation such as restaurants and theatres.

As for the schools a Swedish prototype was created which was used repeatedly afterwards for many kinds of educational institutions, and that was the secondary school at Uppsala (Fig. 71) designed by F. W. Scholander and built in 1863. The plan is the shape of a T with classrooms ranged along corridors on each side of the entrance hall, and the lecture hall in the projecting wing at the back. The plan was varied according to the practical needs of individual schools. This school was built on a new street lined with trees in one of the northern outskirts, that is, in imitation of the Continental malls lined with separate public buildings according to the pattern of the Ring in Vienna. The façade had pilasters ornamented in the bourgeois

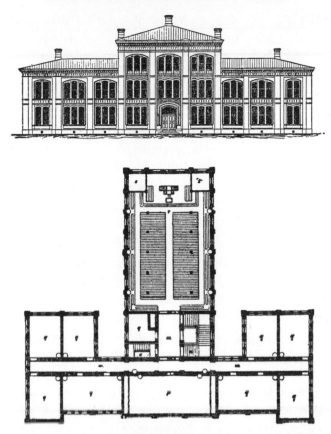

FIG. 71. Secondary school, Uppsala.

spirit, and a strongly accentuated central part which is slightly higher than the rest of the building. In Valand Art School at Gothenburg, the National Gallery in Stockholm, and the old Technical High School in Stockholm, the architects used the same means to achieve a similar architecture.

The educational institutions in Denmark had a less standardized pattern than in Sweden, and well illustrated the many different styles of the last century. In 1822 Peder Malling, a pupil of C. F. Hansen, designed Sorø Akademi. The three-storied building has a pronounced middle part with three doors, and both ends project slightly. The ground floor is treated as a rusticated basement, pilasters flank the projecting ends, and a triglyph frieze crowns the building. Thus articulations and motifs originally used hundreds of years before on Roman palaces were applied in order to enhance the reputation of the building. The same architect designed the University of Copenhagen, but this time the inspiration was early and late Gothic. Here the spirit of medieval times, when education was so carefully fostered by the cathedrals and universities, was more important than the expression of bourgeois prestige. A similarly Gothic environment was provided in Scholander's secondary school at Visby in 1856.

Banks took a prominent part in the urban building programme from the middle of the century onwards. The National Bank in Copenhagen, of 1866–70, by J. D. Herholdt is a classic example of Semper's grammar of style—more Early Florentine even than anything in Florence itself. The later Scandinavian Bank in Stockholm is much more abundantly decorated, but styles changed quickly in those days. A simplified form of Florentine style appeared in the House of the Nobility in Helsinki by G. T. Chiewitz (Pl. 92a), 1859–61, while the Exchange at Gothenburg has a more Roman character.

Restaurants were modelled on those of Paris and Vienna, and a new 'restaurant culture' was introduced with the cafés and verandas that were often connected with billiard-halls. These sprang up where they did as a consequence of the new habit of strolling along the boulevards and esplanades.

Especially in Bern's Restaurant (Pl. 92b) in Stockholm, built in 1862 after plans drawn by J. F. Åbom, Knaust's Hotel at Sundsvall of the 1870's, and the National (Pl. 93) in Copenhagen in the 1880's, lavish and extravagant settings were created which gratified the bourgeois delight in material splendour and abundance. While in such a building the architect piled the historical styles on top of each other, especially in his designs for the interiors, he also had to know all about the latest building materials and ways of construction—that is, how to deal with cast iron. This is evident in the Royal Theatre in Copenhagen with its large iron roof above the auditorium.

As in schools, the expanded functions of restaurants conditioned the plans. A restaurant now had to contain several different rooms for other uses besides billiards. Coffee was not taken in the same room as that in which dinner was served; many restaurants had special rooms for lady guests. The furnishing and decoration of the various rooms were richly differentiated not only to add to the lavish effect but to cater for different levels of expense in the amenities provided. The foremost room in Bern's was naturally the south saloon where the music played and the magnificent chandelier and numerous small lamps shed a glamorous light over the elegant guests. A similarly effulgent décor was created in the foyers and auditoriums of theatres and opera houses, for example in the Dramatiska Teatern and the Opera in Stockholm, while in the Tivoli in Copenhagen fairy-like pleasure gardens were created by means of a 'Moresque' architecture. It is typical of this kind of architecture that critics and reviewers often put the name of the styles, 'Renaissance', 'Romanesque', etc., in quotation marks.

On the outskirts of the growing industrial towns residential districts developed during the middle of the century containing detached houses and villas for the new capitalist class, representing a new habit of leaving the towns to enjoy, not too far away, the sweetness of country life. In plan, elevation, and façade architecture these houses were influenced by local tradition from neighbouring estates of the landed gentry, as well as by aristocratic manor-house and palace design generally.

In the early and mid-nineteenth century, villas were still built in the neoclassic style. In Denmark there appeared a kind of late-classic style, as for instance in a villa designed by N. S. Nebelong called Sølyst at Vedbaeck: the façade is governed by its entirely symmetrical proportions. The Dutch baroque-villa style became especially popular in Denmark. When based on aristocratic ideals this villa architecture became symmetrical and formal, with the living-room facing the garden and the more private rooms on either side of it. Such newcomers regarded themselves as the successors to the county aristocracy.

Towards the middle of the century it was more common to break up the symmetrical, 'classic' façades of Dutch Palladian, French, or Italian origin. The reason was that architects were now abandoning the symmetrical line of rooms in their planning. No special pattern was substituted for the symmetrical; the longing for comfort established the norm. Their clients especially wanted a drawing-room somewhat set apart from the other rooms and this broke up the old symmetry. The grouping of the rooms thus became irregular and somewhat picturesque. This picturesqueness also affected the façade, which was meant to show not only the wealth of the owner by means of elaborately ornamented details but also his isolation from other members of society by the use of 'exclusive' styles. And so 'medieval

Italian' and 'medieval Dutch' styles were introduced into villa architecture.

Fig. 72 shows a reflection of contemporary English taste for picturesque domestic Gothic with a dash of Swiss cottage; there is a stone basement for the kitchen, with timberwork above, and the main floor includes a *blomsterveranda* or greenhouse. Many of these Scandinavian villas, unlike those in England but like many in the United States, were timber-frame houses with decorative weather-boarding in various 'shingle' or 'stick' facings and much elaborate carpentry on turrets and gables and balconies.

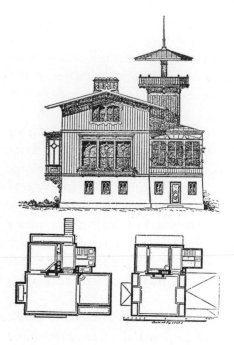

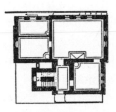

FIG. 72.
Design for a 'villa in the English taste' from *Tidskrift för praktisk byggnadskonst*, 1852.

It is evident that once the principle of a free grouping of the different rooms, and consequently of the different volumes of the villa, was accepted, which early happened in the house that Webb designed for William Morris in 1859 and even in Schinkel's House at Potsdam, this freedom was then frequently imitated. The emphasis on comfortable furnishings for such houses, much publicized by the Dane J. D. Herholdt in the middle of the century, naturally also contributed to the breaking up of the old symmetrical and formal planning. The free grouping of rooms and volumes and the use of so many differing styles in suburban villas were later to develop into a complete anarchy which gave even the more exclusive suburbs a most heterogeneous character.

The English influence that was heralded in the Red House and before was most usual in Sweden along the west coast and especially near Gothenburg. Glasshouses and small orangeries were often connected to these villas and in those the principles laid down by Paxton and others were directly imitated.

To the period of these villas and to the bourgeois field of life also belong the 'recreational' communities that began to spread and develop all over Scandinavia during the middle of the last century: the resorts. Two of the famous ones are Klampenborg near Copenhagen and Gustavsberg in Bohuslän in Sweden. The way of life in these places exactly followed that of the spas on the Continent and was from a modern point of view very exclusive. The bath-houses with the *societetshus,* or pavilion, were the core and ceremonial frame of these communities. The pavilion was the meeting place where everybody went for gossip and concerts. As all this represented a completely new programme, the architects were singularly free to use new materials and principles of construction. But perhaps more important was the lust for festivity and ceremony, expressed by a new kind of glittering decoration, highly imaginative, with exotic flowers and leaves, and pilasters of previously unknown orders all brightly painted. The Scandinavian resorts did not reach the same grandeur as those in England and on the Continent, but they were similar in character. It is, however, noteworthy that Scandinavian seaside resorts never imitated the pattern set by Brighton and other famous places along both sides of the English Channel. When people towards the end of the century took the step to the sea, a real 'sea front' with hotels and piers was never established; people usually stayed in rented fishermen's cottages and moved their entire household to these simpler quarters, changing their mode of living for the summer, a habit even more common today.

The bourgeois culture reached its peak just after the middle of the century, and thereafter it only slowly gave up ground. The bearers of this culture in Scandinavia were, like their Victorian contemporaries, very dominating people. The exploits of the new industrial magnates were tremendous; with industrialization Western man seemed to be on top of the world as never before. Money was earned quickly and much of it was spent to give life a festive, splendid, and glamorous setting.

The industrial and political achievements of the Great Powers of Europe and the United States reverberated in Scandinavia, and the boom years reached the North in the latter half of the century: rail-roads were built, steam-ships of ever larger size launched, and the enormous riches of Sweden's and Finland's forests were exploited.

This was the material background for bourgeois culture—no wonder that life took on a somewhat boastful quality, an exaggerated self-esteem. So dominant economically, politically, and ideologically were these patrons that for a long time they were imitated by most other classes in society and set the pattern for everybody. The latter half of the century saw the arrival of several styles of architecture and interior decoration, neo-rococo, neo-baroque, exotic styles of various sorts succeeding or paralleling each other at high speed. This phenomenon has often been characterized as the decline of taste—an expression only partly true.

With the arrival of industry the populations of the towns grew as never before. Most towns expanded rapidly. In the 1870's the Östermalm quarters began to be built up in Stockholm and a few years earlier the last resistance to an expansion of Copenhagen, put up by the military authorities because of the existence of the fortified walls, had been given up and the city could march out of its old boundaries. In a pattern set by Vienna the former fortified walls were soon taken up by residential buildings. The new blocks of flats that filled these spaces clearly illustrate how vivid and strong the old tradition was (Pl. 99a). The back yards were filled with back-houses cramped together. The architects only designed the façades but hardly ever went behind them.

With the emancipation of the new classes and the gradual change towards a democratic society the bourgeois society was bound to disappear and new bourgeois architecture became scarcer and scarcer towards the end of the nineteenth century. But the fact that fewer and fewer individual private patrons appeared on the bourgeois scene did not automatically mean that this kind of architecture was no longer built at all. A reminiscence of bourgeois culture was towards the turn of the century enacted by other patrons, by governmental and municipal institutions.

The architectural situation of the end of the nineteenth century and the beginning of the twentieth was not less complicated than it had been during the middle of the nineteenth century. There was a clear conflict between the 'engineers' and the 'architects'. The discussion of style was as intense as it had been during the nineteenth century; from the point of view of style, buildings of entirely different character were being erected. A cleaning out of the most bombastic ornaments was already beginning, according to the aesthetic tenets of Art Nouveau, but this did not mean that neoclassicism was dead nor that purely national values were being done away with. A wave of national romanticism succeeded by a severe classicism swept all over western Europe at the turning of the century. At the same time there was beginning a more realistic architecture, to be dealt with here in the last chapter.

The sweeping away of certain old styles—first of their details and ornamental features—was taking place under the banner of Art Nouveau or Jugendstil, a style which within art was inspired by the painter Seurat, and was based on a linear surface ornament in which the lines were interpreted as conveying different emotions. Simultaneously, within architecture there sprang up the wish to create new kinds of space, dependent on the dynamic play between forces that the lines were thought to illustrate. The Scot Mackintosh created an entirely new experience of the depth dimension at the Glasgow School of Art by the way his wall was broken through and by the way his iron railings accented it between the windows, a movement already begun outside the building itself, in the iron railings on the street. Other examples were the designs for the Hochbahn in Vienna, where the supporting duty of the consoles is filled with tension, or the early sketches by Eric Mendelsohn for various factories.

This new concept of space was especially fertile in Scandinavian church architecture. The foremost examples are the Grundtvig Mindekirke (Memorial Church) in Copenhagen (Pl. 100a) by P. V. J. Klint, built 1913–40, and the Engelbrektskyrkan in Stockholm by L. I. Wahlman, built in 1911 with details in the *art decoratif* spirit, and Berghäll Church in Helsinki by L. Sonck, built in 1908. The Grundtvig Mindekirke has an interior characterized by its purely pictorial quality, a feature achieved by the handling of light and shade. All details are suppressed in the great areas of wall which have the blurred edges of pure tone rather than the precision of stone, so that the boundaries of the interior space are equally indistinct.

Klint became the leader of a group of architects who broke away from the Danish Academy. As a teacher he again and again stressed the need for genuineness, which was to him, in theory at least, the ethical basis of good architecture. This insistence upon genuineness and authenticity, at the time made only on the purely aesthetic level, was necessary for the emergence and development of modern archi⁄ tecture although it cannot be regarded as solely responsible.

Klint's interpretation of architecture as conveying ethical values is expressive of the turn of the century. I have earlier described the architecture of the nineteenth century as a tension between the norm and the individual. Art Nouveau proved to have no permanent solution of the problem of style, although it left some clearly notice⁄ able traces, and the discussion flared up afresh. The development from norm towards individual, which earlier on could be traced as a dominant trend, came to a standstill at the end of the century and again there appeared simultaneously a variety of building styles: the neoclassicism of the twenties, national romanticism, and realism.

Examples of the neoclassic of our century are the little Museum at Faaborg (Pl. 100b) in Denmark by Carl Petersen, 1912, and the Politibyggnaden in Copenhagen by Hack Kampmann, 1918, the interior of Stockholm City Hall by Ragnar Östberg, finished in 1923, and the chapel Skogskapellet in Stockholm by Gunnar Asplund, 1919. In Finland the line is represented by the Finnish House of Parliament, designed by J. S. Sirén. The national⁄ romantic temper created buildings like the Town Hall (Rådhuset) in Stockholm by Carl Westman, 1912–15, inspired by Vadstena Castle; the Town Hall in Copenhagen by Martin Nyrop, 1892–1905, and the Library at Bergen by Olof Nordhagen, built in 1906. One could also mention Eliel Saarinen's Bank Hall in Helsinki or his Town Hall at Lahti in Finland. Among early realistic buildings, the factory buildings for A.S.E.A. (Pl. 101) at Västerås in Sweden by Erik Hahr and the power stations by Oswald Almquist occupy a leading position.

These three kinds of architecture must be characterized by finding the factors which decided the design. In classicizing architecture the factor was the norm, or ideal type; in romanticism it was the national spirit; in realistic architecture the factor was function according to the slogan of Louis Sullivan: form follows function.

The picture is simplified if the two first groups are regarded as one, the anti-realistic. Admittedly it was a question of great importance for the design whether inspiration was found in the eternal values of the classical arts or in the history of the home country, but in general this search for inspiration outside contemporary society meant an anti-realism. This repudiation of one's own community and the contemporary life which often had to determine the interiors of plans, can also be said to illustrate aesthetic values in the early years of this century. Façade architecture showed how, often enough, a functional plan and interior were screened by a loosely attached decorative style; beauty was added as an extra dimension objectively comparable to any of the others.

Part Six

INDUSTRIAL SOCIETY AND ITS ENVIRONMENT

Pl. 101. A.S.E.A. factory, Västeras, Sweden (pp. 204, 218).

(a) Exhibition of 1930, Stockholm (p. 220).

(b) 'Elementhus', Gothenburg, Sweden (p. 222).

Pl. 102. 1930 and after.

Pl. 103. Flat designed for 1930 exhibition (p. 221).

(a) Kvarnholmen house, near Stockholm (p. 231).

(b) 'Open-air city', Malmö (p. 231

Pl. 104. Neighbourhood planning, Sweden.

(a) Cottage at Ordrup, Denmark (p. 242).

(b) House at Hälsingborg Exhibition (p. 225).

Pl. 105.

(a) Årsta Centre (p. 232).

(b) Lamella blocks, Hjörthagen (p. 223

Pl. 106.

(*a*) Residential area.

(*b*) Shopping centre.

Pl. 107. Vällingby, near Stockholm (p. 236).

Pl. 108. Tower block, Södra Gulheden, Gothenburg, Sweden (p. 224).

109. Tower block, Örebro, Sweden (see Pl. 110, left).

(b) Bellahøj, Copenhagen (p. 238).

(a) Gustavsberg, Stockholm (p. 224).

Pl. III. Recent blocks of flats.

Pl. 112. Paimio Sanatorium, Finland (p. 241).

Pl. 113. School for girls, Stockholm (p. 239).

Pl. 114. Aarhus University, Denmark (p. 239).

(*a*) Radio House, Copenhagen (p. 240).

(*b*) Concert Hall, Gothenburg (p. 241).

Pl. 115.

Pl. 116. Crematorium chapel, Skogskyrkogården, Stockholm (p. 242).

117. Burial chapel, Turku, Finland (p. 242).

Pl. 118 (*a*, *b*). Chapel, Otaniemi, Finland (p. 242).

Pl. 119 (*a*, *b*). Kudeneule Factory, Hanko, Finland (p. 242).

(*a*). Vällingby under-
ground station, detail
(p. 236).

Pl. 120.

(*b*) Bus garage at Hornsberg, Stockholm (p. 243).

XXII

PRODUCTION AND COMMERCE

THE forms of production in the new community demanded new things from architecture, among which production, distribution, and commerce were the most important elements to be considered besides accommodation for the workers.

In many cases the transition from handicraft to industrialized pro-duction, with specialization and the splitting up of the different stages of manufacture, was a relatively lengthy progress and consequently it was not until the 1870's that a completely industrialized environ-ment emerged. The first radical departures from handicraft in Scandinavia were taken in the engineering and the textile industries, which were mainly situated in the towns. In some cases there were whole regions with factories and dwellings for the workers in the vicinity, such as at Norrköping and Hälsingborg in Sweden, and sometimes entirely new towns were built, in which the factories and the new railways were the most outstanding elements.

The new metal industry was mainly to be found at Eskilstuna in Sweden, where since the sixteenth century a forging trade had been firmly established in the famous Radermacher forges along the river. Complete industrialization grew and developed out of these shops at Eskilstuna only very slowly, for the first factories were set up among the dwelling houses wherever space was to be found. Thus an early form of industrial environment was created there, much resembling that of the first industrial towns in England, characterized by a mixture of factories, handicraft shops, and dwellings for workers and others.

The heavier metal industry and its factories were given a specific character by processes and machines that demanded considerable space. To start with, this environment was relatively undifferentiated and consisted of large factory halls in which the machinery was put up. The size of such halls necessitated a new way of construction with cast iron and glass, which permitted increased roof spans and ampler daylight with a minimum of vertical supports.

P

A considerably more developed functionalism was created in the textile industry, with its more highly standardized production. To start with, the mechanization of textile production only involved the introduction of two kinds of machines, the spinning machine and the mechanized loom. Their working period was preceded by dyeing, mixing, and carding, and followed by the processing of the material, but the introduction of the two machines was radical enough. They were placed alongside each other in long rows in the halls, the architecture of which followed the rows of machinery. Thus in the textile industry one can trace one of the roots of modern functionalist architecture.

In 1832 this pattern of operations was introduced into Sweden with the Jonsered canvas factory outside Gothenburg. The prototype was Scottish; as a matter of fact the factory was founded by an emigrated Scot, one William Gibson. This factory was given a saw-tooth roof for even lighting of the hall. For many years the Jonsered Factory was an exception in Sweden, as most textile factories, mainly at Norrköping, Alingsås, and Borås, only slowly developed out of the old handicraft system. But towards the 1870's and later, this factory had many followers.

Designers of many of the newly established factories allowed the structure to dictate the form of the interiors, making considerable use of cast iron and glass. Their predecessors in this respect were the glass halls on the Continent, market halls and exhibition buildings, and also the railway stations. The foremost examples of market halls in Sweden are the Klarahallen in Stockholm, built in 1865, and the market hall on the square Kungstorget in Gothenburg, built in 1867. The hall in Stockholm has many features in common with the halls by Baltard in Paris, while the Gothenburg hall in form and construction was somewhat like the Crystal Palace in London. It had a rectangular plan and was covered by an extensive barrel vault of cast-iron arches and glass with smaller transverse barrel vaults. Such a building presented a rather radical example of a plan and elevation following the structural functions. It is only in the details that one can see an adjustment to the stylistic ideals in vogue at the time of construction.

Before the emergence of industrialism, and even before it came to dominate the structure of Scandinavian communities, exhibitions were arranged for the products of industry and handicraft. This happened for the first time in the 1820's, but a specific showplace was not set up until 1852 with the exhibition in Copenhagen, or until 1866 in Stockholm. The exhibition buildings themselves displayed many new features from a structural point of view. The one in Copenhagen had a neoclassic façade, but its elevation and inner lighting were distinct results of the conquests of new problems by engineers and architects. The exhibition in Stockholm (Pl. 94) was designed by A. W. Edelswärd and was placed in Kungsträdgården, a former royal park opposite the palace. It was planned with a central quadrangular middle part with two projecting wings, one in the shape of a T, the other with a semicircular end. The middle was crowned by a polyhedral dome entirely of glass, high over the roofs of adjacent parts of the building, and in it the architect excelled in what were, for Scandinavia, new methods of construction. Each projecting wing was triple-aisled and covered by a simple roof.

Under the dome a gigantic model in plaster of Molin's fountain dominated the exhibition (it can now be seen in its finished form on the same spot), and for the rest all the Scandinavian countries had contributions on show from their handicraft and industrial production. The spectators came to admire the industrial design, and perhaps above all to be fascinated by the numerous new machines which were put up and could be seen working daily to the intense satisfaction of all concerned.

The structural problem in this hall was to create large covered areas for the exhibition of all the different objects. The problem was the same in the train sheds built in the 1850's. According to foreign prototypes, extensive terminals consisting of large train sheds and station halls were built in many large towns. The foremost Scandinavian architect in this field was the earlier mentioned Swede, A. W. Edelswärd, who was ably adapting the railway architecture of England and France. The railway station at Gothenburg built in 1856 was one of the finest examples of his architecture in this field. A Danish example from the same time is the Fredericia railway station built in 1868 by Bottger in medieval style (Pl. 97b).

An interesting, unfortunately never realized, Danish project was the design by Hetsch for a winter garden in the Customs House in Copenhagen—an almost greenhouse-like construction. The Industriforeningen, the industrial association, built in 1870, was, however, entirely in wood. In 1889 an exhibition hall by Nyrop was built, also in wood, based entirely on structural principles.

This hall architecture, whether for factories, railway stations, or exhibition buildings, could not be allowed to expose too clearly and unabashedly the new structural architecture. Both client and architect were proud of their results in this line, especially when they broke new records in the width of spans or managed to create new sensations of space in their buildings. But the way in which factories and stations were valued was too complex to let the structural features appear too nakedly. Numerous enthusiastic contemporary descriptions of the new industrialized community go to prove that the factories and stations and so on were valued very highly in a symbolic way, as well as for their utility. The steam engine, the trains, and the numerous products on the market were too magnificent as manifestations of human progress to be allowed to remain 'merely' functional and structural in character. It filled a human need to make them symbolical in form; in short, people were proud of their achievements.

Thus the railway became part of the bourgeois town, and in those cases where a station for topographical reasons had to be outside the centre of town it was linked with the centre by new residential districts growing up along the streets leading out to the station. Ways of setting off the new stations included giving the buildings formal façades and creating parks in front of them. The latter also served the practical purpose of stopping fires that were started by the engines, a common danger especially in Swedish wooden towns. The numerous railway stations that were being built in Scandinavia just after 1850 were soon equipped with façades which concealed their purely structural elements. Often the middle of such a façade or perhaps the two ends were made to project in an arbitrary monumental way. As in England where stations were built by private enterprise and in a competitive spirit, and one station was designed in the Greek spirit, another in the Gothic, similar means to surpass each predecessor were used in Scandinavia. A direct effect on Scandinavian railway architecture from England appeared in the second station in Copenhagen, which was strongly influenced by King's Cross in London, while the station at Klampenborg, the resort just outside Copenhagen, was built in 'Swiss cottage' style.

The enhancement of the purely structural was practised in the industrial world as well. The industrialist regarded his factories with proud admiration; they were to express the 'new deal' of the new era. They had to be adorned, often by ornament borrowed from Roman architecture, and friezes, pilaster strips, and attached columns became common features of factory façades. The high chimneys necessitated by steam engines showed more freedom, and in designing them the architects usually followed their own personal taste; chimneys were quadrangular, octagonal, or round, and their pedestals especially were designed in a truly monumental spirit.

In the same endeavour the grouping together of the different elements of an establishment became an important factor. The extensive factory hall was given monumental scale by being surrounded with smaller buildings, often arranged as symmetrical wings. The power of invention varied as is shown by the three illustrations given here (Pl. 96, 97a). Similarities with country estates were especially frequent, but other prototypes can be traced as well.

The desire to give the exterior a worthy façade while building the interior in accordance with new structural principles shows clearly the conflict that existed between 'engineers' and 'architects' during and after the middle of the century, a conflict that in Scandinavia often resulted in clashes similar to that between the Académie des Beaux-Arts and the École de Polytechnique in Paris. In Edelswärd's exhibition building in Stockholm it is difficult to decide which school is dominating, the 'structural' or 'academic'. The ornamental features both inside and out are in balance with the frankly structural roofs and walls because the ornament is subordinated to these elements. The decoration is restricted to a frieze in the dome and a monumentalizing of the entrance porches. One must not regard this building as a unique phenomenon. Its effect then actually lay with the objects exhibited therein, so that it stood in the same class as the bourgeois residential neighbourhood, for example, or the contemporary schools. In most factories the interior did control the decorations of the exterior; the order of the windows was a direct consequence of lighting that was determined from the point of view of techniques and working conditions and the vertical stress in the exterior followed supports in the interior. In the railway stations on the other hand, there was usually no connection whatever between the inner functions and the façade of the exterior.

To start with, the 'architects' were nearly always the victors, but the history of the emergence of modern architecture shows that the victory never lasted very long. The effort to create a monumental and symbolizing façade architecture continued to be strong, but more and more it was subordinated to practical suitability. In certain categories such as railway stations, this suitability to a purpose did not act creatively upon the façade architecture, as the façade was merely a screen in front of the shed over the railway lines, and the ticket offices, waiting rooms, and so on contained within the façade could adapt themselves to its architecture but did not condition it. In the factories, on the other hand, and more especially in the market halls, emphasis upon technical functions became stronger and the symbolic values were expressed only in the scale of a building, the essential relations between buildings, or with the aid of ornaments added on to an already finished building.

XXIII

BETTER HOMES FOR EVERYBODY

AT first the growing population of industrial workers had no power to create their own environment, mainly because they had no economic power. When towards the middle of the nineteenth century the immigration to the industrial towns began to take on the proportions of an invasion, the question of housing these new strata of the urban population became a real problem. In the old market towns, where the residential quarters still had the form of the surrounded yard, the yard houses were let to the workers. This became possible when the old household establishment was being split up. This was one aspect among many of the transition from the almost medieval habit of bartering to a money market. The foremost merchants became specialized wholesale dealers, whose businesses were no longer connected with their residences. Industrialism was breaking up the old unity of residence and workshop. And so the houses across the yards became empty and were rebuilt or extended to serve as dwellings for the clustering workers. This solution to the problem of housing the proletariat, which from the beginning marked a difference in value between the old distinguished house in the street and the considerably smaller house across the yard, could only be a temporary solution. Soon the influx became such that all houses available were occupied. At the rapidly expanding railway junctions, moreover, it must be remembered that there were no old settlements to absorb the first comers. The result of this new usage of the back houses was a high density and very poor sanitary conditions.

Therefore the housing question had to be solved either by the building of apartment houses or of detached houses. The first real tenement houses built as such were influenced by the blocks of flats built by the bourgeoisie according to French ideals. The enormous increase in population of large towns and cities forced an intensive exploitation of living space. Following models in Berlin, Scandinavian houses were equipped with wings projecting into the yards,

215

which were sometimes entirely surrounded by houses. Such new yard houses were occupied by the working classes, and so the difference in value continued in analogy with the old reorganized merchant houses.

In Copenhagen there had earlier emerged the picture of more distinguished houses facing the streets and less attractive houses at the back. At least two rooms were placed facing the street in the front house, where often an oval dining-room formed the transition to the wing towards the yard (Pl. 98), which was occupied by bedrooms, kitchen, and maid's room, the last of which was often without direct light. The yards, or rather the light wells, were sometimes less than three feet in width, a flagrant proof of insufficient legislation (Pl. 99a).

The façades revealed nothing of the cramped yards behind them. Up to the 1850's in Denmark, neoclassic façades were the most common on blocks of flats with smooth walls and a simple moulding between the stories. The back houses were appallingly poor. A law requiring that flats should be reached from two different staircases gave birth to the so-called corridor house.

The laisser-faire industrial town was a free creation, its design allowed to evolve by the free working of economic laws. The legislation already in existence in Scandinavia was quite insufficient and could not prevent the emergence of incongruities, which generally resulted in the lower classes paying a greater proportion of their income for an obviously insufficient home than the upper classes paid for one that was more than sufficient. The dwellings of the lower classes were not only cramped but lacked the most elementary sanitary equipment, secondary rooms for different needs, and so on.

Such enormous incongruities and misery roused a growing opposition against prevailing urban conditions. After the middle of the nineteenth century a reform movement started with an increased concern for better hygienic conditions in the towns and this resulted in better sanitary laws, and the gas, water, and sewage systems were enlarged and firmly established. In Denmark this happened in the 1850's and Sweden followed about ten years later. The aim of the reform movement was to detect all incongruities and to eliminate them by means of new laws and prevent their emergence. These reforms went on in many different fields, most of which are outside the compass of this book. Here it will be sufficient to mention the two most important aspects, both concerned with housing. One is the technical-economic question: how to create better and less expensive houses with the aid of the new achievements in technology; the other is the social-economic question: how to give a reasonable dwelling standard to the lower classes. These two problems are the roots of modern domestic architecture.

Houses built on free speculation had shown beyond all doubt that the lower social classes were the hardest hit by a laisser-faire housing policy. Towards the end of the nineteenth century there emerged in Scandinavia a co-operative movement dealing with housing problems, which tried to balance the relations between the production of housing on the one hand and rents, site-prices, costs of building, supply of work, and so on on the other. The first co-operative movement to be established in Scandinavia was the one in Copenhagen, as early as 1865, which built tenement houses containing flats of two rooms and a kitchen, an achievement that was far better than anything the speculators had to offer. Later the state and the municipalities started similar building enterprises, and these have limited the scope of private enterprise. Since 1933, when co-operative societies were forbidden in Germany, the Scandinavian countries have occupied a leading position within this field.

The road to the modern block of low-cost flats was not easy. In order to bring about better houses for all social classes, architects began to realize that they must concern themselves with low-cost housing, which during the nineteenth century was treated in a fairly stepmotherly fashion, and to a great extent was entirely in the hands of builders without professional supervision. The gradual reversal of this situation has meant a complete change of the architects' profession in Scandinavia; from being only an exclusive occupation it has become a large body embracing all kinds of building activities in a community. There was also a great need for better legislation and better hygienic conditions and technical equipment for houses. This social awareness and concern came to life in earnest towards the 1920's.

Art Nouveau played an important part in the creation of new plans for houses and flats. Architecturally the style was born when in 1893 Victor Horta designed a house in the Rue de Turin in Brussels, and as used by Horta it meant more than just a new fashion. Art Nouveau decoration was based on a new and free ornamental rhythm of lines, covering walls and ceilings in bold ornaments. Starting from the tectonic members, such ornament came to be freely developed. Horta was one of the first to draw the consequences of the new structural principles made possible through iron and steel. The interior of his building was no longer tied to the old structural system; he could present a new and freer composition of the rooms. Horta's plan is dynamic, and this was in fact the embryo of plans to come. The dissolution of the formal plan of the residential house and flat had begun.

Horta's architecture could not in itself create an entirely new attitude. But when Le Corbusier developed it by adding his cubistic ideas architecture was emancipated. Le Corbusier has hardly ever been socially engaged, at least not very successfully, but after the First World War he created his famous principle of the Dom-i-no, a standardized house made of three horizontal slabs of reinforced concrete carried by six vertical supports, and with it he planned to rebuild ravaged northern France. The Dom-i-no principle made all interior walls unnecessary from a structural point of view; the architect could place them wherever he wanted them. Only a few houses were ever built strictly according to this method, but the idea was now clear that rooms and plan could follow the actual needs of the inhabitants of a house more closely than ever before.

As, however, Le Corbusier's achievements have to a certain extent gone astray in a queer and rather artificial mass of conflicting theory, the analysing of the actual needs of common man had to come from somewhere else. The fact that a livable house plan had to be based on real needs emerged in the Germany of the Weimar Republic, but before talking about the evolution there something has to be said about the improvements in town planning up to this period, as town planning played an integrated part in the creation of better homes for everybody.

The initiators in Scandinavia for better town planning were the Dane Povl Baumann and the Swede Albert Lilienberg. Their aim was twofold: to create low-cost blocks of flats with a higher technical standard and to achieve a more hygienic town plan. A result of their effort can be seen on Struenseegade in Copenhagen (Pl. 99b), where Baumann built blocks of flats between 1918 and 1920. Lilienberg worked mostly at Gothenburg and in Stockholm. They had a kindred spirit at Västerås in Sweden, where Eric Hahr during the First World War was designing both factories (Pl. 101) and houses.

The ideology fostered by these architects came from Vienna, where at the end of the nineteenth century Camillo Sitte had published his far-reaching book on the building of cities, in which the medieval, intimate spirit of organic growth was emphasized. But of still greater importance was the work of another architect and town planner, Otto Wagner. It was he who in 1896 coined the phrase *Nutzstil* (utility style) and in 1911 published a book *Die Grosstadt* in which he discussed town planning. One must not, however, draw too many conclusions from the particular plans appearing in this book, which should be valued more for its spirit than its form. The form has little in common with Sitte and does in fact often emphasize axiality and a regularity and formality which Sitte had so stubbornly tried to fight. But Wagner's ambition was to create healthy towns with every part of the town adapted to the typical and practical needs of its population. Wagner underlined with all his strength that it was necessary for building sites to be owned by the community, that in no other way could the evil powers behind malignant growth and oppressive exploitation be stopped. The starting point, then, for Wagner was modern urban life. Through his personal initiative he came to mean much for European town planning.

Baumann's blocks of flats on Struenseegade (Pl. 99b) were built under municipal supervision and this was a necessary condition to keep down private exploitation. Private enterprise would undoubtedly have regarded the ratio of profit to the utilization of space as much too low. All back yards were thrown together and made into large shared spaces equipped with lawns and trees, and a similarly unified approach is evident on the blocks themselves, where hardly any exterior decorations are to be found. A healthier environment was here created and the aesthetic impression was healthier as well. Such housing meant an enormous step towards breaking up the old tradition of cramped towns, but this was only one step on the road towards the modern flat.

Otto Wagner's *Nutzstil* slogan meant that everything not necessary in architecture and town planning should be abandoned. In a way his work displayed many parallels with Louis Sullivan's although they had quite different starting points. What Otto Wagner had begun was followed up by a distinguished generation of architects in the Weimar Republic. In 1927 an exhibition was held in Stuttgart, in the Siedlung Weissenhof planned by the

German architect Ludwig Mies van der Rohe with the participation of the world's élite, Walter Gropius, J. J. P. Oud, Le Corbusier, and others. New demands and new ideas had ripened and now became fruitful for the benefit of the rest of the world. The architects also based their work on the German slogan *Sachlichkeit* (practicality), in many ways a continuation of Wagner's utility style, and consequently focused their interest on the technical and practical sides of life and architecture. That they underlined the importance of standardization of houses as well as furniture was entirely along this line. They also analysed carefully the actual needs of the common family and the functioning of houses. Three years later, in 1930, the German ideas as developed in their Scandinavian evolution appeared in the Stockholm Exhibition. A new era had started.

A large number of Swedish architects participated in this exhibition, with whole villas, terrace houses, flats, etc., in a unified environment. The framework of the whole, the arrangement of the exhibition and the restaurant with the large exhibition halls were designed by Gunnar Asplund, the pioneer of modern architecture in Scandinavia. Among the many villas and flats exhibited, a flat designed by Gustaf Clason attracted much attention. It was designed for a family of three to four members. The bedrooms, bathroom and wardrobes, that is everything connected with sleep and hygiene, were placed in one part of the flat, separated from the part containing the kitchen and the dining recess. These two parts were linked by the large living-room, which runs across the entire width of the house. A similar solution was presented by Eric Friberger. The new solutions for housing problems presented here were direct results of the new planning concepts, with the addition of better hygienic accommodation. The desire was to give each function its right and separate space and it resulted in three main cores in these two flats; for sleep and hygiene, for the preparation of food and eating it, and for the family's being together.

The analysing of the new functions of a home—house or flat—and also of the technical aspects, which gave the flats more efficient kitchen equipment among other things, had shown beyond doubt the disadvantage of the old town plans, even if the yards were built as clean and free of back houses as in Baumann's example. The demand for direct daylight into each room saw the birth of the narrow type of house, or 'lamella' house, a free-standing rectangular block, usually of three stories—a form which was made use of by the Swede Uno Åhrén, when in 1931 he designed a plan for Ladugårds-gärde in Stockholm. All houses were lamella houses and no back yards existed. The houses were also oriented to give all rooms a maximum of sunshine. The scheme was rejected; the planning authorities did not yet understand the necessity for narrow houses replacing the old, where so many rooms faced the wrong way. I

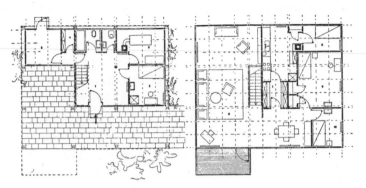

FIG. 73. The 'Elementhus' or expanding house.

will return to this scheme when talking about town plans. It was not until the next year that the advantages were acknowledged in a competition arranged by the city of Stockholm. The advantages of the winning projects were too obvious not to make a deep impression.

At the Stockholm Exhibition the problem was not only to create new low-cost blocks of flats but also row houses and villas, which were meant to break up the compact built-up areas of the towns. The villas designed by Sven Markelius and Kurt von Schmalensee showed the architects' desire to work with the free plan once intro-duced by Victor Horta and developed by Mies van der Rohe and others, but here the free plan appeared with the practical functions fully considered. These houses also showed how some activities were held together while others were kept apart. The living-rooms with built-in balconies (Pl. 103) are expressions of the accent on being together, which was felt to be a desirable factor at that time. Another expression of the same idea is the collectivism which appeared within many other fields. One need only think of the new Russian towns of this age or the villas designed by Le Corbusier with his dynamic and free planning which often included one large living-room where all members of the family could live together. Among the row houses on show at the Exhibition those designed by Uno Åhrén and Oswald Almquist were the best ones. The ideas were soon copied in small houses all over Scandinavia.

In 1937 Eric Friberger constructed his 'L-house', or *elementhus*, in order to lower building costs (Pl. 102*b*, Fig. 73). It was a pre-fabricated house which was erected in as short a time as two months outside Gothenburg. Apart from the flexibility of construction with prefabricated components, this house was also meant to be flexible according to the size of the family. By using identically the same components in varying quantities, four different houses could be built providing from about 30 to 148 square feet in floor area, the largest house being developed out of the smallest by successive additions.

Apart from new technique and methods of construction and the analysis of functions, the architecture of the early thirties showed a strong aesthetic urge towards purity and clarity. This was not only a result of the new structural ideals, but was regarded as a desirable thing in itself. The new materials, glass, steel, and concrete, easily lent themselves to this purity. The exterior of the pioneer creations show many similarities to the cubist paintings of the 1920's. On the other hand the architect of the Exhibition itself, Gunnar Asplund, proved that modern architecture in the hands of a good architect could easily lend itself to the creation of a festive and gay background (Pl. 102*a*) for the strictly functional and technical exhibits without using any of the formal elements of older exhibitions. Asplund's exhibition architecture conveys much of the feeling of triumph with which the new ideas were launched in Scandinavia.

It has been said that when functionalism was carried further into the main stream of architecture, the purity was sometimes exag-gerated. The stress on certain technical aspects was quite natural, however, as a number of new factors had been found which were unknown earlier. The demand for fresh air and sunshine made most town plans rather alike, whether in Denmark, Norway, or Sweden. The long narrow unit of the lamella block was victorious all over Europe with the exception of England, and the parallel lines of white-plastered units marched along without regard to topo-graphical variations. In some parts of Scandinavia this kind of housing is still very much in use.

This victory for the uniform lamella slab was due to the fact that the hygienic and technical aspects of housing had been over-emphasized and isolated. But towards the middle of the 1930's much was done to repair this one-sidedness and the programme was widened. Many architectural competitions and investigations have since then been carried out in order to acquire still more knowledge about housing conditions and living habits. The most important were the competition arranged by the city of Stockholm in 1933,

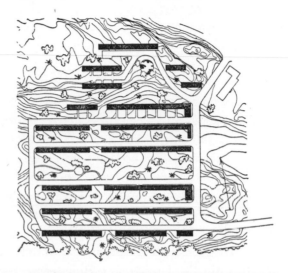

FIG. 74.
Hjorthagen, layout of
lamella blocks of flats.

and a housing investigation arranged by the Swedish Arts and Crafts Society, to mention only two. This activity was carried out in the other Scandinavian countries as well, but Sweden has had a leading position in this field, which is why mostly Swedish examples are dis-cussed in this chapter. With the help of all these investigations and a large number of exhibitions, some of them regularly reappearing in the Scandinavian countries, the purely technical aspects have gradually been deepened and the new social perspective has enriched architecture. Simultaneously the municipal and co-operative housing production has been immensely increased at the cost of private enter-prise. In an attempt to lower the costs of housing, or at least to lighten the burden on the tenant, the communities and government today give loans for the construction of houses and have thereby gained control over the standard of the houses.

A good lamella housing scheme was created by Hakon Ahlberg at Hjorthagen in Stockholm for the workers at the Stockholm gas works (Pl. 106b, Fig. 74). Each block is only twenty-three feet wide and thus also the secondary spaces have direct daylight. Each flat contains two rooms and a kitchen. The lamellas appear as bright linear slabs surrounded by nature. The Danish architects P. Baumann and K. Hansen have created in the Storgård in Copenhagen a lamella block on a much larger scale. By means of standardized balconies a rhythmic pattern appears over the façades, which breaks up the somewhat massive character of the buildings.

In an attempt to break up the town plans, which tended to become rather monotonous by the sole use of the lamella house, a monotony for which the housing production industries were partly to blame, and in order to create other types of apartment houses for other categories of families, the tall block or point block was introduced a few years before the Second World War. That some of the flats in these houses should face east or north seemed unavoidable, and in an attempt to solve this problem the Swedish architects Sven Backström and Leif Reinius produced at Örebro a new variety, which consisted of three blocks radiating from a communal staircase (Pl. 110). By linking these blocks in different ways the town plan could be quite attractively varied; apart from giving all flats a maximum of sunshine the creation of closed-in yards free from traffic was made possible. In Denmark Arne Jacobsen has used another method of breaking up the monotony of the conventional lamella type by putting the flats in a saw-tooth pattern. Still another solution is found at Gustavsberg a few miles outside Stockholm (Pl. 111a, Fig. 75), where Olof Thunström joined two quadrangular blocks of flats by means of the staircase, but with one of the blocks appearing higher than the other as it was put on pylons, which gives the building a certain lightness. It should also be noted that these flats have a very intimate contact with the surrounding nature, lawns are laid out right up to the building line, and the small scale is a correct approach in this rather small community. Through Thunström, Gustavsberg has become very much a model community.

A related plan is found at Södra Guldheden in Gothenburg where Sven Brolid and Jan Wallinder designed some tower blocks in 1950 (Pl. 108, Fig. 76). Two narrow blocks containing two flats to each story with kitchen, dining recess, hall, and three to four rooms, have common stairs and lifts, a fact that of course reduced the building costs. The plans of these flats show some interesting features. The kitchen and dining recess are separated by means of cupboards, which can be opened from either side, but what is more important is the 'open' character of the flats, with passages practically non-existent and the openings between the rooms large and light. The piling of flats on top of each other has received adequate expression in the emphasized horizontality of the narrow concrete slabs.

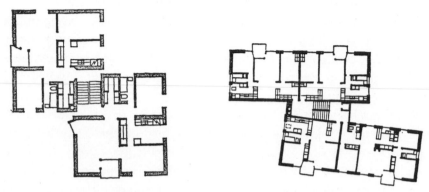

FIG. 75. Gustavsberg flats.   FIG. 76. Södra Guldheden flats.
(Not to same scale).

Among the latest contributions to the everlasting discussion about the planning of the one-family house, the villas designed by Erik Ahnborg and Anders Trygg (Pl. 105b) on one hand and Mårten Larsson and Anders William-Olsson (Fig. 77) on the other, are worth mentioning. They were both exhibited at the Hälsingborg

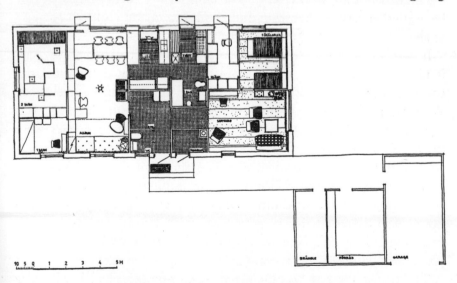

FIG. 77. One-family house, Hälsingborg Exhibition.

Exhibition in 1955. Personal isolation on one side of the house and the family being together on the other is the principle behind the plans: the bedroom of the parents and the children's bedrooms are situated in different parts of the house, and the parents also have a private drawing-room or study, while the room for the whole family is a large all-in-one room in connection with the kitchen.

The apartment houses at Sorgenfri in Malmö in Sweden by Samuelson and Janecke can be mentioned as one of the latest examples of modern blocks of flats, conspicuous for their new building technique in concrete using standardized elements, which has contributed to produce the new and unconventional exterior.

All these houses and flats can be regarded as results of numerous investigations of housing and living habits in the Scandinavian countries, results of a widened basis of knowledge, especially of the social foundation of architecture. Domestic architecture is being tackled from a much wider angle of approach than earlier and at the same time the plans of flats have tended to become less rigid and locked in layout—for example, the all-in-one room at the Hälsingborg Exhibition, or the open plan at Guldheden in Gothenburg. The possibilities of creating flats with a changeable plan have occupied the two architects Tage and Anders William-Olsson. The results can be seen in their experimental house at Gothenburg, where the inner walls are movable, so that families with small children can have another form of flat from those with grown-up children or none at all.

It goes without saying that the family residence in a block of flats is not the only type of urban housing. Especially in our modern community other demands have arisen and insisted upon a solution. A special problem emerges in a household where both parents go out to work and for such families the so-called collective houses were designed, which apart from flats contain a collective kitchen and restaurant, nurseries, laundries, etc. The pioneer in Sweden was Sven Markelius and his first collective house, built in 1935, is on John Erikssonsgatan in Stockholm. Another, at Marieberg in Stockholm, was designed in 1944 by Sven Ivar Lind. In the last few years other forms of 'special category' houses have been built for pensioners, young people, etc.

The rented flat has become the most common type of family residence in Scandinavia. The demand for detached one-family houses has always been present, however, but as the building costs for these are considerably higher than for blocks of flats, quite contrary to the situation in England, great difficulties have arisen when the architects have tried to design detached houses available for all social classes. Standardized prefabricated houses have developed very rapidly since the war in order to lower the building costs and in addition certain simplifications have been made: the cellar is discarded, the laundry is placed in connection with the kitchen and the bathroom, which reduces the costs of plumbing. It is yet too early to say whether the rents for these one-family houses are going to stay below the rents in blocks of flats.

The Danish architects have many times been the leaders in Scandi-navia in designing the one-family house and the row house. Their ability to create a harmonious unity with the house and the garden or park is remarkable. Viggo Möller Jensen, for his Artists' House at Utterslev, deserves special mention.

Needless to say, war caused an interval in building activity in Finland and Norway and to a large extent in Denmark, while in Sweden building was limited mainly to domestic work.

XXIV

TWENTIETH-CENTURY
TOWN PLANNING

THE nineteenth century saw the emergence of the special bourgeois districts in towns and cities along the new and fashionable boulevards. Other parts of the towns were taken up by industry, factories, working-class houses; still other areas were occupied by institutions, schools, law courts, etc. This erratic transformation of different parts of a town into 'specialized' regions was as regrettable a result of uncontrolled urban development as it was unexpected, and it put its hallmark upon the nineteenth-century city to such an extent that it exists today as a phenomenon all too familiar to everyone.

With the advent of industrialism in Scandinavia, as everywhere else, the building of towns became an extremely complicated affair, with all the technical factors of urban existence such as gas and water mains, sewage disposal, communication systems, etc. To deal with this technical complexity the town engineer took over planning leadership from the surveyor, whose one commission then was to stake out the lots and sites.

The town created by the engineer did function from a technical point of view—admittedly with some screeching—but the main problems remained unsolved. Levellings of distinctions in the older regional character of towns, the emergence of slums, traffic chaos, and social misery were some of the blighting symptoms of urban decay that the technically competent hardly observed, much less cured. As the social situation of the architects in the twentieth century was changed from an earlier involvement only with capitalistic and governmental commissions to include nearly all kinds of buildings and their setting, town planning inevitably became part of the work of architects.

Reform of the unplanned industrial town took many forms and the prescriptions that were worked out varied greatly in content and in effect. Independently and simultaneously two schools emerged

228

for the beautifying of towns. The so-called 'City Beautiful' movement had emerged in the United States in an effort to create the civic centre in a form different from that of the commercial area of the town. The Chicago Exhibition of 1893 was intended to express this theme by creating a beautiful entrance to the town from the lake and a worthy water-front. The plans of Louis Sullivan were put aside in favour of those of Beaux-Arts architects and a return to pompous classicism and baroque was made. In our day the Exhibition is better known for Sullivan's criticism of it, but its concept of spacious city planning spread abroad and to Scandinavia. The other school was that of Camillo Sitte in Vienna and Wagner's continuation of it as I have already mentioned (see p. 219).

In Scandinavia the foremost exponents of the 'City Beautiful' were the Industrial Exhibition in Stockholm in 1897 (Pl. 95) designed by Ferdinand Boberg, and the Gothenburg Exhibition of 1923. By means of the large, light dome-vaulted building that Boberg designed as foil to the Nordiska Museum, a fairy-like, almost romantic effect was achieved, an effect quite in the Chicago tradition of 1893. In Gothenburg the most important aspect was the symmetry which created a monumental street ending in the Göta-platsen where the Art Gallery formed the background. An offshoot of this principle was the design for a replanning of Helsinki by Eliel Saarinen, an unexecuted plan which was characterized by many wide boulevards and vistas and a severe axiality.

The new kinds of apartment blocks introduced by Povl Baumann in Denmark and Albert Lilienberg in Sweden (described above, p. 218) meant in reality that the town planner had started to use a larger unit than earlier, the block rather than the individual house. With the continuation of these ideas in the lamella house the closed block was, as earlier mentioned, completely broken up if at first in an all too regular way. If one can speak of exaggerated technical aspects in the earliest modern architecture, it is here that they are to be found and a peril was latent in this form of planning. Some town plans were contemplated as consisting of nothing but such lamella houses. At least they allowed for the newly understood functions of the home together with the hygienic aspects that were now at last appreciated. An advantage was that all houses were equal—the difference between front house and back house was gone for ever. And the inhabitants had good opportunities to use parks and playgrounds, and sunshine was justly distributed. But in all this hygienic and democratic ardour, factors such as over-uniformity and the human need for individuality were forgotten, so that the overall impression of such a plan sometimes became a bit dismal. This was of course not always the case, far from it, but such neighbourhoods do exist. The very extensive building programme since the thirties has sometimes had this mechanical effect when planning had to race against time. The planners had gathered that the needs for all families were on the whole equal, so that their homes could be standardized and even whole neighbourhood areas could be standardized to contain similar if not equal types of homes.

When the social aspects of architecture and especially the individual demands of particular families upon their homes and neighbourhoods were brought into the discussion, the picture became entirely changed. These new themes were partly brought into Scandinavia from abroad, and partly originated in the discussion that followed on the Stockholm Exhibition of 1930. It is very difficult to say exactly what came from abroad and what ripened in the Scandinavian countries, neither is it necessary to isolate this, for modern architecture in the western world is to a higher extent than in earlier days an international movement.

Two new concepts were introduced into the planning discussion during the 1920's and were put into practice about a decade later: regionalism and zoning. They emerged in Germany and in Anglo-American discussions and planning. Both had a similar goal, with different starting points.

Foresighted policy in regard to the price of land and excellent legislation fostered as early as the end of the nineteenth century a town administration of an extremely high standard in Germany. The towns were divided into zones, each with entirely different contents and form, industrial zones, residential zones, administrative zones, and so on. When building new towns or when extending already existing towns the functions of future zones were kept well apart from each other. A direct result of this thinking was the building of the Siedlungen or housing estates in the time of the Weimar Republic.

This principle was adopted by Uno Åhrén in Sweden and further extended in his draft plan for a residential area at Ladugårdsgärde in Stockholm. The area was treated as one unit but within it differences were made in the types of houses, suitable for different kinds of families, and in the exploitation of space. Parks, playgrounds, and open space in general were treated as integral parts of the whole and not as mere left-over areas remaining after the houses were planned. In general the houses were rather narrow to allow better solutions for the plans of the flats. The time was not ripe for these ideas and the plan was rejected, but just the same it had a great impact upon later planning.

The first impact of regionalism therefore came in Scandinavia when the Kvarnholmen (Pl. 104a) in Stockholm was built in 1934. The plan was made possible by the fact that the patron, the Co-operative Society and Wholesale Association, early employed archi-tects who were prepared to engage themselves in modern planning, and also because the Association owned the land. The community forms an entity which is more or less independent; the aim was to make it independent as regards residences and work-places, mainly the flour mills. The area thus contains two functions, work and dwellings for the workers, the two parts of the community kept well apart by the use of zoning. Apartment houses, in the shape of lamella blocks, and row houses complement each other.

Similar planning can be seen in the Friluftsstaden at Malmö in Sweden by Erik Bülow-Hübe and Erik Sigfrid Persson, built in 1944 (Pl. 104b), with the exception that this area contains row houses only, and is only a residential area. Literally Friluftsstaden means the 'Fresh Air Community' and emphasis was laid upon the interdependence of houses, private gardens, and common parks. The plans of the rows of houses form a kind of zigzag pattern which provides a certain privacy and at the same time an intimate connec-tion between homes and nature. Many other examples of this kind of planning could be given from the different Scandinavian countries. Scandinavia's contributions to this discussion have undoubtedly inspired many foreign planners.

The Anglo-American ingredient of the discussion could perhaps be best characterized as an American modification and enrichment of Ebenezer Howard's concept of the satellite town. As Howard said, the increase in population of a town should come about in such a way that complete communities with their own centres, administra-tion, industries, shops, and houses should evolve quite separately from the old towns. The new town should be dependent upon the old one for certain qualified services only, and be separated from it by means of wide agricultural areas, for the goal was the self-sufficient and independent community of a limited size.

In reality Ebenezer Howard's mother town and satellite towns consisted of several self-sufficient precincts containing local shopping centres. Howard never called these units neighbourhood units although that was what he meant. This concept was introduced by the American sociologist Clarence Perry, one of the planners behind Radburn, N.J., near New York City. Perry was much stimulated by the Chicago sociologists who during the first decades of our century had found that all towns for social-ecologic reasons became divided into what they called natural areas, with certain cultural, economic, and ethnic characteristics of their own. Clarence Perry thought that this natural development was good and should be encouraged and the neighbourhood unit could be used not only in the new towns or new parts of a town, but also when clearing slums in already built-up areas. In his book *Culture of Cities* Lewis Mumford carried Perry's ideas further; by making the school the centre of the unit he decided the size of the population and also gave the unit an organic background.

For various reasons the Garden City neighbourhood community idea had little impact on Scandinavian thought until the time of the last World War. One reason was the translation of Mumford's book which appeared in Sweden in 1940; another was that the war raged in Europe. This is part of the background for the planning of Årsta (Pl. 106a) in Stockholm, the foremost Swedish expression of all these ideas.

The guiding principle for Årsta was to put a community centre in the middle of the residential area for the benefit of its population. From the beginning the centre was intended to be accentuated by means of a somewhat higher density and by placing the bus terminal there. This principle formed the background not only for Årsta but for many other residential areas and suburbs built in the same period, but because of the war and the building restrictions which followed as a consequence Årsta was the only one to be fully built.

The centre itself at Årsta complements the residential community with shops, health clinics, recreational facilities such as a cinema-cum-theatre, clubrooms of different kinds, assembly rooms, cafés, library, etc., all placed around a square designed for markets and leisurely strolling. The guiding principle for the planning of this community centre was not only to create a visual and practical focus for the residential area, but also to design an interesting and stimulating spiritual centre for the community, a centre that would have an inspiring effect on the activities of those who used it, fostering their desire to be together in an active communal way. It was meant to guard democratic principles, to raise young people in this spirit, and to encourage everyone to be democratic citizens. This aim has produced, specifically, a most varied design, with many different materials used both indoors and out as well as decorative murals, painted windowframes, and so on.

It is difficult to say to what extent Mumford's ideals and similar principles have inspired the brothers Erik and Tore Ahlsén, the designers behind this centre. Undoubtedly Mumford's slightly romantic conceptions have favoured a rather small scale, and certainly Årsta has in common with Mumford's principles a certain undertone of antiurbanism: the big city should be divided into small parts because the democratic ideals tend to get lost in the massive city— an idea that was also behind the architects' wish to enliven the architecture at Årsta.

Årsta community centre is the culmination of the idea of the neighbourhood unit in Scandinavia. Whether or not it provides the final answer to the problems of the city is too early yet to decide. Its lack of local industry and offices providing work for the inhabitants has, however, caused it to function more or less as a dormitory suburb, and therefore it does not function as well as the planners had hoped; a fact that is not to be blamed on the Ahlsén brothers but on the Stockholm County Council. So Årsta has become a residential suburb with a wellequipped centre, not a satellite town.

Generally speaking, one can say that the neighbourhood unit, whether in its English, American, or Scandinavian version, stands in sharp contrast to the conception of a city. In order to create a neighbourhood unit in its true sociological sense, the scale must be kept so small that its economic stability must be sacrificed. If on the other hand it is allowed to grow, it loses its human basis and dimension. This is not at all strange if one bears in mind the fact that the neighbourhood unit was born as a direct result of the antiurban school in English town planning, which originally had its roots in the fear the industrialists felt that made them move out of the towns.

On the other hand, the bringing in of the sociological concepts has enriched the discussion by bringing in new dimensions. But one must remember that the discussion at the beginning of the 1940's was not formulated on a broad enough basis. The neighbourhood unit does not cover more than a small part of an extremely complex reality, and approaches just one aspect of modern life. The large city, as well as the small, exists to a great extent in the fluctuating play of a variety of forces and these are not only economic, or social, or technical. Other forces are those only partly calculable valuations that people make of their surroundings, their world. These valua, tions and forces are not yet fully comprehended. The result is that the town and city has a structure of a much more complicated nature than we have understood until quite recently. We stand here only at the beginning of a vast undertaking, that of analysing the city and its structure.

It is impossible to know whether Årsta Centre and similar creations provide a solution. With the years that have passed since its comple, tion experience and knowledge have grown and have affected the picture of the latest contributions to Scandinavian town planing.

Due to the increased immigration to the Scandinavian towns after the Second World War the extensions of the towns have been built on a really large scale. Among the new areas around the capitals I can mention the Olympic Village in Helsinki, planned before the war by Hilding Ekelund and Martti Välikangas, and Tapiola (Hagalund) by Aarne Ervi and associates, rendered possible by the introduction of a government fund A.R.A.V.A. in 1949. The fore, most Danish example is Bellahøj in Copenhagen and among the Swedish examples I have chosen Vällingby, finished in 1955, and Farsta, which is at present being built.

All these town plans have many features in common, but there are differences of course. Principally, Vällingby is a continuation of Årsta, and Farsta is developed out of Vällingby. The aim when creating Vällingby was to design a frame for three functions, work, dwellings, and community centre. By increasing the scale the town was given a more solid economic basis, a variation as regards work, places was made possible, and the community centre was to serve not only the population of Vällingby proper but also the surrounding communities. The scale is still larger at Farsta and here a centre is intended that is to compete with that of inner Stockholm.

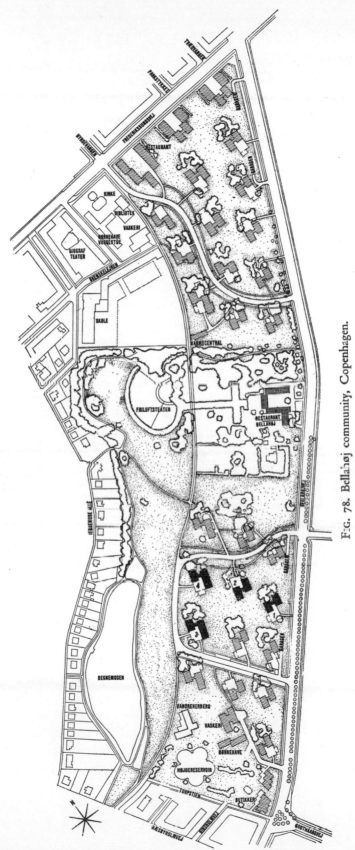

FIG. 78. Bellahøj community, Copenhagen.

The principles of Årsta reappear at Vällingby (Pl. 107, 120a) and the community centre is planned at the underground station, or rather on top of it. Here the majority of shops are to be found as well as offices, banks, restaurants, etc., while the industry is situated east of the centre. It is consequently a question of zoning. The density is highest at the centre with a number of tower blocks; further away there are three-storied lamella houses often grouped together forming traffic-free yards. Furthest out the residences become detached houses, and row houses. From an aesthetic viewpoint Vällingby also displays a certain inheritance from Årsta. Thus there is a contrast between the grand scale of the tower blocks and the engineering works of the Stockholm Tramway Co. on one hand and the execution of the details of the community centre which, emphasized by gaudy neon signs and restless changes in material, makes one think of fun-fair architecture. Without doubt Vällingby is an enormous achieve-ment and the enthusiasm of both the planning authorities and the public is justified, but so far as the details are concerned I think the enthusiasm is being carried just a little bit too far. The stringent and sober temperance which is the hallmark of the architecture now being created by Sven Markelius and David Helldén in central Stockholm is missing. The homogeneity in the latter work is more profound and so better architecture.

The Danish and Finnish town plans outside the capitals do not include any work-places for the inhabitants at all. The distance between Tapiola and Helsinki is so short that this has not been regarded as necessary. In Copenhagen they intend to keep the old-established city centre and, by a gradually performed slum-clearance, renew it. This is in a way contrary to the policy in Stockholm and is partly due to historical reasons. Apart from this the new Scandi-navian town plans show many similarities. Both Tapiola and Bellahøj display principles that can be found also at Vällingby and Farsta, namely to give the inhabitants a community centre with opportunities for leisure-time activities, schools, health centres, etc.

The Finns themselves regard the standard at Bellahaøj is hgher than that at Tapiola. It would be unfair, however, not to mention the outstandingly good design of Tapiola centre, consisting of a high block surrounded by lower buildings at right angles to each other forming yards which are free of traffic. There is a fine contrast between the restful character of the lower houses and the vertical

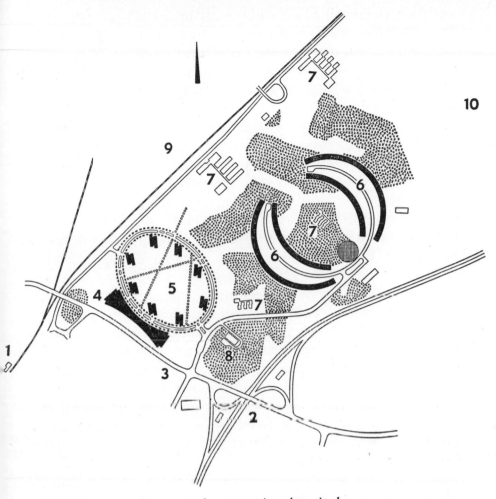

FIG. 79. Täby community, schematic plan.

1. Railway station.
2. Trunk road from Stockholm.
3. Road linking trunk road to centre.
4. Regional shopping centre.
5. Näsbydal, fifteen-stories blocks.
6. Grinthorp, blocks of flats, of eleven or four stories.
7. School
8. District heating centre.
9. Industrial area.
10. Suggested race-course.

aspiration of the tall block. But in its unity Bellahøj (Pl. 111b, Fig. 78) shows superior planning. The uniform separation of functions within the neighbourhood has reduced the length of roads and other forms of communications to a minimum. The blocks of flats consist of rather narrow high blocks linked in pairs and resemble those of Brolid and Wallinder at Gothenburg. They are divided into two areas separated by a restaurant and an open-air theatre in a large park. Each residential district has its own local centre with laundry, nursery, district heating control, and so on, but one of these local centres—the north one—serves the whole unit with its school, cinema/theatre, library, and a church. The line of thought behind this dividing of functions and its consequence, zoning, is clear and unsubtle, but at the same time one must remember that the communal life of the inhabitants was given much importance.

Another theme is struck in the master plan for Täby community north of Stockholm (Fig. 79), outlined by the architects of the Vattenbyggnadsbyrån, literally Water Construction Department, in Stockholm. The plan consists of three large residential districts completed by a centre, the influence of which is planned to reach far outside the surrounding area. It will be placed very near an arterial highway, and will be easily accessible to people in other communities. An industrial region is to be laid out north of the residential areas, providing work for at least part of the population. What is new in this plan and what distinguishes it from the others is, on one hand, the separation of residential areas of different character—the personally owned homes and the blocks of flats—whereby the structures in each area are homogeneous, and on the other hand the great concentration in the two ellipsoidal point-block or skyscraper areas, giving the districts an urban intensity and character. This concentration offers quite a new townscape.

XXV

PUBLIC BUILDINGS

ONLY two of the problems of twentieth-century architects have been discussed—housing and town planning. But a town must contain other things besides houses in order to become a functioning whole: schools, hospitals, the environment of production and trade, communication and, last but not least, recreational facilities.

Scandinavian architects have carried out this vast programme on a broad front. At times one kind of building has inspired others through its form or contents, at other times buildings within other categories have served as inspiration sources, but the new architecture in all its manifestations is an integrated whole. The reason for dealing first with domestic architecture and town planning as separate chapters has not been that domestic architecture, for instance, should have held a leading position in the development of modern architecture, but only that these two problems—the house and the town—are to most of us questions of everlasting interest and importance.

The same analytical way of looking at the problems of domestic architecture began to be used in other directions. The elementary school for girls on Sveaplan in Stockholm (Pl. 113) by Nils Ahrbom and Helge Zimdahl, built in 1932–35, can stand as a good example. With the new methods the school was designed as several buildings put together, each housing different activities: the class-rooms facing south, the large hall to be used when bad weather prevents the girls from spending the breaks outside, lecture rooms for physics, chemistry, etc., a gymnasium and a speech room projecting towards the north, and the different parts of the building communicating with the entrance hall and its staircases. As parts of the school are raised on pillars, a rain-shelter is created, and by referring different functions to different buildings the architects have been able to group these freely and create a relationship between the school and its surrounding yard. An equally good illustration of this is at Aarhus University in Denmark (Pl. 114) by Kay Fisker, C. F. Møller and Povl Stegmann,

239

where the connection between the buildings and the university parks by C. T. Sørensen is still more intimate (see also p. 242). Still another example of this kind of school architecture is the school designed by H. E. Langkilde and I. M. Jensen in Gentofte in Denmark, built 1949–51, where one part of the school is reserved for small children and the other for bigger children.

With Arne Jacobsen's and Erik Møller's Town Hall at Aarhus, built 1938–42, this town has become one of the most advanced architecturally in Denmark. The building is divided into two parts for offices and court room and has an open and very unconventional tower, wherein the architects have translated the old medieval symbol of town halls into an inspiring system of horizontal and vertical slabs of reinforced concrete, demonstrating at the same time both boldness in construction and the power in modern architecture for renewal of old concepts.

Fine results were achieved fairly soon after 1930 with department stores and office buildings. Radio House in Copenhagen (interior, Pl. 115a) by Vilhelm Lauritzen, 1934, was given a horizontal stress by assembling the windows in bands. As in the case of Bredenberg's Store in Stockholm by Gunnar Asplund, 1933, this façade presupposes the use of an interior structural framework of reinforced concrete; the walls are mere screens and so could be greatly varied in design. The same effect re-occurs in Oslo where Ove Bang designed the Samfunnshus, or Community House, in 1940. A foil for its block-like character is the recessed balcony on the third floor.

Functionalist architecture was in its youth in Scandinavia then and, as in many other parts of the world, it stressed a bit too strongly the purely technical aspects. At first Scandinavian architecture became more international—or rather, un-national—in its attitude, working with elements like steel, glass, and concrete and in its youthful delirium not taking into consideration any national or climatic factors. After a few years a so-called national functionalism appeared, subduing and modifying the impersonal international approach without either abandoning the original ideals or looking to past epochs for inspiration. Such Finnish buildings as Paimio Sanatorium, 1929–33, by Alvar Aalto, and the Olympic Stadium of 1934–39 and 1942 by Y. Lindegren, and Swedish buildings such as the Concert Hall in Gothenburg, 1931–35, by Nils Ejnar Eriksson, and the burial chapels at Skogskyrkogården outside

Stockholm, 1935–40, by Gunnar Asplund, are examples of this new personal and national approach. These are a few selected examples of high international reputation that show how the new technical gains have been boldly exploited to make possible quite new and untraditional forms.

In Aalto's Sanatorium (Pl. 112) the concrete frame and struc- ture together with the provision of balconies facing the sun were the factors deciding the form. The vertical members of this building rise

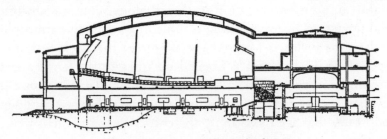

FIG. 80. Concert hall, Gothenburg.

like thin slabs and there is a clear and logical difference between the supporting elements of walls and roofs, and the spaces of the rooms. This building is an early work of Aalto's; his forms have since be- come less hard, perhaps inspired by his bent-wood technique in the fabrication of furniture. With the reappearance of wood in his and other Finnish architects' buildings the texture of surfaces has become more interesting than the naked concrete surfaces. The main practical problem in designing the Olympic Stadium—to accommodate as many spectators as possible—was not the only goal for its architect. Out of the stadium tower he made a kind of concrete fanfare to celebrate the Olympic games for which the stadium was once designed and to set up at the same time a dialectic between the low principal construction and this vertical accent.

In the Gothenburg Concert Hall (Pl. 115b, Fig. 80) quite another effect is made. All practical arrangements, entrance, stairs, foyers, etc., are extremely well solved, but the culmination is naturally reached in the large hall, which has a quiet and concentrated charac- ter. The wooden panelled walls are not strictly vertical, and a series of small balconies are drawn in along the walls. This together with the balanced proportions of the hall gives an impression of quivering equilibrium.

The last but also the greatest work of Gunnar Asplund—the three burial chapels at Skogskyrkogården (Pl. 116) in Stockholm—gives us yet another example of the national and personal functional archi‑ tecture of this time. Here the architect has designed not only the buildings but also the landscape surrounding them. Before reaching the entrance the visitor's eye is caught by the free‑standing monu‑ mental wooden cross and a tone of restful contemplation is struck. The stillness becomes enriched by the reposeful nature of the low chapels in which a secluded world is created and each detail empha‑ sizes and supports participation in the religious act that constitutes a funeral service. The leave‑taking is done in a meditative atmosphere, but when the coffin is lowered the whole of the back wall in the Chapel of the Holy Cross is opened up towards the landscape and its peaceful air penetrates and fills the contemplative room. The atmosphere is changed from grievous sorrow to a liberated confidence.

Such buildings well exemplify the entirely original quality of this architecture. The list of Finnish examples would be incomplete without some mention of such buildings as the Burial Chapel at Turku (Pl. 117) by Erik Bryggman in 1940, and the Kudenuele Factory (Pl. 119) by Viljo Rewell in 1956. Smooth, unbroken areas of wall in concrete or glass, wood or bricks, stand in needle‑ sharp contrast to slender supporting elements, roof‑trusses or columns, in the latter building. Thanks to this structural logic all details are given their distinct functions and fixed places in the layout of the buildings, and at the same time they are treated with the utmost refinement for their purely ornamental character. In addition the Finns have an almost unerring ability to put buildings into their landscape by making dramatic use of the dialectic between two kinds of beauty—that of nature and that which is created by man. A striking instance of this is the chapel at Otaniemi (Pl. 118) built in 1956 by Heikki and Kaja Sirén.

Compared to Finland, Denmark has sought more idyllic values. In his house at Ordrup (Pl. 105a) of 1943, the architect Finn Juhl has given the bedroom wing a 'romantic' touch by means of window shutters, and at Aarhus University (Pl. 114), a few years older, there is a tendency towards almost playful decorativism in the large win‑ dow, where the bars originally necessary for the construction have been emphasized by placing them on the outside of the window as part of the exterior design. In Denmark there is as well an old tradi‑ tion of creating a harmonious relationship between the landscape and the buildings, but it is done with other means than in Finland, one might say by ingratiation rather than by tension. The scales are more even between buildings and nature, so that the contrast is less apparent. Sometimes a building is subordinated to nature by its small scale. In recent years the scale has once more been increased in Denmark, as is clearly visible in the apartment houses at Bellahøj (Pl. 111*b*) and the new office buildings near the Raadhusplads in the centre of Copenhagen.

In Sweden both the 'romantic' and a bolder scale can be found. The skyscrapers at Sveaplatsen in Stockholm by David Helldén, now under construction (1957), and the designs for blocks of flats at Täby north of Stockholm both show a return to a more purely structural, coherent architecture on a grand scale with all details subdued so as not to interfere with the main effect. Further examples are the blocks of flats at Södra Guldheden at Gothenburg (Pl. 108) by Brolid and Wallinder, and the staff quarters at the hospital Södersjukhuset in Stockholm. A bold construction is the bus garage by Eskil Sundahl (Pl. 120*b*).

As has been mentioned, the community centre at Vällingby (Pl. 107) shows another trend. Its contrasting colour schemes with similarly contrasting volumes, roof angles, and materials are developments of its inheritance from the Årsta community centre (Pl. 106*a*). Behind this kind of architecture lies a refusal to make it merely a neutral background for human life—an affirmation, rather, that architecture plays an active part and carries its own actively intervening values. Here also details of construction and material give expression to the rising standard of living, and the use of rich and expensive material is in great contrast to the utilitarian work which characterizes more 'structural' architecture.

Even such a short survey as this shows not only the continuous renewal of modern Scandinavian architecture but also how it has been able to cover all the many different fields of life included in the modern community, and how in the different Scandinavian countries there have been different goals, different themes, with varied effects on their architecture.

Since the Stockholm Exhibition in 1930, functional architecture has been victorious in all types of buildings in Scandinavia. The quality of the best work is impressive, even if the severe Nordic climate, together with other national factors, sometimes restricts the forms and gives them a rather closed character. That a very limited number of outstanding buildings has been mentioned here should not make one forget all the architecture that daily and in a quiet way is being created for all levels of Scandinavian life, making even the average standard of architecture admirable.

SELECTIVE LIST OF BOOKS

(Books in each sub-section are roughly in order of general usefulness)

SCANDINAVIA AS A WHOLE
General History

Rasmussen, S. E. *Nordische baukunst.* Copenhagen, 1940. A short, well-written introduction to Danish and Swedish architecture.

Specialized Works

Nordisk kultur. About 25 vols., in progress. Stockholm, publ. irregularly. A comprehensive work on Scandinavian culture as a whole with articles on architecture included.

Books on Contemporary Architecture

Lettström, G., and others. *Nordisk arkitektur, 1946–49.* Stockholm, 1950. The first years of post-war architecture in Scandinavia.

Var tids konst och diktning i Skandinavien. Copenhagen, 1948. In this book there are, among other essays, three specialists' views on twentieth-century architecture in Denmark, Norway, and Sweden.

Paulsson, T. *Ny arkitektur.* Stockholm, 1958. A recent analysis of the emergence of modern architecture with special regard to the development in Sweden. *Ny stad,* 1958, deals similarly with town planning.

DENMARK
General History

Beckett, F. *Danmarks kunst.* 2 vols. Copenhagen, 1924, 1927. A general introduction to Danish art and architecture.

Specialized Works

Langberg, H. *Danmarks bygningskultur.* 2 vols. Copenhagen, 1955. Very well illustrated and with numerous plans, sections, etc., this is the most exhaustive book there is on Danish architecture from the beginning until 1930. The distinguished author has based his work on thorough primary research work and gives an excellent bibliography.

Wanscher, V. *Danmarks arkitektur.* Copenhagen, 1943. This book covers some important milestones in Danish architecture with a personal touch. Illustrated with sketches by the author.

245

Langberg, H. *Dansk byggesaet, 1792–1942.* Copenhagen, 1942. A general survey of Danish building activity during one and a half centuries.

Weilbach, F. *Dansk bygningskunst i det 18 aarhunderte.* Copenhagen, 1930. A comprehensive study of one of the peaks in Danish architecture.

Millech, K. *Danske arkitekturstrømninger, 1850–1950.* Copenhagen, 1951. The work of a learned 'style historian' about Danish architecture during the past century.

Danmarks kyrkor. Series in progress. Copenhagen. Inventory of Danish churches based on measurements and archives.

Mackeprang, M. *Vore landsbykirker.* 2nd ed. Copenhagen, 1944. A classification of Danish cathedrals and churches in terms of building techniques, plans, and ornamentation.

Lorenzen, V. *De danske klostres bygningshistorie.* 11 vols. Copenhagen, 1912–41. An inventory of Danish monasteries based on measurements and archives.

Roussell, A. *Danmarks middelalderborge.* Copenhagen, 1942. A description of fortified castles and manor-houses in the Middle Ages.

Lorenzen, V., and others. *Danske slotte og herregaarde.* 4 vols. Copenhagen, 1943. An extensive work on castles and manor-houses.

Lorenzen, V. *Vore byer.* 2 vols. Copenhagen, 1947–52.

——, and others. *Christian den fjerdes byanlaeg.* Copenhagen, 1937. These two books are of special interest to those who wish to study Danish towns and town planning.

Rasmussen, S. E. *Byer og bygninger.* Copenhagen, 1949 (publ. in England and U.S. as *Towns and buildings,* 1951). In this general analysis of some milestones in the history of town planning and architecture, the most important Danish examples are included, as seen against their historical and social background. Richly illustrated with line drawings by the author.

Wanscher, V. *Christian IV's bygninger.* Copenhagen, 1937. The building activity of the foremost royal builder of Scandinavia.

Elling, C. *Danske borgerhuse.* Copenhagen, 1943. A complete history of the burghers' domestic architecture from its emergence until the end of the nineteenth century.

Thurah, L. L. de. *Hafnia hodierna.* Copenhagen, 1748.

—— *Den danske Vitruvius.* Copenhagen, 1749. These are two important volumes of engravings by this great architect of the buildings of his time.

Books on Contemporary Architecture
Architecture of Denmark. London, 1949. Reprinted with added material from a special number of *Architectural Review.*

Hiort, E. *Ny dansk arkitektur.* Copenhagen, 1950. An introduction to modern Danish architecture with good illustrations. Also his *Danish architecture of today,* exhibition catalogue. London, 1950.

Fisker, K., and F. R. Yeobury. *Modern Danish architecture.* London, 1927. Nineteenth-century romanticism and the classicism of the twenties.

Periodical

Arkitekten. A monthly journal published by the national association of Danish architects in Copenhagen. It publishes competitions, new architecture of all kinds, and articles on architects and the history of architecture.

FINLAND

General Histories

Wennervirte, L. *Finlands konst.* Stockholm, 1926. A general introduction to Finnish art and architecture.

Ekelund, H. *Byggnadskonst i Finland.* Helsinki, 1932. A general work on Finnish architecture which is especially useful because it includes an English text.

Specialized Works

Vikstedt, J. *De finska städernas byggnadskonst.* Helsinki, 1926. An inventory of Finnish town architecture with many illustrations and plans.

Meissner, C. *Carl Ludwig Engel.* Berlin, 1937. A thorough work dealing with all the buildings by this German architect who practised in Finland, with many illustrations and plans.

Waasastjerna, N. *Finsk arkitektur, exteriörer och interiörer.* Helsinki, 1904. Mainly a picture book dealing with the architecture of the turn of the century.

Books on Contemporary Architecture

Industriarkitektur i Finland. Helsinki, 1952. An exhibition catalogue on modern industrial architecture, with an introduction and including an English text.

Finland bygger. Helsinki, 1953.

Architecture in Finland. London, 1957. These two exhibition catalogues, the latter for an exhibition at the Royal Institute of British Architects, have introductions and illustrations dealing with modern Finnish architecture and its background.

Neuenschwander, E. and C. *Alvar Aalto and Finnish architecture.* London and New York, 1954.

Labò, Giorgio. *Alvar Aalto.* Milan, 1948. Two well-written books on modern Finnish architecture and its foremost representative, both well illustrated.

Periodical

Arkitekti. Published in Helsinki, a Finnish equivalent to the Danish *Arkitekten.*

NORWAY

General History

Lexow, E. *Norges kunst.* 2nd ed. Oslo, 1942. A general introduction to Norwegian art and architecture.

Specialized Works

Bugge, A., and others. *Norsk byggningskunst fra Urnes til Universitetet.* Oslo, 1927. Written by a number of specialists in different fields of architecture, this book offers a complete picture of Norwegian archi‚ tecture up to about 1850.

Brochmann, Odd. *Gjenreisningen og det Norske i var byggeskikke.* Oslo, 1940. An analysis of Norwegian building traditions with the emphasis on the purely Norwegian.

Vreim, H. *Norsk trearkitektur.* Oslo, 1947 (rev. ed.). Norwegian wooden architecture with special regard to ornamental wood‚carving.

Alnaes and others. *Norske hus, en billedbok.* Oslo, 1950. An exhaustive picture book with many and good illustrations. Also as *Norwegian architecture throughout the ages,* in English. Oslo, 1950.

Bugge, A. *Norske stavkirker.* Oslo, 1953. This is the best book yet about the stave churches, well illustrated, with many plans and sections.

Fett, H. *Norges kirker i middelalderen.* Kristiania, 1909.

——— *Norges kirker i 16 og 17 aarhundrede.* Kristiania, 1911.

——— *Norges kirker i nyere tid.* Kristiania, 1911. These three books are still the most complete inventory of religious architecture in Norway, written by a well‚known specialist.

Kielland, J. *Norske hus og hjem, byggningskunst og bohave.* Kristiania, 1919. Of interest to those who wish to study domestic architecture.

Periodical

Bonytt. A monthly periodical, published in Oslo, with articles on arts and crafts and architecture.

SWEDEN

General Histories

Cornell, H. *Den svenska konstens historia.* 2 vols. Stockholm, 1944–46.

Hahr, A. *Architecture in Sweden.* Stockholm, 1938. These two books are introductions to Swedish architecture, the first being the more thorough and dealing with painting and sculpture as well. Cornell gives an exhaustive list of literature.

LIST OF BOOKS

Specialized Works

Lundberg, E. *Byggnadskonsten i Sverige under medeltiden, 1000–1400.* Stockholm, 1940.

―――― *Byggnadskonsten i Sverige, senmedeltid och renässans.* Stockholm, 1948. This compendious work in two parts is written by the foremost scholar of Swedish architectural history. Richly illustrated and with numerous sketches, plans, drawings, etc.

Sveriges kyrkor. Series in progress. Stockholm. An inventory of Swedish churches based on measurements and archives.

Svenska slott och herresäten, Stockholm, 1908–14, 1918–33, 1931–34. An inventory of Swedish castles and manor-houses based on measurements and archives.

Hahr, A. *Vasatidens borgar.* Uppsala, 1917. A comprehensive survey of the Vasa castles with numerous plans and sections and good illustrations.

Lundberg, E. *Herremannens bostad.* Stockholm, 1935.

―――― *Svensk bostad.* Stockholm, 1942. Two complete histories (roughly similar in content) of mainly Swedish domestic architecture from ancient times to functionalism, seen against a background of foreign influences.

Paulsson, G. *Svensk stad.* 3 vols. Stockholm, 1950, 1953. An analysis of the emergence of modern Swedish towns and town structures (buildings, furnishings, town plans, etc.), well illustrated with photographs, diagrams, and maps.

Karling, S. *Trädgårdskonstens historia i Sverige intill Le Notre-stilens genombrott.* Stockholm, 1931. A comprehensive study of baroque gardens.

Åström, L. E. *Skånska slott.* Stockholm, 1948. A short history of the fortified castles and manor-houses in Skåne from the Renaissance to the eighteenth century.

Dahlberg, E. *Suecia antiqua et hodierna.* Stockholm, 1716. A great series of engravings begun in the latter seventeenth century (separate engravings from 1661) from drawings by this Swedish architect of old and new buildings all over Sweden. A reprint was published, 3 vols. in two, in Stockholm in 1924.

Books on Contemporary Architecture

Smith, G. E. Kidder. *Sweden builds.* Rev. ed. London and New York, 1957. This book is most useful for its illustrations and for its bibliography.

Ahlberg, H. *Swedish architecture of the twentieth century.* London, 1925.

249

Johansson, C. *Funktionalismen i verkligheten.* Stockholm, 1931. An analysis of the architecture of functionalism written by one of its foremost advocates.

Jacobson, T. P., and Silow, S., eds. *Ten lectures on Swedish architecture.* Stockholm, 1949. These lectures were given to a group of architectural students from England in 1946 by ten specialists in different fields of architecture and town planning.

New Swedish architecture. Stockholm, 1940. A picture book with an introduction by Gregor Paulsson.

Cornell, E. *Ny svensk byggnadskonst.* Stockholm, 1950. A short description of modern Swedish architecture.

Periodicals
Arkitektur, 1901–21.
Byggmästaren, 1922 ff. Monthly journals, published in Stockholm, of the same character as the Danish *Arkitekten.*

INDEX

(Note for non-Scandinavians: Å-, Ö-, Ø-words appear at the end)

INDEX

INDEX